Endorsements

We can only live where we've died. This reality as a Jesus follower is beautifully unpacked on these pages in a way that is both challenging and hopeful. *Accessing the Greater Glory* by Larry Sparks and Ana Werner will be a great treasure to the church for many years to come. With clarity of heart and mind, they present brilliant insights to enable the reader to see where we are as a church and where we're going. Through wisdom, they've laid out a prophetic vision in very practical ways. Read this book, and accept the challenge to step into your reason for being—on earth as it is in heaven.

—Bill Johnson
Bethel Church, Redding, California
Author of *The Way of Life* and *Raising Giant-Killers*

Larry Sparks and Ana Werner rightly emphasize not human techniques or honor but sacrifice and surrender. Are we desperate for God? Do we want the Spirit as much as the Spirit wants us? The Lord is worth everything. May He consume us—first individually, and then to be His agents in a needy world.

—Dr. Craig Keener
www.craigkeener.com
F.M. and Ada Thompson Professor of the New Testament at Asbury Theological Seminary
Author of *Acts: An Exegetical Commentary* and *Miracles*

One of the most destructive lies of all times is that, "In the last days the church will get brighter and brighter while the world gets darker and darker!" People speak of darkness as if it is the most dominant force in the world. Yet Isaiah prophesied in Isaiah 60: *"Arise, shine; for your light has come, and the glory of the Lord has risen upon you."*

The world should look different because people filled with glory are present in every sphere of society. Light always overcomes darkness! It is incumbent upon us as the people of God to not curse the darkness but, instead, stand boldly in the midst of the thick gloom and shine!

Accessing the Greater Glory is a prophetic blueprint and practical invitation on how to do just that. It will show you that the glory within you is superior to the darkness around you. When you discover how to partner with Christ in you, the Hope of Glory, you will be positioned to bring radical change to whatever sphere God has placed you in. I believe this book will catalyze its readers into exponentially greater levels of cultural transformation and revival on the earth!

—Kris Vallotton
Leader, Bethel Church, Redding, California
Co-Founder of Bethel School of Supernatural Ministry
Author of thirteen books, including *The Supernatural Ways of Royalty, Heavy Rain,* and *Poverty, Riches and Wealth*

Is there a greater move of the Holy Spirit coming in a worldwide fashion? Across the globe believers are hungering for a greater access to the greater glory of God. Larry Sparks and Ana Werner believe the key to the question is being released in this hour. Wisdom, knowledge, faith, hunger are all a part. But do you want the key to greater access for yourself? Then dig into this treasure chest! Keys of the Glory are contained within!

—James W. Goll
God Encounters Ministries
GOLL Ideation LLC

A book that provides a synergy of biblical teaching, supernatural stories, revival history, and prophetic perspective on where we are right now and how to access the greater glory available to us through the Holy Spirit is my kind of book. I recommend *Accessing the Greater Glory* by Larry Sparks and Ana Werner.

—Randy Clark, D. Min.
Overseer of the Apostolic Network of Global Awakening
President of Global Awakening Theological Seminary

I can think of no one who burns with a passion to experience the fullness of God more than my friend, Larry Sparks. But I also know his passion goes beyond any encounter; Larry is divinely charged to equip and lead others into desiring and accessing more, too. I, for one, am a grateful product of his life's mission. Now, in *Accessing the Greater Glory*, Larry profoundly draws upon his years of pursuing God's Presence and a fascinating encounter in the place of God's Presence to deliver a handbook for us all to experience the greatest glories of God's Presence. Prepare to never be the same! Coupled with the awe-inspiring contributions of Ana Werner, you'll be lifted to new levels of supernatural (normal) faith.

—Kyle Winkler
Author of *Silence Satan* and *Activating the Power of God's Word*
Creator of the Shut Up, Devil! app
www.kylewinkler.org

Out of incredible personal experiences with God, Larry Sparks and Ana Werner are calling the church to the final endless revival that will usher in the Kingdom of God. I highly recommend this book to everyone who is praying for a great move of God in our time.

—Dr. Vinson Synan
Oral Roberts University
Author of *Century of the Holy Spirit*

My heart leapt with joy as I began to read *Accessing the Greater Glory*. I believe that Larry and Ana have been given a supernatural prompting from the Holy Spirit to spur God's people on to the greater works they have been called to. There is a divine awakening happening as the church is stirring from a complacent slumber and beginning to recognize the invitation to partner with the Holy Spirit for things "exceedingly, abundantly above all we can ask, hope or imagine." Open your heart to hear what the Lord is saying through these pages, and as you apply the wisdom you find here I believe together we can all step into a greater glory and a glorious new era for the church worldwide.

—Katherine Ruonala
Senior Leader of Glory City Brisbane
Founder and facilitator of the Australian Prophetic Council
Author of *Living in the Miraculous, Wilderness to Wonders,
Life with the Holy Spirit, Speak Life: Creating Your World with Your Words*
www.katherineruonala.com

Birthed in a divine encounter while in Israel, Larry Sparks and Ana Werner will take you by the hand and help you in *Accessing the Greater Glory*! As I read through this book, my body trembled and my spirit came alive. I can't remember reading a book that contained more power and more insight into the activity of Holy Spirit. Be prepared to burn with the sacred flame of Holy Spirit as you turn the pages of this book. You will end up crying out for more. Listen to their words: "Some people need a message, some people need an encounter. Some people need a sermon from a pulpit; some people simply need to meet God on the carpet." For me, I simply need to meet God face down on the carpet! Read this and you may find yourself in the middle of your own personal revival!

—Brian Simmons
The Passion Translation Project

My friends Larry Sparks and Ana Werner have written more than a prophetic invitation to step into the glory of God—they have declared a prophetic summons. We are being summoned by the Holy Spirit to move into the next levels of glory. We cannot be satisfied with what we have had, no matter how good it might have been. We must move from glory to glory. The literal destiny of nations hangs in the balance concerning these transitions. Only the weighty glory of God can reclaim nations and cultures to the Lord's purpose for them. Let's join our friends and respond to this heavenly summons and partake and be carriers of this glory of God. We have seen but the edge of Him.

—Robert Henderson
Bestselling author of the *Courts of Heaven* series

As I read through *Accessing the Greater Glory*, I experienced wave after wave of the Holy Spirit's Presence and confirmation of what I was reading. Larry Sparks and Ana Werner blend the experiential and biblical components of the Greater Glory that issues an invitation to the "hungry and desperate." They reveal that two of our greatest adversaries are "religion and tradition." But they also present to us new paradigms and wineskins to hold the new wine of the Holy Spirit as we continually access His glory. This book is not only refreshing, but it is also a landmark scholarly treatise on revival and the glory of God. It is exciting and convicting and a must read! Thank you, Ana Werner and Larry Sparks.

—Norman Benz, D.Min.
Lead pastor, Covenant Centre International
Co-founder, Renewing South Florida
Palm Beach Gardens, Florida

There is a sense of excitement in the air as our generation has observed many biblical prophecies fulfilled. We are quickly coming to a time when the fire that is burning on the heavenly alter will be visible in the lives of believers in Jesus everywhere. These believers are His "burning ones" who have consecrated their lives on the holy altar of the Most High God. Romans 12:1 (AMP) says, *"Therefore I urge you, brothers and sisters, by the mercies of God, to present your bodies [dedicating all of yourselves, set apart] as a living sacrifice, holy and well-pleasing to God, which is your rational (logical, intelligent) act of worship."*

Once this phase of our worship on God's holy altar is consummated, we will not need to wait long for the visible glory of God to come upon us individually and on the Ecclesia as a whole. This process will eventually usher in the coming of our Lord Jesus. Are you ready to position yourself for this move of the glory of God? My good friends Ana Werner and Larry Sparks are assigned to give you the keys to this mighty move of God that is right around the corner in their new book, *Accessing the Greater Glory*! Allow the Lord Jesus, by His Spirit, to speak to you concerning your life as you become a resting place for the *Greater Glory*.

—Dr. Kevin L. Zadai
Founder and president of Warrior Notes
and Warrior Notes School of Ministry

Accessing the Greater Glory by my friends Larry Sparks and Ana Werner is nothing short of a gift to the body of Christ and the earth. This book will not only create hunger in you to see Him and see His Glory, but awaken and activate you to the accessibility to moving and flowing in His Presence and Glory that is already yours in Christ. Full of biblical truths and wisdom, these pages are full of impartation for deeper encounter. Expect to be impacted, transformed, and changed by the hand of God through this book. It's a divine impartation specifically for you to prepare you for the greatest revealing and demonstration of His Glory upon the earth that we have ever seen.

—Lana Vawser
Author of *The Prophetic Voice of God*
lanavawser.com

This book will reveal some of the main things that Jesus is having the Holy Spirit impress upon church leaders today. Everywhere I travel throughout the world the prophets and apostles are saying the same things using similar terminology. God is about to release the greatest glory upon and through the church that has ever been recorded in church history. We have entered the Third Reformation, which will raise up a people who will fill the earth with the glory of the Lord as the waters cover the sea. Read this book to gather some insight and inspiration to manifest God's glory to the world.

—Bishop Bill Hamon
Bishop, Christian International Apostolic-Global Network
Author: *The Eternal Church, Prophets & Personal Prophecy, Apostles/ Prophets & the Coming Moves of God, The Day of the Saints,* and *God's Weapons of War*

The true Bride of Christ is beginning to emerge out of the present darkness covering the earth. She is rising still. Many of these sons and daughters are invisible now but they will be invincible in the days ahead, clothed with the radiant light of God!

Larry Sparks and Ana Werner are on the cutting edge of not only declaring this reality but articulating the next move of God with clarity and power. Now is not the time to fear or get discouraged, but to grab hold of the visions and words contained in the book and run with them. You will be empowered and greatly encouraged!

—Jeremiah Johnson
Jeremiahjohnson.tv
Heart of the Father Ministries
Maranatha School of Ministry
Author of *Cleansing and Igniting the Prophetic* and *The Power of Consecration*

"Lord, remember David and all his afflictions; how he swore to the Lord, and vowed to the Mighty One of Jacob: 'Surely I will not go into the chamber of my house, or go up to the comfort of my bed; I will not give sleep to my eyes or slumber to my eyelids, until I find a place for the Lord, a dwelling place for the Mighty One of Jacob'" (Psalm 132:1-5 NKJV).

David was desperate for the Glory of God to rest on him. He understood there was no higher experience. This book asks, "What are you waiting for? Why do you need another hand laid on you or another 'word' when the Great God Himself waits to rest on you and then, through you, change the world?"

A classic kind of Christian is about to appear on the world stage. Believers with unstoppable passion, speaking words that the world cannot counter, confirmed by undeniable miracles. *Accessing the Greater Glory* will help drag the church out of Sesame Street and back to Azusa Street.

—Mario Murillo
International evangelist
Author of *Fresh Fire*

I know the word "Wow" is not a very professional way to communicate within an endorsement, but honestly it is the best word I can think of to describe my elation after reading *Accessing the Greater Glory* by Larry Sparks and Ana Werner! This book is powerfully and profoundly prophetic but also reveals historical and biblical insights that literally turn the lights on with your heart to an invitation of God to engage in His feast in this season. My faith and expectancy are soaring, and I'm confident that yours will too after you read *Accessing the Greater Glory*! Thank you, Larry and Ana, for the glorious impact you have made on my life through this wonderful book!

—Dr. Patricia King
Author, television host, minister

I am thrilled to endorse Larry Sparks' and Ana Werner's new book, *Accessing the Greater Glory*. We are hearing a lot these days about glory. I'm grateful for everyone seeking it as well as pressing into it; however, many times the books I've read and the messages I've heard haven't given me the keys to accessing the glory. What I love about this book is that Larry and Ana call us to the age-old truth—the fire and the glory always falls on a sacrifice. We must learn in this hour to accommodate the Presence and learn the protocol of hosting Him, and if we continue to go about business as usual I'm afraid we will continue to see the limited fruit that we've become accustomed to. I'm so grateful to God for Larry and Ana and their "press" into God and His fullness, and I believe that this book will help all of us as we access the greater glory.

—Corey Russell
Upper Room Dallas
Speaker, author of *Glory Within*

In the late '90s I was attending a women's event hosted by Ruth Ward Heflin and Brenda Kilpatrick at the Brownsville Assembly of God during the Pensacola Revival. One evening the glory that descended and rested in that room was beyond description of human words. As I lay prostrate and surrendered, once again crying out to the Lord from my heart and surrendering my life as a living sacrifice, He spoke a truth to me that remains alive in me and that continues to increase and carry me throughout my ministry and life. His words, "In the glory is everything needed to sustain life." That was an altar moment, a gate of opening, a heavenly revelatory connection in my life of a deeper awakening of His greater glory. It carries, empowers, and sustains me. Friends, the truth is, we can have as much of God as we want. We are not waiting on Him; He is waiting on us. Ones who will say, "Lord, here I am. Take me as a living sacrifice for You." And from this place we become the glory carriers to see His light and Kingdom made known throughout the world in every sphere He leads us in. *Accessing the Greater Glory* is not just a book to read for knowledge; it is a now word enveloped in His glory that will bring you into a place of awakening and transformation. Thank you, Larry and Ana, for this now word. It is my prayer that all who read this manuscript will have a deep hunger awakened to the truth of His great glory and revival and reformation will sweep through the church and the land.

— Rebecca Greenwood
President,
Christian Harvest International
Author of *Authority to Tread, Destined to Rule, Let Our Children Go, Defeating Strongholds of the Mind, Glory Warfare: How the Presence of God Empowers You to Destroy Works of Darkness*

Riveting! Magnificent! Supernatural! Larry and Ana had a divine encounter with God while visiting the Holy Land and are now sharing it with the world! *Accessing the Greater Glory* includes ancient secrets to living saturated in God's glory. Discover how you can access this greater glory now and start releasing it into your sphere of influence. Understand the one thing that the fire of God is drawn and attracted to in your life and learn how to demonstrate God's glory! The greater glory is your destiny *now!*

— Ward Simpson
CEO, God TV

My heart was stirred when I read this prophetic summons to access the greater glory. I've been crying out for the same at Awakening House of Prayer. Surely, this book will awaken spirits all over the church to press in to the present season — a season in which God is knocking on the doors of our hearts and inviting us into supernatural encounters that most eyes have not seen and most ears have not heard. In *Accessing the Greater Glory*, Larry Sparks and Ana Werner write with authority, stir you, and guide you into understanding and accessing these dimensions because they have studied and experienced what they are writing about—and yet long for more.

—Jennifer LeClaire
Bestselling author of *Mornings with the Holy Spirit*
Founder of Awakening House of Prayer

We access the greater glory of God when we humble ourselves, surrender to Him, and are willing to pay the price to step into His will. We offer ourselves wholeheartedly to God—not half-heartedly. We do that through being secure in our identity as sons and daughters of the Almighty God and being willing to serve as the Lord directs us. This book will encourage you to do just that. When we give God our "yes," we make a way for Him to move and release His glory!

—Dawna De Silva
Founder and Co-leader of Bethel Sozo Ministries
Bestselling author of *Shifting Atmospheres*, *Sozo*, and
Overcoming Fear

Accessing the Greater Glory is a present word for the new era Holy Spirit is now revealing. It is a guidebook for this tipping-point moment in history.

Thankfully, there is more to be accessed and lived in. Ana and Larry have written with excellence the crucial answers as to why and how to enter in to the greatest days in church history. I highly recommend this book. Read it prayerfully and enter new levels of glory.

—Dr. Tim Sheets
Bestselling author of *Angel Armies* and *The New Era of Glory*

Larry Sparks and Ana Werner have put forth a prophetic word that has resonated in my spirit for a number of years. I am delighted that it can now go to the breadth of audience it deserves. What they have written is where God wants to take the church in these coming days. It redefines what we have known of revival and prepares us for the real thing. How many will listen and respond? How many will awaken to the call? Read this book and take seriously its message!

—R. Loren Sandford
Founder and pastor, New Song Fellowship
Author of Understanding Prophetic People and
Visions of the Coming Days

It seems to me that each generation since Adam and Eve in the garden has had to decide what to do about God desiring to walk in the midst of them. God's Presence and glory continue to mark each cycle of history in a way that invites and provokes men and women to have to respond in some way. The testimony of the ages is that when a generation responds to the Presence and glory of God with hunger, submission, and engagement, the goodness of God is evidenced through peace, prosperity, and human flourishing. In retrospect, when the invitation to respond to God's glory is rejected or ignored that generation usually sees war, poverty, and human suffering abound. In *Accessing the Greater Glory*, both Larry Sparks and Ana Werner have captured a fresh invitation of God to this current generation, to discover and engage with God's glory in a fresh way. The prophetic encounters coupled with the biblical principles outlined in this book will inspire and equip you to powerfully engage with this invitation from the Lord. The nations, unbeknownst to them, are waiting for the church to engage into the greater glory so that God's destiny and answers can be translated from heavenly realms into the earth. I trust this book will stir you toward the great works that Jesus promised that we would enter into in this coming hour!

—David Balestri
Executive Leader, Hope Unlimited Church Sydney Australia
New Prophetic Dimension

Larry Sparks' and Ana Werner's enlightening book, *Accessing the Greater Glory*, is a wonderful presentation of the Christian journey from the new birth to the throne room of God with a focus on the process of transformation that must take place in every believer. This road map of the supernatural, glory-saturated pilgrimage is exactly what the body of Christ needs today. Soak in the message of this book and move into the glory realm.

—Joan Hunter
Author/Healing Evangelist
TV host *Miracles Happen!*

Kudos to Larry and Ana for writing a book on how believers should prepare their hearts for awakening so they will be ready for the glorious season that is even now coming upon the church. Prophecy in and of itself is good, of course, but *Accessing the Greater Glory* adds the key practical element of necessary heart preparation on our part. The Lord rewards those who "diligently seek Him." God is searching for individuals who will become committed partners with Him and heed His invitation and plea—"present your bodies a living sacrifice." It is our responsibility to position our hearts and say, "Yes, Lord!" Larry and Ana not only stir up our hunger for more of God, they underscore their prophetic insights by sharing personal God-encounters, explaining scriptural principles and historical background, and revealing the vital connection between Israel and the greater glory. We heartily endorse their book!

—Drs. Dennis and Jennifer Clark
Full Stature Ministries
Authors of *Releasing the Divine Healer Within: Self-Deliverance Made Simple* and *Flowing in the River of God's Will*

"Larry and Ana are going on this trip for one thing, but I have something else for them to receive as well." These were the softly whispered words I believe I heard the Lord say when I saw that my friends, Larry Sparks and Ana Werner, were travelling to Israel. It was, therefore, with great joy that I heard about their God encounters that birthed this timely blueprint for *Accessing the Greater Glory.*

This is more than a book; it is a spiritual roadmap in which Larry and Ana highlight the spiritual signposts they have discovered in their quest to see God's glory cover the earth and His Kingdom manifested in our world. In these pages, they unpack a clear understanding of our current condition as the church, providing valuable insights into the underlying reasons for our delay in realizing the promises of God. What I loved about this book is that they do not leave us there.

Drawing on their prophetic engagements with the Lord, they share how we can begin to move from where we are to the place of the divine promise of greater glory. Walk with Larry and Ana as they unveil prophetic signposts in the Scriptures that mark our journey to *Accessing the Greater Glory.* This book is a fresh invitation from the Father to the church to come into the place that He has prepared for her. The invitation is for today and the invitation is for you!

—Beverley Watkins,
Author of *The Trading Floors of Heaven*

Having had the privilege of being with Larry Sparks and Ana Werner recently in Israel, I witnessed firsthand the dramatic encounters they had with the Lord that led to the incredible revelation that has been captured in this prophetic book. You will literally feel the fire and glory of God as you read and meditate on *Accessing the Greater Glory*!

—Ryan Bruss
Author, *Carrying the Presence*
reviveus.org
Producer, *It's Supernatural!*

This book not only pinpoints issues facing modern-day believers but also provides much-needed solutions on how to access and carry the greater glory of God in our everyday lives. Larry and Ana have created an invaluable tool that speaks to the heart of those wanting to walk in the authority that comes with being a true son or daughter of God.

— Catherine Mullins
Worship leader and recording artist

Accessing the Greater Glory is a book for those who carry an insatiable hunger for the "the More" of God. This book will awaken the reader into the unprecedented journey of the pursuit of the Holy, of the Glory, and the Presence of God in the now. It masterfully draws a revelatory grid and paradigm in understanding the progression of the past, present, and future and our role in this divine intercession that we stand in as a church today, giving language to the potential of the Bride so that she can enter into the promise of the Greater Glory that will inevitably manifest a greater and transformative future.

— Fiorella Giordano
Prophetic voice and founder of 8th Ocean

I couldn't stop reading *Accessing the Greater Glory*! Very few books have an attached tangible anointing on them; this one does! I literally felt the Presence of God come upon me as I was reading it. Thank you, Larry and Ana, for capturing the true heartbeat of our Father!

— Todd Smith
Lead pastor, Christ Fellowship Church, Dawsonville, Georgia
Host pastor to the North Georgia Revival

My good friend, Larry Sparks, and Ana Werner have managed to transform hunger into words. Their new collaboration, Accessing the Greater Glory, is not a book that you would have found on Christian booksellers' shelves in days passed. It simply wasn't time for it yet. As I read the manuscript, I could feel the volley of two hungry hearts flowing in the same current of a glory that is yet to be revealed. One thing is for sure—Larry and Ana are forerunners of the "Greater Glory!"

—John Kilpatrick
Founder and Senior Pastor
Church of His Presence
Daphne, AL

The Holy Spirit is emphasizing the impact that His glory has on our lives. While many people sing about the Glory of God, many do not really understand it. This book is an invitation to come up higher into His glorious Presence.

—Dr. Cindy Jacobs
Generals International
Bestselling author of *Possessing the Gates of the Enemy*

I've had this strange recurring vision of God pulling back huge curtains which have hidden a degree of glory previously unseen. We are in that time when God is going to fling back those curtains. I love this book because it prepares us for that greater revelation of glory. It also relates it to the big picture including Israel. Get ready for the glory tsunami going to overtake the earth by buying a copy of the book and processing it fully!

—Barbara Yoder
Bestselling author of *The Breaker Anointing*

Accessing

THE

Greater
Glory

A Prophetic Invitation to New Realms
of Holy Spirit Encounter

Larry Sparks & Ana Werner

DESTINY IMAGE® PUBLISHERS, INC.
P.O. Box 310, Shippensburg, PA 17257-0310
"Promoting Inspired Lives."

This book and all other Destiny Image and Destiny Image Fiction books are available at Christian bookstores and distributors worldwide.

Cover design by Eileen Rockwell

For more information on foreign distributors, call 717-532-3040.

Reach us on the Internet: www.destinyimage.com.

ISBN 13 TP: 978-0-7684-5293-8

ISBN 13 eBook: 978-0-7684-5294-5

ISBN 13 HC: 978-0-7684-5296-9

ISBN 13 LP: 978-0-7684-5295-2

For Worldwide Distribution, Printed in the U.S.A.

1 2 3 4 5 6 7 8 / 23 22 21 20 19

*The Heavenly Father does not ask for golden vessels.
He does not ask for silver vessels. God asks for yielded
vessels — those who will submit their will to the will of
the Father. And the greatest human attainment in all
the world is for a life to be so surrendered to him that the
name of God almighty will be glorified through that life.*

Kathryn Kuhlman

Dedication

from Larry Sparks

I DEDICATE THIS BOOK to my wife, Mercedes Sparks. Mercedes, you show me what "carrying God's glory" looks like as you live to make the *move of God* tangible, accessible, and transformational. You're my hero and it's the great honor of my life to call you my wife.

Dedication

from Ana Werner

I DEDICATE THIS BOOK to my husband, Sam Werner. Your love is what always carries me through the birthing process of writing a book. You support our family in so many ways that most people don't realize. You are my rock and the backbone to our family and the ministry. You encourage me in every way possible so that I can fly! I am one very blessed woman to be your wife!

Acknowledgments

from Ana Werner

THIS MESSAGE WAS BIRTHED IN ISRAEL, but accessing the glory of God and walking in it daily is something I carried for years really. Israel is a thin place between Heaven and earth and I can't encourage enough for every believer to make a trip there. There is nothing like walking in the very places Jesus walked. It will change your life!

I would like to acknowledge and thank Mr. Sid Roth for inviting me on his Israel tour of 2019 to be a host. What an amazing and life-changing trip that was for so many, including me! Thank you for the way you pursue the supernatural power of God with all your being. You have broken ground that many of us probably don't even realize.

The power of my intercessors who surround and cover me in prayer when I travel and minister is something I cannot go on without recognizing. Thank you for every time you press in to the Lord and pray for me and my family. Your prayers go before me, break ground, and shift the atmosphere to prepare the environment for the move of the Holy Spirit.

Brian Simmons, thank you for the countless hours of research and study you put into translating the Bible into *The Passion Translation*. (I use it many times throughout this book, as I believe it is soaking with revelation!)

I would like to acknowledge my spiritual parents—James Goll, Patricia King, and Tony Kemp. Thank you so much for the ways you have poured into my life, believed in me, encouraged my dreams, and have instilled into me nuggets of Holy Spirit and God-given wisdom. Also, I have to recognize Jill Austin who has passed on to glory. Although I never got to personally meet her when she was alive, her ministry continues to breathe into me freedom with Holy Spirit.

I bless and thank my ministry team that travels with me when their schedule allows—Melissa Shirley, Josiah and Hannah Wyatt. You guys are such warriors for the Lord and I believe the Lord has so much more to birth through you guys!

I acknowledge my husband Sam and his dedication to help me on this project. There were many late nights when I was up writing, and he helped me the following days with our children as I walked around in a zombie-like slumber.

Larry, you are a dear friend. Your heart burns for revival and the glory of God. There is no other person I would want to co-author this book with, and I can't thank you enough.

Destiny Image and team, thank you for editing and putting together our two writings. I have never seen a publishing house work as quickly as this to produce a book in such a short time frame! Way to go guys! Shall we do another?

Acknowledgements

from Larry Sparks

I HAD TWO BOOKS I was in the middle of writing; I thought they were both pretty good, actually! By "good," I sensed a mandate of the Lord to be writing them. Both were sovereignly put on hold, though. Then, this assignment came up as a divine interruption. The Lord had me and my friend, Ana, ministering with Sid Roth on an Israel tour where the Holy Spirit burned into our hearts what's coming and what's possible.

Sid Roth, the Lord has given you language for what this "greater glory" outpouring will look like. Keep describing it. Keep prophesying. It's coming, it's at the door. And every time you talk about it, hearts burn to experience it.

Ana Werner, so grateful for your friendship and your example. As I read through your amazing contribution to this book, you provided clarity and practical instruction on how to make a lifestyle of glory possible. You lived these words long before writing them.

Norman Benz, we have been learning these principles in the "trenches." What an honor to consider you and Judy my spiritual parents and ministry covering.

Ed Silvoso, for your revolutionary book *Ekklesia* that has significantly influenced my perspective on our assignment as the church.

Ryan Bruss, for giving me this amazing assignment.

Bill Johnson, thank you for teaching us how to steward the glory that has come while also faithfully crying out for more. You don't simply teach this; you live this.

Finally, I wish to give honor to Dr. Martyn Lloyd-Jones who I believe wrote one of the definitive books on the subject of experiencing God's glory — *Revival*. Sometimes the "new" is in the old; the greater is in what's been already released. This book is a prophetic blueprint that if read and heeded would get us back on track.

Contents

Foreword

by Sid Roth

I AM SO AMAZED at how many of the same people go on every tour to Israel with me. I understand one time, but not every tour! I began to ask, "Why?" They all say, "Every time I come to Israel with Sid, I hear from God!" The authors of this book, Larry Sparks and Ana Werner, were no exception. What they heard from God in Israel changed their lives forever! Imagine, the publisher of Destiny Image, a major Christian publishing company, saying that this word from God was the most life-changing revelation in his life! It not only profoundly changed Larry's life but also the life of a major prophetess, Ana Werner, too!

Now get ready for the most significant game changer to invade your world. It's called *Accessing the Greater Glory!* Why have I been calling it the "greater glory" for the last three years? Because the display of God's Presence will be greater than any glory the world has ever seen! Smith Wigglesworth, the great signs and wonders evangelist, saw this *greater glory* in a vision. He said it was a thousand-times greater power than anything he had ever seen in his ministry—and he saw the dead rise, the blind see, the deaf hear, and the lame walk! Why is this happening now? Because Jesus wants everyone to know Him quickly. Why? Because He's coming back soon!

—Sid Roth
Host, *It's Supernatural!*

Introduction

From Spiritual Concept to Supernatural Encounter

This book is written by me (Larry Sparks) and my trusted friend, Ana Werner. When it comes to Ana writing something specifically, I will identify it as such. Otherwise, when I reference "I" or "me," it's referring to Larry. The teaching content, however, represents both of our perspectives.

AT SIXTEEN YEARS OLD, I encountered the glory of God's Presence—and have never since recovered. It was not a dramatic or spectacular experience; it was very subtle but profoundly supernatural. Up until that destined summer evening in Palm Beach Gardens, Florida in 1999, I had a spiritual concept of God; however, following that encounter, I was convinced that God was a real Person. He was not a distant, detached cosmic deity; He was real and very near. And if this was indeed true, this meant that I would need to radically reconfigure how I lived my life.

You have to understand, at the time of this encounter, I was intentionally avoiding environments where His Presence might show up (although I didn't have a grid for it quite yet). During this season of spiritual seeking, I would attend the local megachurch because I really enjoyed the practical teaching. However, I really didn't mind if I missed the "praise and worship" segment. Truth be told, I thought the singing, accompanied by enthusiasm and uplifted hands, was a little, well, creepy. Just being honest. But this was a critical juncture in my life where God was sovereignly stirring a hunger and thirst in me for more. I believe that even as you read these pages, your hunger for God is going to intensify. You might be thinking, "Larry, Ana, I *want* to be hungry for God but I am not there yet. I want to pursue Him, but I'm not where I should be." I speak over you right now that the very God you desire to pursue and hunger after is the One who placed the desire within you. So, the good news is that the "want to" is God-planted. If you want to be hungry and thirsty for Him, that's a sure sign He is already moving in your life and summoning you to new places with Him.

Something happens when we simply talk about His glory, His Presence, His power. Whether in conversation or through written word, when we share stories and testimonies of what happens.

From fourth grade onward, I attended a strict Christian school that provoked me to do two things: not to go to hell when I die, and not to miss the rapture if I am alive when Jesus comes back. So basically, I wanted enough of God to miss hell and make the rapture. Otherwise, I wasn't a big fan of the Christian life. I always believed in Jesus (to some degree), but it was at sixteen when everything shifted for me and I became absolutely driven by *One Thing*.

What happened?

One night, I just happened to be present in the church gathering for the praise and worship segment. I'll never forget that during one worship song, I started to feel electricity in my hands and burning in my heart. I so desperately wanted to experience what the lyrics were describing.

So close I believe
You're holding me now
In Your hands I belong
You'll never let me go

As I tangibly felt the Presence of God touch my hands and burn in my chest, from that one, single encounter, I recognized that God was a real Person who could be experienced. I had years and years of informational knowledge about God, but Jesus didn't come to simply give us information *about God*; He came to show us what God the Father was like and then, through the redemptive work of the Cross, provide a bridge to reconnect us to relationship with Him. Jesus actually describes eternal life as an invitation to a present walk of experiential knowledge of God.

In John 17:3, this is how Jesus defines eternal life: *"And this is eternal life, that they know you, the only true God, and Jesus Christ whom you have sent."* This is not intellectual knowledge; this is knowledge that comes through intimate experiential encounter.

In this one moment, I was marked by God. My experience with His Presence, although subtle, launched me into a lifestyle and, ultimately, a ministry that has become dedicated to helping connect people with power encounters with the Holy Spirit. However, my pursuit was new, pure, and yet immature. For many years I sought a "formula" to access this amazing, weighty Presence of God and, furthermore, help bring other people into a similar encounter. It was in April of 2019 when the Holy Spirit gave me a definitive answer on what the "secret formula" was to accessing the glory of God. In short, there was no formula; there was simply an invitation extended from Heaven to Earth. Would I receive this invitation?

No Formulas for the Glory: An Encounter in Israel

In April 2019, I had the honor of serving as a ministry leader on a trip to Israel hosted by Sid Roth, along with my friend Ana Werner. It was my second time being in the Holy Land, and quite truthfully I had no idea what to expect. All of the marketing language leading up to the trip used the phraseology, "An Appointment in Israel." More than catchy marketing, I believe this was a prophetic summons—especially to the authors of the book you are currently reading.

Time prevents me from detailing all of the encounters we had with the Lord while in the Holy Land, but one of the most unusual was while I was lying in bed, simply scrolling through my phone. Nothing particularly spiritual about the setup to this experience, and yet God walked in the room and touched me powerfully. I stumbled upon a worship song I had never heard before. I couldn't even tell you the title or lyrics, but all of a sudden it was as though the lightning of God struck me. I felt something like spiritual fire and force strike my body and I began to shake violently as if I were being electrocuted. Although it was intense, I knew it was the Lord. I just didn't know what He was up to. The power of God surged through me and ultimately knocked me off the bed and onto the floor. As I tried to get up, I felt like I was being pressed down—like my body was too heavy to move. Only in retrospect do I realize that God was depositing something into me, because unusual and intense supernatural encounters are often signposts that we are receiving major deposits from God. This is why they are often so intense— God Himself is literally putting something into you (or awakening something within you).

I wasn't on the floor all that long, but when I did get up, I was quite confused. I had no idea what God was actually doing, as it seemed like quite the random experience. That week, as a group, we enjoyed encounter after encounter with God, from a Holy Spirit-filled boat ride in the Sea of Galilee to a supernatural Passover Seder that closed out the week. It was an hour or so after the encounter, however, that I sat at the hotel desk and started going through several chapters of the Bible that, I believe, the Holy Spirit was highlighting to me. Most of that week, there was one verse I could not escape from. This passage is a key catalyst behind this book. Furthermore, I believe that if we as a church community and as individual followers of Messiah Jesus adhere to the simple principle in this passage, we would absolutely witness the manifestation of God's powerful Presence released into the earth through a glory-filled people.

So, let's start at the end, work our way back, and seek to discover the *protocol* to experiencing His glory. God has a target: *all the earth.* Throughout the whole of Scripture, God reveals His agenda, which is obviously driven by His heart of love. His agenda is to fill the whole earth with His glory. Such statements can be seen throughout the Old Testament, but the real inauguration of their fulfillment came on the Day of Pentecost. Joel prophesied of a day when *all flesh* would experience the outpouring of the Spirit. Not *all church.* Not *all religious people.* Not even *all Pentecostals and Charismatics.* God's agenda for the ages is to fill the entire planet with His glory.

Practically, how will this happen? Simple. It begins with the sons and daughters of God giving their lives to accommodate His movement in the earth.

Two scriptures that have been burning in my spirit on the subject of God's glory and the hour in which we are living:

> *David arranged for Asaph and his fellow Levites to serve regularly before the Ark of the Lord's Covenant, doing whatever needed to be done each day* (1 Chronicles 16:37 NLT).

> *Therefore, I urge you, brothers and sisters, in view of God's mercy, to offer your bodies as a living sacrifice, holy and pleasing to God—this is your true and proper worship* (Romans 12:1 NIV).

You may not think these two passages of Scripture have any level of relationship, but trust me, they do. How do we "serve regularly before the Ark" of God's Presence, doing whatever needs to be done each day? We continually offer up our lives as *living sacrifices.* We are here to please God, not ourselves. And yet, it's in laying down our lives to serve His story that we will experience a fulfillment and satisfaction beyond comprehension. How? When we live for *ourselves*, we are living small lives because *we* are at the center of everything we do; when we live for God and the unveiling of His glory in the earth, we are participating in something that is epic, monumental, and world-changing.

God is seeking people who continually offer up their lives as living sacrifices to Him, recognizing their lives are not their own, they have been bought with the precious blood of Jesus, and they are giving their lives to participating with the movement of God in the earth.

The glory realm of God is exclusive. Yes, highly exclusive. But the invitation to enter into this realm is extended to all believers. It's exclusive because all believers do not receive or accept this invitation to come and give up their lives so that *His life* would be revealed and released in the earth. May we be such a people. Not perfect; perfection is not possible. But may we be a process-able people, ever yielded and submitted to the Master. When we live this way, we become attractive to the fire of God. For many years, the church has been waiting for anointed leaders and ministers to lay hands on us, impart a supernatural gifting, and empower us for greater levels of ministry or effectiveness. The season is shifting. I prophesy this is the hour in which *God Himself* is going to fall upon His people; *He* will begin laying hands on His people, commissioning them as ambassadors and agents of reconciliation into every sphere of influence.

God Is Making His Appeal Through You!

For I hear the Lord say, "I am making My appeal through you! Yes, you are filled with My Spirit, not for conferences and events, but you are filled up so you can be spilled out. You are filled up to be poured out. You are filled and empowered so you can run toward every person, place, and sphere of society that is unredeemed. As one filled with My Spirit, you should be drawn to everything unredeemed. My blood has made provision for every person, place, and thing to be redeemed — brought back to Myself. My blood has paid the price, but I have filled you, I have commissioned you, I have empowered and appointed you to serve as My agents in the earth to facilitate this process." The Lord is calling us to be agents of reconciliation, bringing everything that is disconnected from God back into relationship with Him and agreement with His original purpose.

> *And God has given us this task of reconciling people to him. For God was in Christ, reconciling the world to himself, no longer counting people's sins against them. And he gave us this wonderful message of reconciliation. So we are Christ's ambassadors; God is making his appeal through us. We speak for Christ when we plead, "Come back to God!" For God made Christ, who never sinned, to be the offering for our sin, so that we could be made right with God through Christ* (2 Corinthians 5:18-21 NLT).

Our assignment is to boldly proclaim: "Come back to God!" For the prodigals who have run away from home, *come back to God!* For spheres of influence like the arts, entertainment, science, education, and medicine that were meant to reveal the wisdom, beauty, and goodness of God, we prophesy: *come back to God!* For the ones who are wandering hopelessly through life, not knowing their purpose and furthermore believing they have no hope and are condemned to a life of separation from God because of their sins — *come back to God!*

When a people filled with glory step onto the scene, they push back darkness and simultaneously confront everything that is disconnected from God. Glory reminds people and creation itself of its original state — a state that the blood of Jesus has made full provision to bring us back into.

Our prayer is that as you read this book, you would be provoked.

A Vision of the Coming Glory

During our Supernatural Passover Seder in Israel (April 2019), Ana and I both had a stirring in our spirit. As the meeting escalated and became anything but traditional, I had this vision of God falling upon every person in that building (roughly 400). If the scene in my head would have come to pass, it would have been earthly chaos (AKA: heavenly order). I saw the weighty kabod glory of God falling on each person, increasing and intensifying. I saw people falling on their backs and people falling on their faces, depending on how the Spirit was touching them. I saw tables crashing down, chairs flipping over, and people being absolutely overwhelmed by God.

This didn't happen as I saw in my mind. But it's coming. These scenes will become increasingly common, not because a powerful minister went around laying hands on everyone, praying for spiritual impartation. No. I see the greatest days of glory ahead for us as the people of God, individually and corporately, offer their lives as living sacrifices to God, basically saying: "Lord, use me. I submit and yield to You. It's on Your terms, not mine."

What will happen as we do this?

> *Fire flashed down from heaven and burned up the burnt offerings and sacrifices, and the glorious presence of the Lord filled the Temple* (2 Chronicles 7:1 NLT).

The fire of God always gloriously fills temples that present sacrifices. What happens when the temple *becomes* a sacrifice? A people filled with glory who embrace and fulfill the mandate of God to fill the earth with His glory.

Part One

The Promise

Heaven's original plan was for the people of God to live in the glory, both positionally and experientially. The glory is both Heaven's perfect standard and supernatural atmosphere. When sin took place, humanity fell from the glory. Traditionally, we interpret this as mankind missing the mark through sin and falling from God's standard of perfection. This is one dimension. The other dimension, which must be recaptured, is the experiential realm of glory that mankind was meant to dwell in. The cross restored the standard of glory by putting humanity in right relationship with God; it also restored the realm of glory by filling redeemed humanity with the Person of the Holy Spirit!

1

"Order in My Church"

IN THE SPIRIT, I saw a judge's gavel slamming down with force. We've all seen the movies where, in the classic courtroom scenes, there is an unruly crowd making a ruckus, and in order for the judge to bring a sense of sanity he would slam his gavel down, declaring: "Order in the court." I sense there is a parallel taking place in the spirit realm, as God is presently calling His church into *Holy Spirit order.*

We are in a season of exciting, yet urgent transition. In this catalyst moment, I believe the gavel is slamming down in the courtroom of Heaven. I don't see the Father doing this in a spirt of anger, but more so beckoning us to partake of His banqueting table when, for too long, we've settled for crumbs. He's calling us to feast when we've lived content—and yet, dissatisfied—on religious morsels.

What brand of order is the Lord looking for? An order that accommodates the unrestrained, uninhibited movement of His Holy Spirit. The Scriptures urge us: *"Do not quench the Spirit"* (1 Thess. 5:19). This means that the movement of the Spirit can indeed be quenched or stifled. I know His movement is unusual. I know when the Spirit touches people, their reactions are often uncomfortable. Loud. Emotional. Sometimes dramatic. We often ask, *is that person just acting in the flesh?*

Can I be real with you? It's *always* the flesh. When people laugh, cry, shake, tremble, or fall down when being touched by the Spirit, it is always a response of the flesh. It's an evidence of a flesh and blood person being touched by the Spirit's power. The flesh is always responding to God's movement. Here's where we need to evaluate and be pastoral: either the flesh is responding or manufacturing. We either authentically respond to a genuine touch of God, or we try to make something up to appear spiritual. Regardless of the good, bad, and ugly, we cannot shut down the Spirit in fear of the few who will either manufacture an experience or be offended by the experience. I promise, it's always the minority; the majority is either curious or absolutely desperate for an encounter with God.

A Vision of Holy Spirit Order

More than simply teaching me this concept, the Lord decided to personally illustrate it to me. In doing so, I am convinced that He gave me a clear vision of what the coming revival will look like.

During a conference me and my spiritual father, Dr. Norman Benz, hosted in Florida, I experienced something very unusual. After praise and worship, there was a strong sense of God's manifest Presence — one of those glorious moments where the Omnipresent One decides to localize Himself in our midst. The Holy Spirit was moving among us in great power, touching people very deeply. I was the person responsible for facilitating the meeting, so I was consulting with the Holy Spirit as this scenario unfolded.

God started to fall upon people — not in an extremely demonstrative manner, but through beautiful yet powerful subtle touches. I could discern that the Holy Spirit was moving in personal, profound ways across the group. I opened the front of the church for whoever sensed the Holy Spirit's Presence was moving upon them. Several came forward. Some knelt. Some wept. Some simply laid down on the ground. God was at work and it was beautiful. Here is where I caught Heaven's vision for the coming revival.

I assumed I knew what to do next. Never assume you know what God wants to do. In fact, the greatest place to "arrive at" in the middle of the Spirit's movement is a place of feeling completely unschooled. It's amazing the level of education God offers us in these sacred moments, as we commit to trust His leading each step of the way. Even so, I started to assume. Surely I had facilitated enough renewal services to know that this is where we "throw out the program" and yield to the Holy Spirit, right? *Wrong.*

Give the Spirit Space...
and He Will Fill It!

The Lord told me to keep the meeting going. Keep preaching. Continue on with the program. Nothing changed, except one key, integral element—the very thing that will either mean Holy Spirit outpouring or a continued deluge into dead religion. Even though I continued with the preaching segment, the Lord instructed me to encourage the people who were at the altar to stay there as long as the Spirit was touching them. Even further, I gave an invitation for people to come forward *during the message* as the Lord was touching them. So, I preached *while* people continued to be touched by God and come forward. This is where our paradigm needs to shift. Most of us would consider this kind of "interruption" distracting. However, we need to allow what was once distracting to become celebrated.

I see the Lord creating this same atmosphere in churches across the United States, as He ushers us into embracing an unrestricted move of His Spirit.

Some people need a message; some people need an encounter.

Some people need a sermon from a pulpit; some people simply need to meet God on the carpet.

This is a beautiful picture of the coming revival. There are many churches where both leaders and communities are desperate for a fresh outpouring of the Spirit. They desire God to move powerfully in their unique contexts, even with multiple services, parking lot attendees to navigate, children's ministry to facilitate, and programs to maintain. I believe the Lord is saying that *programs are not the enemy*. Preaching and sermons are not bad. Hosting multiple services is not the issue, either.

Programs are not bad; however, programs (or anything else) can become deadly when they serve as substitutes for the Spirit's Presence. No atmosphere that man can create — top-notch sanctuaries, impressive lights, the latest high-tech media, the best kids' programs — can substitute for the Holy Spirit.

This is where the invitation becomes increasingly uncomfortable. Yet, I believe it is being extended in this hour with great mercy and tremendous urgency. The Lord is *not* looking for you to abandon preaching, program, and protocol. No. Rather, the Lord is asking you to give the Holy Spirit space. This is order from Heaven's vantage point. Will we hear and respond to the gavel of Heaven, as God calls us into *His order*?

What Did Paul Really Mean by "Decently and in Order"?

For too long, Paul's instructions at the conclusion of First Corinthians 14 have been used to restrain, not release the Holy Spirit. Even in classical Pentecostal or Charismatic churches, we are witnessing more and more of an unbiblical sensitivity to the uncomfortable movements of the Spirit. As soon as the unusual begins to take place, someone brings up First Corinthians 14:40, "*But all things should be done decently and in order*," as a wet blanket to throw over the Spirit's fire.

Make no mistake, this is a very valid principle, but I sense that the Lord is looking for those on earth who would embrace what order looks like from a heavenly perspective. In the verse right before the "decently and in order" instruction, Paul boldly admonishes: "*So, my brothers, earnestly desire to prophesy, and do not forbid speaking in tongues"* (1 Cor. 14:39).

Order from Heaven's vantage point looks very different from our earthly, comfortable, neat and tidy concept of order.

Creating Atmospheres Where Life Is Birthed

A birthing room in a hospital does not really communicate the pristine, clean image of "decently and in order." Nevertheless, the beauty of the life that comes forth on the other side of the often-chaotic delivery process is totally worth it. The Lord is looking for those, in this hour, who want to see birth take place. Yes, the birth of souls, but also the birth and advancement of the Kingdom. I sense that as we give the Spirit space to release the power of the Kingdom— signs and wonders, healing, miracles, deliverance, gifts of the Spirit, touches from Heaven, visions, dreams, and supernatural encounters—a thirsty *world* will take notice. People who don't know God are not looking for the world repackaged when they come to our churches and gatherings; quite the opposite, they are looking for the otherworldly and supernatural. The problem is that the supernatural has been unnatural for so long that what *should* be "decently and in order" has become seen as chaotic, messy, and disorderly. This needs to change.

God's invitation to His church right now is to freely give the Holy Spirit space; when we give the Spirit space, He *will* fill it. Where are those who would put out the *welcome* mat for Him? Where are those who refuse to merely *tolerate* manifestations of His Presence but celebrate them?

We can keep the protocol, but I believe God wants to move within this infrastructure. Are we okay with giving Him space to do this? Are we okay with people coming to the altars during praise and worship? During our sermons? Are we okay with welcoming this phenomenon and not stifling it? Are we okay with celebrating the unique and unusual ways the Spirit might be touching people? Some may laugh. Others might cry. Some may dance, shake, or tremble, while others fall or lay down. God is not asking for some Charismatic free-for-all; He is, however, looking for those willing to welcome and navigate the movement of the Spirit, as *He* is ultimately the Guest of Honor. If there is indeed a "seeker" in our gatherings, it is the Holy Spirit, as He is seeking out people to radically touch and transform.

Are you hungry for outpouring?

Desperate for revival?

Praying for another Pentecost?

Look no further than the sacred Treasure of Heaven you house in the temple of your mortal body. I've got good news. The Holy Spirit is not coming down from Heaven again. Jesus is, yes, but the Spirit has already been given. Our job is to steward His Presence well.

We will experience revival in the church and release outpouring to the world around us to the degree that we say an unqualified "Yes" to the order of the Holy Spirit. Let's all commit to welcome the Spirit's activity on God's terms, not our own.

A Glimpse of What's Coming

I saw a glimpse of what's coming to the church. This was not through some kind of ethereal open-heaven vision or dream of the night.

During the meeting I described at the beginning of this chapter, I'll never forget how people started coming forward to the altar. They knelt, laid down, fell prostrate—there were many different physical postures of divine encounter taking place in that moment. *This is where I saw a glimpse of the coming revival.* This is where God showed me what's on the horizon. God wants His visitation to be welcome during our meetings, gatherings, and church services. We need to make sacred space for divine encounters not to be tolerated, but celebrated. Even for Charismatic/Spirit-empowered churches, there has been the tendency to marginalize the Spirit's move because of the "mess" it can cause. Therefore, we have "encounter" services or back rooms we take people into if they are being touched by God (and there is a place for both of these!). I say it again—God wants both. He wants the protocol, yes. He is totally okay with the program. But if protocol and program distract us from experiencing His Presence, what can be life-giving will become an agent of death. At the day's end, our meetings do Christians a grave injustice if we leave them with concepts instead of encounters. Your Monday morning—your job, your school, your family, your gym—doesn't need a concept, it needs an encounter. Your Sunday must remind you of what—and more importantly, *who*—you carry into your 9 to 5, 24/7 life. God is giving us a powerful new picture of what He is expecting out of "Sunday." I saw this before my eyes and was absolutely gripped.

For the weeks and months leading up to our event, I had a sense in my spirit that the conference (I have been describing in this chapter) would be a "history making" event. Granted, we want to believe that all of our conferences, events, and meetings will fit this description, but I legitimately sensed something unusual about what God was going to accomplish during this time. Thus, my eyes and ears were open. When you have an unusual sense and stirring about God getting ready to do something extraordinary, live in a state of spiritual readiness. Most likely, the Holy Spirit has something very specific He wants to do and share.

For me, it was this: We are living in a day when church has been programmed down to the millisecond. The worship team's next note can be predicted and timed out. The next service is a mirror image of the previous five services. Our order and structure is upheld as supreme and standard. And yet, in the midst of all the evangelical hustle and bustle, a generation is left discontent and disenfranchised with "church as usual." Even with our impressive sanctuaries, elaborate set designs, light shows, Broadway-caliber productions, and trimmings, there is a significant gap that can only be filled by the Presence of a Person. Remember, the details are not problematic *if* accommodating the Holy Spirit is our supreme objective. If, on the other hand, adapting the Spirit's agenda to suit our needs becomes our driving motivation, things are severely out of order. Even though there is a common perspective that motivates the contemporary church urging, "You'll win a generation when you mirror contemporary culture with Christian packaging," I do believe that such a thought process is deceiving—no, destructive.

What Do We Really Offer?

Even this idea that the church needs to appeal to the "world" in order to *bring the world in* is outlandish. The world is not seeking the "world repackaged"; the world is seeking the otherworldly, and they are desperately searching for its expression in our sanctuaries. There used to be something otherworldly about stained-glass sanctuaries. Now, in an age of technology, innovation, and progressive thinking, we've exchanged the stained-glass for a hipper, cooler model. The implications are infinitely deeper than traditional versus modern; in the same way traditional churches can be labeled as "dead," I would contend that many modern churches are equally devoid of Holy Spirit life. It's not the sermon series. It's not the media. It's not the coffee shop. It's not the children's program. It's not the size of the sanctuary. It's not if the pastor has a New York Times bestselling book or his program is one of the top ten on Christian television. None of it matters; these things are neither forces for good or evil. Things become distorted when we exchange Holy Spirit manifestation for man-crafted entertainment. When the center of our gatherings is offering people a church experience instead of a dynamic encounter with a Person called God, we truly need what we call *revival*. Remember, a concept that we learn about during a Sunday morning lesson will not sustain people on Monday. If we are going to truly *tell the world* about Jesus, mere words will not suffice. Jesus is not a concept that we've been commissioned to argue people into accepting. No, He is a Person who we've been given the distinct honor of representing and *introducing*. We simply do the introduction, step back, and watch Holy Spirit do the rest.

This is not so much a book directed to people outside of the church as it is to the Christians—the pastors, leaders, and believers—who know that we need *more* than we currently are experiencing and offering. This is true. We, as people, have so little to offer; He, on the other hand, is the One who satisfies every need. Amazing how we give our lives to preserving a culture that offers crumbs from the table when, in fact, the Master has set before us a banqueting table. Problem? For too long, we've been made nervous by what takes place when people actually *taste and see that the Lord is good* (see Ps. 34:8).

Are We Waiting for a "Suddenly" from Heaven?

During the Friday night meeting I've been describing so far, I caught a vision for the coming glory. In short, God is not saying that we are to throw out our methods, programs, agendas and protocols. Some radically preach this, and while I see where they are coming from—a call to return to the supernatural simplicity of the primitive church—I do truly see merit in what many contemporary churches are doing. Maybe I don't agree with certain focuses or points of emphasis—doesn't matter. I am not God's appointed heresy-hunter or church critic. I never want to be known as the guy who points out the flaws of every minister, leader, or church, as we all have issues. The goal of this book is not to be some kind of "dig" at the church; far from it. These words are purposed to call the community of God to embrace the *more* He has made available. It's not magical or mystical. It's not some sovereign happening that will fall upon us *suddenly* without provocation. While God does often work in "suddenly" ways, the outpouring of the Spirit is *no longer* a suddenly. His first coming was a "suddenly" moment on the Day of Pentecost so that you and I could freely walk in the fullness of His power today.

I saw a vision of how God wants to actually take the existing "wineskin" of church culture and revolutionize it, *without* absolutely dismantling everything. So I ask you, please receive this book for what it is — one invitation among many that the Lord is raising up in this hour. The purpose is not to criticize or condemn, but to *call*. Criticism and complaint only agree with the devil, as they do nothing to proactively change the problem at hand. My heart is to simply be a voice that calls us *all* into new heights, depths, and realms of encounter with the Holy Spirit. Criticism will never be the catalyst that summons us into the unimaginable glories that Heaven desires the Bride of Christ to walk in during this hour that is pregnant with opportunity. Criticism complains, but the call summons. Criticism continues to focus on the problem, while the call gives a picture of Heaven's solution. May we all, individually and corporately, pursue Heaven's full inheritance in the days that lay ahead.

After all, these are days that God *Himself* prophesied about.

Ana Werner

The Throne Room

Standing before the throne room, there was only one thing I could do in response, and that was to cry out *holy*. I had the opportunity this past year to be baptized in the Jordan River in Israel, and what took place that day at the Jordan was unlike any experience I have had before. Although this was not my first time to get glimpses and walk into places in Heaven, the amount of fire I felt that day that radiated from the throne of God almost took me out.

As I came out of the water and stood there shaking under the power of God, I had to lean on my two brothers in Christ who were there to hold me up. Although I knew I was present with them, all I could do was see the light that was so bright and fire falling from that throne. The power of God that fell felt like literal electricity was pulsating through my body from head to toe. The combination of the fire and glory of God left me physically shaking for days. I was unable to stop it, even if I wanted to. Even now, as I ponder on what happened to me that day, I feel the thick and weighty Presence of God come over me. I pray you, beloved reader, will feel it too.

While I believe that we have stepped into a wonderful time in church history where we are getting a greater understanding of just how accessible the glory realm of God is and what it means to carry the Spirit of Jesus inside of us, the fear of the Lord does need to come back to the church.

As Moses encountered the Presence and glory of God as the Lord descended in a cloud and stood there with him on Mount Sinai, we have to look at Moses' response in that moment.

> *Moses made haste to bow low toward the earth and worship. He said, "If now I have found favor in Your sight, O Lord, I pray, let the Lord go along in our midst, even*

though the people are so obstinate, and pardon our iniquity and our sin, and take us as Your own possession" (Exodus 34:8-9 NASB).

And then, God responds to Moses' heart posture: *"Behold, I am going to make a covenant"* (Exod. 34:10 NASB). Here we see God making covenant with man, which is actually pretty amazing! Moses' bowing down and worshiping God when His Presence fell, and the humility he carried, causes a covenant to be made that would change the course of history. So then, the question is, can we move God's heart? The importance of our heart's posture does matter to God.

He is holy. I remember as I stood there at the Jordan shaking and the fire, light, and power of God was pulsating through my body that day, although I was right up there in Heaven, somewhere off in the distance I could hear my own voice crying out, "Holy, holy, holy! He is so holy!" The revelation of how holy God is and how impure I was before Him in that moment marked me. He is the purest of *pure*, spotless and without sin. He is *love*. The revelation of just how much I needed Him also hit me.

When you get a taste of glory, it burns away all your flesh. He requires everything. He takes possession. Often we think of "possession" as a negative thing in the church, when actually it is to be a beautiful interlocked relationship with *Love* Himself.

> *Abide in Me, and I in you. As the branch cannot bear fruit of itself unless it abides in the vine so neither can you unless you abide in Me. I am the vine, you are the branches; he who abides in Me and I in him, he bears much fruit, for apart from Me you can do nothing* (John 15:4-5).

2

The Altar: A Place of Living Sacrifice

Therefore, I urge you, brothers and sisters, in view of God's mercy, to offer your bodies as a living sacrifice, holy and pleasing to God — this is your true and proper worship (Romans 12:1 NIV).

Fire doesn't fall on empty alters. There has to be a sacrifice on the altar for the fire to fall. If you want the fire of God, you must become the fuel of God. —Tommy Tenney

I Got Kicked Off of Mount Carmel…

DURING OUR TRIP TO ISRAEL in 2019, one of my favorite places to visit was Mount Carmel, the site of the epic confrontation between the impotent prophets of Baal and the Living God. The part of the mountain we visited was home to a monastery and church. The grounds were beautifully manicured, the view was stunning, and the atmosphere was spiritually rich. I'm convinced that the altar Elijah rebuilt thousands of years ago still creates a *thin place* between Heaven and earth, for God has historically responded to altars.

Along with the forty-four people who were on my bus, we were looking for a place where I could share what the Lord was stirring in my spirit. That whole trip, He was placing an unusual emphasis on the power of an altar. The tour guide encouraged me to lead the group into a little room that seemed made for a mini church service.

It had a pulpit, along with pew-like seating. Perfect! Everyone gathered together, we adjusted the frequencies of our headsets, and then I started to share what I felt the Holy Spirit was saying. All of a sudden, the Spirit of the Lord filled that mini church. I began walking around praying for people, prophesying over them, and enjoying the intensifying glory that was filling that room.

Then, all of a sudden, a very perturbed-looking man came running in, pointing to the sign right behind me: *No Explanations!*

What's the point of this humorous story? There was still a powerful residue of God's Presence on this mountain. I know we typically recognize Carmel for the confrontation between Elijah and the prophets of Baal, but I want to propose to you a much grander significance to this sacred place:

> *Then Elijah said to all the people, "Come near to me." And all the people came near to him. And he repaired the altar of the Lord that had been thrown down* (1 Kings 18:30).

I am convinced that right here in this passage, we witness the *secret* of creating a lifestyle that is attractive to the glory and fire of God. Many people are waiting for prayers of impartation and hands to be laid on them—all of which is good and helpful—when in fact, the fire of God is waiting for lives that become altars.

Altar. It's a word we don't use too much in twenty-first century society, outside of religious language. Even when it comes to contemporary Christianity, the concept of an "altar" is often relegated to a period of time during an evangelistic service or outreach when an "altar call" is given for people to come forward and respond to the message. Most often, this would involve people surrendering their lives to Jesus, either for the first time or in rededication. In short, we have narrowly defined an "altar" as a place in the front of a church sanctuary where we make a spiritual decision. While this is an incomplete definition, the concept of *making a decision* is very much tied to what takes place at the altar. Who are we giving our lives to? And furthermore, whose influence do we want to live under?

In the weeks prior to writing this chapter, I was provoked to reconsider the transaction that occurs at an altar. I remember hearing Robert Henderson teach something very unusual, and yet it made perfect sense to me. He said that there are certain people or places that seem to have "easy access" to the Presence of God. As a result, they make it easy for other people around them to experience this glory. *The reason for this is because they have built altars.* And there is no shortcut to building a life that is saturated in the glory of God. You cannot fast-forward past the altar. There are people who minister out of the anointing, which contains a level of power. This is in the indwelling Holy Spirit who inhabits every single believer. They lay hands on the sick, cast out demons, and move in signs and wonders because the gift of God, the Holy Spirit, is working through them. This is one level. However, these people typically don't have the ability to seamlessly usher people into transformational encounters with God's glory. You can't microwave or fast track this. You can have all of the impartation you want and attend every single crusade, conference, or revival service, but without the altar this lifestyle is unattainable and unsustainable.

What does this look like?

People Who Build Altars

To simplify further, maybe there are people you know personally, or ministry leaders you've admired, who seem to "carry" an undeniable Presence of God that makes it easy for those sitting under their ministry to connect with the Holy Spirit. I am so grateful for all of the heroes of the faith who have served as catalysts for Holy Spirit encounter—but their examples are meant to invite all believers to *become the altar.*

This is what we are moving toward collectively—a culture where it's no longer *this minister* or *that leader* who exudes this precious anointing. Every believer can be and should be a resting place for the Holy Spirit. The question is, what creates this? A lifestyle of building altars. In other words, a continuous death to self and further yielding to God. Those who are living now, or those who have lived in generations past, who seem to carry that unusual ability to connect people with God's Presence easily are those who paid the price, saying yes to God and no to their own preferences and priorities. As you will discover reading this volume, there are no shortcuts to living saturated by His glory. Fire is always drawn to sacrifice.

Every great leader who has helped shape church history had to die to themselves and say an unqualified yes to God.

The Protestant Reformation catalyzed by Luther and Calvin was met with tremendous resistance by the religious establishment. The reformers were branded heretics and any semblance of a reputation they had was demolished.

In the Great Awakenings, the revivalists had to often preach outside in open-air fields because the traditional churches rejected them.

The Azusa Street Revival of 1906, which birthed the Pentecostal movement, confronted racial tensions and stirred global controversy for the rediscovery of Holy Spirit baptism, particularly with the gift of speaking in tongues.

Brownsville and Toronto, the great revival movements of the mid-1990s, were met with tremendous controversy because of the "manifestations" that occurred while people were touched by the Holy Spirit. Yet, the leaders continued to say "Yes" to what God was doing. Resultantly, millions around the globe were renewed and transformed.

Kathryn Kuhlman has been quoted saying that she "died a thousand deaths" prior to operating in the healing anointing that she was recognized for. She immediately rejected any notion that she was a faith healer or that she had any supernatural powers in and of herself. More than being known in the earth for her dynamic miracle ministry, Kuhlman was known in Heaven for being a friend of the Holy Spirit. That friendship made the sacrifices bearable. *My Utmost for His Highest* author, Oswald Chambers, captures the essence of this: "You must be willing to be placed on the altar and go through the fire; willing to experience what the altar represents—burning, purification, and separation for only one purpose—the elimination of every desire and affection not grounded in or directed toward God. But you don't eliminate it, God does."

Any notable leader who is operating with integrity and purity and also bringing people into encounters with the Holy Spirit has given their lives to building altars for the Lord. Don't let the language of the altar offend your New Covenant paradigm. Jesus forever will be the eternal, sufficient sacrifice for the sins of the world. We are not building altars to make atonement for our sins. We are not building altars to try to make ourselves more acceptable to God.

Places of Sacrifices, Portals of Passage

What are two functions of contemporary, New Covenant altars? They are places of sacrifice and portals of passage. Sacrifices are not just us laying something down; they involve transactions where people in the natural realm grant a right of passage for invisible entities to transition from the invisible realm into the visible. This is obviously something that those in other nations understand, as you will often hear of people establishing altars in front of their cities dedicated to all manner of demonic deities. There is no neutral middle ground when it comes to the forces that we grant passage to through altars. We either open heavenly gates, partnering with God and all of His angelic forces to bring His purposes to pass in the earth, or we open demonic gates, partnering with Satan and evil spirits causing their agenda to be enforced in the earth. Both realms seek a sacrifice, for it's a sacrifice that opens a spiritual right of passage.

While there are nations where people are providing primitive "blood" sacrifices to these demonic entities, the more common (and perhaps more insidious) reality in modern society is an everyday person giving their lives either to the service of God or the service of self. "Service of self" doesn't sound as destructive or malignant as building an altar to a demonic entity, but it's just as dangerous. Remember, there is no middle ground. We either partner with God or we partner with darkness through the altars we build and the sacrifices we make.

Places That Are Altars

Moments ago, I referenced people who create altars and, in turn, make it easy for others to experience the Holy Spirit. As living sacrifices, these individuals have made their lives attractive to and compatible with the fire of God. Plain and simple. The good news is that every believer can do this!

Furthermore, there are also "thin places," like Israel and specifically Mount Carmel, where one can still experience a residue of the manifestation of God's glory that was present there at one time because it was so powerfully pronounced. That place was saturated by divine Presence, and as a result it still carriers a "lingering glory." We are never to treat places like shrines, as if they have power in and of themselves. They don't. Any residue of Holy Spirit Presence on a place has everything to do with the move of God that took place there. It carries residue because it hosted the person of the Holy Spirit. To the degree that we host the Holy Spirit, we too can become saturated in the glory of God. Later in the book, we will give you practical instruction on what it looks like to *host* the Holy Spirit in your everyday life.

When People Become Places

I pray that the Holy Spirit stirs an anticipation within you— what your life could look like if it was given wholly and completely to God. I heard a minister recently say he preferred the word "antic-ipation" because expectation is limited. We expect God to move, but often our expectations come with parameters and limitations. We expect Him to do something specific, and if He moves contrarily to our expectations, we are apt to write off what God did or miss what He is doing. He didn't move in accordance with our expectations, and thus we second guess whether He moved to begin with.

Right now, I pray the Holy Spirit stirs within you an anticipation for what a yielded, surrendered life could look like. We are mov-ing toward this. The visions and experiences shared in this volume are meant to whet your spiritual appetite for what's possible. God doesn't dangle carrots in front of His people; if He reveals some-thing to us, then He fully intends on bringing what He reveals to pass. The key is we don't become idle following His revelation. When God reveals His intentions to us, it's an invitation to partner with Him in intercession and action.

I was anticipating something that I thought I would see…but have not yet. While in Israel, Sid Roth hosted a supernatural Passover Seder, perhaps the most unusual and wonderful of its kind. In the spirit, I sensed that the evening was moving toward some kind of big Holy Spirit crescendo. I thought something was going to happen. I had this vision of God powerfully falling on the people who were gath-ered there. No need for hands to be laid on them—just boom, the Spirit of God falling and wonderful holy chaos erupting. We tasted it in part, but did not see the full manifestation. Why? It might be the very thing holding back people and churches from experiencing this manifestation of greater glory. We are waiting for God when God is waiting for us.

Two Dimensions of Outpouring

Before moving on, you need to understand two dimensions about Holy Spirit outpouring and revival. One dimension is personal; one is corporate. The vision of this book is to ignite *personal* revival in you so you can become a contributor to what God is doing corporately.

When I write about "not waiting" on God for outpouring, I am referring to your life personally. *We* become the altar. *We*, like the woman with the issue of blood, reach out to touch Jesus. *We* draw near to God and approach His throne boldly, praying for the Spirit to ignite our hearts with His fire.

When it comes to corporate revival, there is a very important sovereign element that we cannot manufacture. When a church or region experiences what we typically define as "revival," there is a "suddenly" that God releases from Heaven. Pastor John Kilpatrick, who hosted and led two globally impacting moves of God—the Brownsville Revival and the Bay Revival—put it this way: "You cannot and must not kick start a revival." Every major move of the Spirit that has shaped history was the result of a divine collision of God's sovereignty and man's stewardship, ultimately producing a "suddenly" outpouring. Kilpatrick further expressed to me that "when it comes to a move of God, you must have the following: 1) prayer, 2) preparation of a people, 3) positioning of the correct leadership, and 4) waiting for the set time."

Now, I bring you to the other side of the spiritual tension of revival. We wait, but we also press in right now. I want to see the "Big *R*" revival. Also, I want to see everyday people press in to experience new levels of God's glory. We are often waiting for a person to pray for us or an event's hype to "take us to that place" spiritually, when in fact God is waiting for a life that completely yields to Him. There is no formula or shortcut to this in your personal life. Fire has and will always be attracted to that which was slain on the altar. Jesus' ultimate sacrifice made provision for the fire of God to fall from Heaven on the Day of Pentecost; now, in order to walk in this fire on a regular basis, we need to align ourselves with the cross. We offer ourselves, as Paul wrote, as *living sacrifices*, human beings who continue to inhale and exhale oxygen and yet, while doing so, offering every breath we have to the Lord and His service. He's not looking for physically dead people. This is why Paul called it being a *living sacrifice,* people who are physically alive but their lives are not their own.

3

Becoming an Altar

To be a living sacrifice demands all-out surrender to the ways of the Lord. I want Ana to jump in and share about what it looks like to live as a surrendered sacrifice.

Surrendered: Jump in and Swim

NOW, I REALIZE that not everyone reading this has had an encounter with the Presence of God in the same way I did at my baptism in Israel. That is totally fine! He is a personal God who touches us all differently and uniquely. What happened to me at the Jordan River that day as I encountered the throne room left me unable to walk normally for the rest of the trip (three days).

Becoming an Altar Means Surrendering to the Unusual Ways God Moves

I have sat on the skeptical side as well, so if you are reading this and are thinking: "Hold up? What is she talking about! Could this really be real, or is this just her made-up experience?" I reassure you, I have had those thoughts as well before. So, skeptics, I am not offended in the least bit, as I have been there.

I remember being in a revival environment before, and sitting back observing. The tangible Presence of God was very thick in that place. There were some who had true encounters with God's Presence, and others I believe were just making up the hype for some kind of weird self-glorification or spiritual attention. The difference was unmistakable. Heaven encounters are amazing, but I am more interested to see and hear about encounters that result in good fruit and point to Jesus.

Can you relate at all? Or perhaps you have had a similar experience before where you have seen God move. The opportunity is always there to sit on the sidelines and observe in amazement, criticize in disbelief, or jump in the river and swim with the move of God. That being said, I do believe we are to be wise and only engage in things that are the Lord, so being critical is not necessarily a bad thing; we need to be discerning, as the Bereans were in the book of Acts.

Larry jumping in for a moment.

The very reputable Holman Christian Standard Bible translates the Scripture this way: "*The people here* [the Bereans] *were more open-minded than those in Thessalonica, since they welcomed the message with eagerness and examined the Scriptures daily to see if these things were so*" (Acts 17:11). Two interesting factors right there. Yes, they examined the Scriptures to make sure what was being taught was correct, but they were commended for being "open-minded." We need to surrender to the move of the Holy Spirit, being open to the unusual ways He moves and operates. We cannot be quick to shut something down because it challenges the way we've always thought or experienced something. The key litmus test is the Scripture.

Back to Ana.

Being critical is a bad thing if it becomes a hindrance for us to be able to jump into something that the Lord is doing, which we might have no previous experience in.

The disciples experienced this phenomenon regularly with Jesus: He would call them to surrender to some very unusual assignments. "You feed them," Jesus commanded the disciples as they looked over the crowd of over 5,000 people. "But...but...we don't have enough food!" the disciples reasoned with Jesus. "Well, here's what we are going to do," Jesus responded, surely with a twinkle in His eyes (see Matt. 14:16-21).

I know I'm paraphrasing the Scripture a bit, but isn't that how it is for us with God often?

"But God, this is how I prefer You to show up and move! This is what's normal and comfortable!" And Jesus looks at us, "Come on now! Have a little faith? Do you trust Me? Step out of your box."

Trust is the issue at hand when it comes to moving into new realms of glory or new territory with the Lord. "God, I don't understand fully, but I know this is You. I asked You to be the leader of my life, so I relinquish my control right now, and just say have Your way in me!" That's true trust. It's a place of resting even in the unknown, because you know your Father and that He has good things for you.

Becoming an Altar Means Being Undone in His Glory

After I was baptized in the Jordan, my friends had to hold me up by each of my arms as I was seeing only the throne room and was shaking.

Larry writing now.

This is absolutely true, as I was one of the friends summoned to help hold Ana up. What God was doing in her life was holy, pure, and real. It's not new or strange. Both the Old and New Testament accounts are filled with people who encountered God and physically they were changed. Altered. Immobilized. They fell. They shook. If the "hills melt like wax" at His Presence, the earth "trembles" at His gaze, and mountains bow at His Name, surely when frail human flesh encounters His Presence, something is going to happen. It's just spiritual science! (See Psalm 66:4; 97:5; 104:32; Nahum 1:5; Micah 1:4.) Martyn Lloyd-Jones made this observation concerning revival phenomena: "We must not be interested in, nor frightened of phenomena," referring directly to people falling under the power of God. "I am pointing out to you that God himself has said that the glory is so glorious that men's physical frame is inadequate. So don't be surprised when you read the reports of people fainting, or going off into some kind of dead swoon, it is a measure of God's glory."[1] This is what Ana is describing, and this is what the both of us—and countess others throughout church history—have experienced in God's glorious Presence.

Back to Ana.

I even had to have help getting dressed that day by an IDF soldier. Then my friends had to help me walk to the bus, as I was still shaking under the Presence of God. For the following days, I couldn't walk without shaking. If people touched me or would brush up against me, they would often fall back feeling and encountering the Presence of God that was doing a work in me. It was the strangest thing, if I am to be completely honest! It seemed like I had no control and had to humbly rely on my brothers and sisters to help me as God kept moving in waves of power through my body.

I remember having an inner dialogue with God during this encounter. "God this is ridiculous! Can't I just have my legs back so I can walk?" He responded: "Will you really let Me have My way, whatever that may look like, Ana?" "Okay, I surrender," I said as I continued puttering and stumbling along. I remember one sweet lady offered to follow me around the breakfast line and carry my plate of food and water, as she saw all my food sloshing around side to side as I attempted to steady my balance.

Larry here again.

One more thing. One lesson Ana and I both learned in Israel is that a dramatic encounter with God like this is often the sign of a commissioning—the deployment of a new assignment. I believe this is why people need to encounter His glory. To know Him as Moses did, but then, to make Him known.

Ana writing.

Let me put it in perspective. As a seer, I experienced the greatest amount of breakthrough with the seer realm being opened to me when I was a missionary in the country of Brazil. I was living in the drug trafficking slums of Belo Horizonte, mostly working as a missionary with only Brazilians. I didn't have the option of leisurely learning the language—Portuguese. Picking up the language quickly felt like a survival tool! So, there I found myself, struggling just to figure out how explain that I needed to buy more toothpaste, and asking where I could buy that. And toilet paper! Well I won't even go there, but you can imagine that reenactment!

The point is this: Like a baby, I had to relearn everything. It was so humbling. I came to the country with college degrees to my name, years of study and experience behind me, and there I was having to act out my need for toothpaste—like a child! I had to go low and ask people for help every minute, it felt like, and to please teach me how to function in Brazil. Everything was different, even including their hours of sleep and daily schedules. I had to throw out everything I knew about how to survive and thrive in my home country of America and learn their ways and figure out my own heart in the middle of that.

And there, God opened so much to me. The way I had done life had to go on the altar; it had to die, and things had to start over. I had to live in a place of total surrender and dependence on Him, and that's where the biggest breakthrough came. Our ability to fully surrender, become childlike and dependent on God, relinquish our rights and control, is key to walking in the supernatural and experiencing the greater glory of God.

Becoming an Altar Means Putting All Our Confidence in Him

Have you ever been at a meeting where in the room there are some people who carry a lot of weight or authority, and suddenly you feel like a small child in that place? Your confidence is swallowed by the qualifications these people may carry. Maybe it's just me, but I seem to find myself in that situation more often than not.

I remember the first time I was asked to be a guest on a television show. All the other guests and I went out for dinner the night before. I remember as everyone sat around the table and shared about all the other shows they had done, and media experience they had, and who they knew — the more I listened, the smaller I suddenly felt. Little did they know that this was my very first show *ever*. Suddenly God's voice interrupted the enemy's attempts and I heard loud and clear from Him: "You have every right to sit here. You are Mine. Isn't that good enough?"

When you get a taste of God's glory, any confidence you may have had in yourself is stripped away, and suddenly you find yourself operating from a supernatural confidence. It's confidence in Him that gets flipped on, and your confidence in yourself is stripped away. Suddenly you find yourself preaching before crowds, laying hands on complete strangers to pray for the Lord to heal them, prophesying with confidence, etc. You are so undone by the love of God that pulsates through your body, spirit, and soul that nothing else seems to matter anymore or hinder you from sharing what is on God's heart.

> *Humbly we say, Lord, we can do nothing without You. Would you have your way in me. Amen.*

Becoming an Altar Means Keeping the Fire Burning

The tendency of fire is to go out; watch the fire on the altar of your heart. Anyone who has tended a fireplace fire knows that it needs to be stirred up occasionally. — William Booth

Larry finishing up here.

God sometimes speaks to us through the most comical ways. He is sovereign and has the right to do whatever He wants, however He wants. For example, one day, I was listening to the Billy Joel song "We Didn't Start the Fire." The Holy Spirit spoke to me concerning this song, mainly that one lyric, and He said, "That's true, you didn't start the fire." Throughout the course of this interesting discussion with the Lord, I ended up in Leviticus 6. Right here is the secret for sustaining a move of God.

> *The fire on the altar shall be kept burning on it; it shall not go out. The priest shall burn wood on it every morning, and he shall arrange the burnt offering on it and shall burn on it the fat of the peace offerings. Fire shall be kept burning on the altar continually; it shall not go out* (Leviticus 6:12-13).

When we surrender our lives to Jesus, we become a living sacrifice (see Rom. 12:1). In short, we *become the altar*. That altar attracts the fire of God. There is nothing you or I can do to merit the fire of God; it's simply attracted to a yielded life. However, we all have an assignment. As New Covenant priests, which we all are because of Jesus, we are called to keep the fire burning.

4

Surrendered and Beholding

I surrendered unto Him all there was of me; everything! Then for the first time I realized what it meant to have real power.
—Kathryn Kulhman

In this chapter, Ana shares a powerful principle on surrendering to God, while also painting a powerful, vivid, and prophetic picture of who we are laying our lives down for. It's not loss; it's heavenly gain. Yes, we lay down our lives, but what we pick back up makes the sacrifice look small.

Following His Lead Is a Lifestyle

As Jesus was walking beside the Sea of Galilee, he saw two brothers, Simon called Peter and his brother Andrew. They were casting a net into the lake, for they were fishermen. "Come, follow me," Jesus said, "and I will send you out to fish for people." At once they left their nets and followed him (Matthew 4:18-20 NIV).

WALKING IN THE greater things of God and being able to sustain the glory does require a constant letting go and dying of our own flesh and even our own agendas. When Jesus called the disciples into ministry, they laid down their very source of income, or lifestyle, and followed Him.

I find it interesting as well that the disciples' response to being close to God was to become "fishers of men"! We can't just get spiritually fat and full in His Presence. We are to leak the Kingdom of God on the earth. After my dose of Heaven that day in the Jordan, I couldn't stop telling others about Jesus and how much He loved them. Getting close to Him creates a deep desire to want the same things that are on God's own heart, and Jesus is always after the lost!

> *And he said to them, "As you go into all the world, preach openly the wonderful news of the gospel to the entire human race!"* (Mark 16:15 TPT)

No longer am I my own, and no longer is life about my agenda. That's a scary statement for many, I know. But when we are fully yielded and willing for God to take full possession of us, it's never about the loss. This Scripture in Philippians has come alive for me: *"For to me, to live is Christ and to die is gain"* (Phil. 1:21 NIV).

When I think about the goodness of God and what it means to be fully surrendered to Him, it actually brings me joy. You are not missing out on life by being fully surrendered to Him! On the contrary, you are *gaining* everything!

After this life-changing trip to Israel, I was in a restaurant with my best friend catching up. I went to use the restroom and the most bizarre thing happened. I am not one to strike up long conversations while washing my hands in the restroom, but there I found myself face to face with a woman who was completely awestruck. "You will never guess what happened to me. I just experienced one of the most terrifying experiences of my life!" the woman just openly started pouring out. (Have you ever had a similar experience, where a random stranger just starts pouring their heart out on you before you even get a chance to say, "How are you?" They are attracted to the Jesus in you!) The woman continued on, "My husband told me he was going to surprise me tonight with a fun planned date for us. I thought we were going out somewhere nice, so I curled my hair and got all pretty for our night out. He took me to do that indoor skydiving thing, and I had the worst experience of my life! I had one of those Willy Wonka experiences where I just kept floating up and up to the ceiling and they couldn't stop it. It was terrifying and the workers had to do like a special mission to get me down!"

Smiling, I stopped and thought, "Oh, Lord. Obviously you have placed this girl in my path for a reason. What should I say?" So right there in the bathroom, I witnessed to her and told her about the God of Peace and prayed to break trauma off of her. Instantly, her countenance changed and she was full of joy and peace again.

If you are willing, God can and will use you anywhere in whatever sphere of influence you have.

Laying Down Our Platforms to Kiss His Feet

Sometimes the Bible becomes dry after reading a story a thousand times, or perhaps it's from getting lazy and skimming through it without actually connecting our heart to the story. Seek the Lord now for fresh eyes to grasp something new out of this passage of Scripture.

The story of the woman pouring her alabaster vial on the feet of Jesus that we find in Luke 7 has taken on a deeper meaning to me.

> *And there was a woman in the city who was a sinner; and when she learned that He was reclining at the table in the Pharisee's house, she brought an alabaster vial of perfume, and standing behind Him at His feet, weeping, she began to wet His feet with her tears, and kept wiping them with the hair of her head, and kissing His feet and anointing them with the perfume* (Luke 7:37-38 NASB).

You can just feel the tension the disciples must have sensed in that moment. "Who is this woman, whom they call a 'sinner,' and how dare she disturb their dinner meeting with Jesus! What is she doing? Why is she doing that? Somebody just stop her—this is so inappropriate! Why isn't Jesus stopping her? Why is she just wasting such expensive perfume?"—they might have said.

Now, stop and imagine you are this woman for a second. She had every chance to walk away and not do what she felt led to do. Fear could have gripped her, and yet she seized the moment. The cost of the perfume could have held her back from sacrificing it. Pushing through all barriers and comfortable normalcies of that day, she didn't care. Wanting all of Him and nothing more, she pushed past the group of men to reach Him and anoint Jesus before His burial. Jesus said that she will be remembered. What she did was a strategic and prophetic act, marking Jesus for what He was about to endure.

We know that this lady is described as a "sinner," and some scholars agree that this most likely was Mary Magdalene. You see, those who are forgiven much can truly love much. And some of the most loving, passionate and kind people I have ever met, come from the roughest backgrounds and are the most radically transformed by Jesus. The woman with the vial of perfume was desperate to show her love for Jesus because she knew what life was like without Him. Sometimes we need a good reminder of where we would be today without Jesus to grow us and push us into living more humbly and being more adoring of Him.

There was sacrifice. There always is. If we want to taste deeper measures of His glory, we must do as this woman did and lay down our reputations completely. Paul writes this concerning Jesus Himself. It doesn't say He laid down some of His reputation; rather, we read that Jesus made Himself of *no reputation* (Phil. 2:7 NKJV). Result? "*Therefore God also has highly exalted Him and given Him the name which is above every name"* (Phil. 2:9 NKJV). There are no short-cuts to glory.

There are no platforms in Heaven but *one*. I know; I've been there. He is *holy* and He is worthy. There is nothing to lose in God, but everything to gain. You can't take your platform to Heaven. I dare touch on this subject of platforms because we have become a platform-driven society. The very core of our culture has become performance-driven and platform-oriented, and yet Jesus calls us each to counter that. "Come away with Me, Beloved," He says. "I love you no matter what you do." Unconditional love. You don't have to work for His love. He is love, poured out for you. When you think of the sacrifice of the cross—what He went through just to have relationship with you and me—then isn't He worth it all? Who cares about our reputation when we have our eyes fixed on Jesus?

This woman had no plan B, no back up plan. There was no self-promotion or relying on her own capabilities. It was a desper-ate cry: "I need You, *God!* I love You, Jesus!" For this very reason, I believe she was allowed to draw close. Her heart posture was cor-rectly focused on Him.

When God moves on you, it may look silly. It may actually cause you to lose or change some friendships. It may even cost you your job. But look at Jesus' response to the woman's sacrifice: *"Truly I say to you, wherever the gospel is preached in the whole world, what this woman has done will also be spoken of in memory of her"* (Mark 14:9 NASB). God rewards the risks we take for Him. Her life, the beauty of her adoration, the risky move she made to show it—all will be remembered forever.

Correct Posture

Maybe there is a reason Jesus says, *"For everyone who exalts him-self will be humbled, but the one who humbles himself will be exalted"* (Luke 18:14).

As a seer, Jesus has taken me to Heaven before. I've seen bits of different places — the throne room, the garden, the body parts room, the mailer room, the library in Heaven, etc. Often, it astonishes me a little when people ask me to go up to Heaven and get them something. I know they are desperate, and for that reason I have so much compassion for them and intercede on their behalf.

But it doesn't quite work like that. I never go with the attitude that I deserve to be there. Before His eyes, I hope to someday be pure. I am a work in progress, as we all are until we reach Heaven. We need Him.

Every time I have had the privilege of getting to taste a bit of Heaven, it never comes by working myself up there. It's not like I can lace up my army boots and march up to Heaven to make my demands on the King. *He is holy!* Although it does say in Scripture to come boldly before the throne of grace (see Heb. 4:16), the context by which you interpret that scripture will show your understanding of the Father and relationship to Him.

He is Holy. He is Love. He is altogether beautiful. You are His child whom He deeply loves. He loves to play with you and make Himself known every day if you dare to catch Him. I imagine Him like a Father playing hide and seek sometimes with us, His children. He's always speaking, but are we looking for and listening to Him? He calls and summons us.

I enter into the greater measures of Heaven as a worshiper and adorer of Him. Only, and I repeat, *only* out of His sovereign will can I stand in the glory. *He* is *God* and I am merely me. Purity and humility are the absolute requirements for entering into the glory. Matthew 5:8 reminds: *"Blessed are the pure in heart, for they shall see God."*

I don't march up to Heaven. No, Jesus graciously and sovereignly invites me up. I enter into the Holy of Holies lying on my face. Perhaps my place is on my face. Reverently, I enter in. I wait and be still, making no demands. I worship and pour out my "I love

Yous" before the King. I anticipate Him. And then, He speaks. He then touches me with power, glory, and what can only be described as liquid love. Revivalist Charles Finney described his encounter with the Holy Spirit using similar words. As I encounter Him this way, He then opens my eyes to show me things.

It's the only way I know how to enter in. Humbly, laid down, and "lower still" as Mama Heidi Baker would say.

The Eyes of Jesus

His eyes are like a flame of fire, and on his head are many diadems, and he has a name written that no one knows but himself (Revelation 19:12).

As I looked and saw Jesus, knowing He could see all of me, and there He was before me, pure, my own insufficiency was brought up like a huge lump in my throat. And yet, He looked at me with a smile on His face and I heard Him say, "All of Me, for all of you." The love that I experienced falling on me in that moment, mixed with the glory, felt overwhelming. Just when I thought, "I can't take anymore," I beheld His eyes.

Those eyes, I could never describe in enough words. They are more alive than any other eyes that I have ever seen. They look through you and consume you at the same time. They are tender and yet full of fire. Light radiates out of them and shines into your very soul. They pierce you with love like you've never known before. They are full of bubbling joy, peace, healing, and compassion. Those eyes look with potential at you and see the amazing person you are despite your mishaps. They fiercely love.

I pray that right now, as you read about the eyes of Jesus, that you yourself would stop and take a moment and embrace His very Presence that has rested upon you. Whenever I speak about the eyes of Jesus, He comes near. I pray that you would have an encounter right now with His eyes that speak over you: "I love you, My child." Just one look, and your life will be forever changed. One taste of His love like that, and you can't go on the same. He marks you with His love.

When I looked into those eyes, my immediate response was, "How could I not do anything for You? How could I not want to give up my own life, give up everything and lay it down?" There's no other love like that that I can say I have ever experienced. Even deeper than a love a parent has for their own child, this love burns so deep within. One look into His eyes and I am yoked with Him. I realized that I am no longer my own but entirely His. There is no self-will or selfish desire when the eyes of Jesus look at you. All is burnt away and only love remains. Love that purifies, requires everything, and yet is so full. Every unmet need in that moment melts away, and you are full. The love of Jesus meets everything you could possibly need or want. He is all knowing, all seeing, all understanding, and yet He still chooses you! That's the love of the Father. *There is no other sacrificial love you will ever meet like it.*

Love so amazing, so divine demands my soul, my life, my all. — Isaac Watts, "When I Survey the Wondrous Cross"

Beholding, Not Striving

This may seem like a change of subject, but rather, it's an illustration of the power of beholding. In the Old Testament, Jacob finds himself in a precarious situation. He has worked for years for his father-in-law, Laban, and he's ready to branch out and go tackle new land with his own family. "*Send me away, that I may go to my own home and country,*" he says (Gen 30:25).

Laban asks Jacob what he can give him, and Jacob comes up with a plan. He asks to go through Laban's flock and remove every speckled and spotted sheep, goat, and black lamb.

> *Then Jacob took fresh rods of poplar and almond and plane trees, and peeled white stripes in them, exposing the white which was in the rods. He set the rods which he had peeled in front of the flocks in the gutters, even in the watering troughs, where the flocks came to drink; and they mated when they came to drink. So the flocks mated by the rods, and the flocks brought forth striped, speckled, and spotted. Jacob separated the lambs, and made the flocks face toward the striped and all the black in the flock of Laban; and he put his own herds apart, and did not put them with Laban's flock. Moreover, whenever the stronger of the flock were mating, Jacob would place the rods in the sight of the flock in the gutters, so that they might mate by the rods; but when the flock was feeble, he did not put them in; so the feebler were Laban's and the stronger Jacob's. So the man became exceedingly prosperous, and had large flocks and female and male servants and camels and donkeys* (Genesis 30:37-43 NASB).

We see here that what we focus our gaze on, we become. What we behold, we become like. Jacob strategically placed those striped rods in front of the animals. They would see them while they went to drink and mate, and what was produced out of it was striped.

To access glory, we need to simply learn to behold Jesus. It's so easy and tempting to want to encounter God for what we can glean or get from Him. There will always be fruit from encountering Him, but that shouldn't be the motivation behind why we want Him.

One day, I found myself in a room in Heaven. In the very center of the room was a large art easel with two paint brushes and two pallets. Jesus and I began to paint together, but really all I could do was just watch what He was painting. *What will He make?* I kept thinking. *What is He trying to teach me through that picture?* I wondered.

Jesus stopped me. Looking me in the eyes He said, "It's not about the product here, but just be with Me." Then later, "You've been working out of striving even in your relationship with Me. You've lost your joy. That's not living in freedom. Let's do life together. Let's spend time together and just enjoy. That's real relationship."

Beholding isn't striving. We don't strive for or work up an encounter with God. Learning to be still and waiting on Him is perhaps the biggest struggle. The disciple John, whom Jesus loved, leaned against His chest. Mary sat at his feet as Jesus said, *"There is only one thing worth being concerned about. Mary has discovered it"* (Luke 10:42 NLT).

Likewise, we have access to Him. Removing the mentality of performance — that I have to do something to acquire access to God — takes the load off of us and puts it on Jesus. Jesus is the access point.

So, we set our eyes and behold Him. We learn to be still and soak in His Presence. We worship and adore God with our hearts full of thanksgiving. We don't strive or do things out of our own strength because we know we don't have to work for His love or His Presence. We lean into Him, fully dependent on Him to break through. We believe with childlike faith that we have access, to go and sit right up on our Papa's lap. *And then He comes...*

> *He will come to us as the showers, as the spring rains that water the earth* (Hosea 6:3).

5

Why We
Need the Glory

"WE DON'T WANT YOU having *Holy Ghost* meetings!"

These were the strange instructions given to me over the phone by a "Spirit-filled" pastor many years ago. This recommendation was strange for several reasons. First, the church was a self-proclaimed Charismatic church (which, by definition, should be open and receptive to the movement of the Holy Spirit). Second, we had been leading weekly Friday night prayer and intercession meetings where the people were getting powerfully touched by the Lord. That said, some people didn't know what to do with this because even in the context of a "Spirit-filled" church, the actual manifestation of God's Presence was an unusual thing. I seek to make these comments with honor, as I don't want to throw anyone under the bus—just make an observation that even in the Spirit-filled/Spirit-empowered community something seems to be…missing. Was it lost? If we mean "lost" like losing your car keys, no. The more correct word would be *traded*.

Before further discussing this critical topic of trading in the spirit, I want to ensure that you hear my heart for what you are presently reading. I do *not* want to simply "call out" the situation. Anyone can look at the Christian community and point out all the glaring "warts." That doesn't require prophetic vision; it just takes open eyes. The offering of Kingdom solutions and strategies is the fruit of true prophetic ministry. It doesn't take a prophet to say, "Hey, this is a big problem!" The prophetic confronts problems with the intention of presenting strategies that will bring solutions.

Pure, authentic New Testament prophetic ministry does two things: it calls out and calls in. It confronts and consoles. Consider Jeremiah's prophetic assignment for a moment: *"Behold, I have put my words in your mouth. See, I have set you this day over nations and over kingdoms, to pluck up and to break down, to destroy and to overthrow, to build and to plant"* (Jer. 1:9-10). It wasn't *all* building and planting, nor was it all plucking up and breaking down—it's both. In the New Testament, we see prophets like Agabus being confrontational (see Acts 21:10-14), while later on, in First Corinthians 14, we see explicit instruction on how the prophetic is supposed to edify, encourage, and exhort!

The point? Yes, we call out issues and problems, but we also need to call forth supernatural solutions and call the body of Christ, individually and corporately, into Kingdom fullness. Just calling out issues all the time is often the byproduct of a critical spirit, while offering nothing but exhortation and encouragement tends to be motivated by a spirit of slumber. So I present this with fear and trembling. I present this as someone who by no means claims to have all of the answers, but as one gripped by a vision of what could be. I love the Bride of Christ, the body of Messiah Jesus in the earth. I love the church, the glorious Ekklesia—the advancing, binding and loosing community that the Son of God introduced in Matthew 16. I strongly recommend reading Ed Silvoso's amazing book, *Ekklesia,* to give you a biblical and historical perspective on what Jesus envisioned when He birthed the church. Ed captures it beautifully in this statement: "the Ekklesia was a building-less mobile people movement designed to operate 24/7 in the marketplace for the purpose of having an impact on everybody and everything."[1] Jesus did not envision a static temple or tabernacle because He wanted a *moving movement.*

I want to serve Jesus by being one voice (among many) who sows into His beloved bride so she can walk *clothed in the glory* she was destined for!

Two Dimensions of Glory: A Position and an Experience

For all have sinned and fall short of the glory of God (Romans 3:23).

We need to understand the two dimensions of this vital scripture. The glory is both a position of relationship and a dimension of experience—it's a positional reality and an experiential realm. It's a description of the standing you were born again to have with God, positionally, and an invitation into a realm of experiential fellowship that this position in Christ has opened up to you.

Adam had a position with God, but also engaged an experiential dimension. When God fashioned man (and woman), He intentionally created someone who would be compatible with Him. In Genesis 1:26, we see the first dimension of glory displayed—the position that man was meant to occupy.

The Position of Glory

Then God said, "Let us make man in our image, after our likeness. And let them have dominion over the fish of the sea and over the birds of the heavens and over the livestock and over all the earth and over every creeping thing that creeps on the earth" (Genesis 1:26).

The position of being created in the image and likeness of God was the foundation of mankind's place of administration and dominion in the earth. Your position of being in right relationship with God directly impacts your assignment. Even though the fall of mankind deeply disrupted the original intent of Eden, Calvary restored that which was lost, or traded—a people, on the earth, who would rule and reign as those in right relationship with the Creator (see 2 Cor. 5:21). This was not possible until the transaction of Jesus, which made it possible for the redeemed to become the righteousness of God in Christ and, thus, fully step into their original created design once again. God is seeking a people who operate in His likeness to, in turn, release His likeness throughout the earth. We can only fully behave like God by being indwelt by the Spirit. Yes, it's true that even those who don't know the Lord are still created in His image and likeness. They can still exhibit certain traits that are in agreement with who God is. Yet, there is a fullness released through a redeemed people who are in right standing with God, operating from a heavenly-places position of glory, who intentionally set out to see His likeness and image canvas the planet!

The Experience of Glory

Adam was in right standing with the Lord positionally, but he also walked in the cool of the day with Him, representing the *realm of glory* that he fell from (see Gen. 3:8). Many, if not most, Christians are familiar with Romans 3:23 as a fall from a position; this is absolutely true. However, we need to be aware that falling from that position also meant falling from a realm of experience. Right standing with God is not a doctrine to be known; it's an invitation to a lifestyle of intimate encounter with the One who still walks in the cool of the day with His people.

I believe that Jesus Himself reinstated human access to this realm at the Great Commission, where He ended with the following statement: *"And never forget that I am with you every day, even to the completion of this age"* (Matt. 28:20 TPT).

This statement is not meant to simply bring us comfort in times of trial or difficulty. It's not meant to produce "greeting card" feelings of warmth and comfort. It's a dynamic invitation into a realm of continuous encounter with a Person called God. Truly, the Presence of Jesus is with us and will never leave us because of the indwelling Holy Spirit. We have 24-7 access to the glory realm of God by simply stepping in by faith. Jesus was describing an accessible realm for all who believed in Him!

We don't see the church functioning in this experiential dimension of glory for a few reasons. For one, we confine the "glory" to the position we fell from, and thus it remains restricted to a theological concept. Second, we don't fully understand what the "glory" of God is. Third, we are afraid of what "might" happen if this glory or Presence should manifest. The reason we are not functioning in a glory dimension is not because God, in His sovereignty, is withholding this from us. He's not waiting for the "right dispensation" or era to send His glory into the earth again. Likewise, He did not withdraw the dynamic manifestation of His glory following the canonization of Scripture or death of the last apostle. We are not waiting for glory to come *down*; God is waiting for a people to arise in faith and let the glory *come out.*

Just maybe we are not witnessing the fullness of what the church could be and the impact she could have because those who believe in God's glory are not personally experiencing it. The conscious, continuous experience with and in His glory will empower people to do exactly what Jesus commissioned — *make disciples of all nations.* We will see nations discipled to the degree that our discipleship strategies are birthed by and saturated in the glory of God.

Destined to Demonstrate the Glory

If the destiny of the church is outlined in the following passage, it makes logical sense that the "gates of hell/hades" would try to do everything in their deceptive powers to prevent God's people from fulfilling this pivotal assignment.

> *I also say to you that you are Peter, and upon this rock I*
> *will build My church; and the gates of Hades will not over-*
> *power it. I will give you the keys of the kingdom of heaven;*
> *and whatever you bind on earth shall have been bound in*
> *heaven, and whatever you loose on earth shall have been*
> *loosed in heaven* (Matthew 16:18-19 NASB).

Jesus did not come to planet Earth to establish a building. If any-thing, He rendered the former "building-driven system" obsolete. It doesn't mean buildings are bad; it simply means that the church is not a building by identity; it's a community that assembles in a building. He did not die for a country club. As prayer leader Corey Russell has candidly observed: "Jesus didn't die for 45 minutes once a week and 20 bucks."

Jesus fulfilled the Old Covenant sacrificial system and died so that an entire people would become qualified vessels to carry His very Person and Presence into every sphere of culture under hell's tyrannical rule. We've been called to be carriers of His glory with the expectation that what we carry will have a measurable impact on the world around us. After all, Jesus had an impact on the world around Him.

If we are to function as the body of Jesus in the earth, why should our results be any less? Of course, we will not (and could not) oper-ate in His role as Messiah; that identity is forever exclusive to Jesus. What we can do is operate in Kingdom power, thus pointing people to the Messiah and Savior. What we can do is receive innovation from Heaven, strategy from the Spirit, and creativity from the Cre-ator so that as such things are expressed through the people of God, they function as a sign and wonder to the onlooking world. Cre-ative, entrepreneurial strategies that supernaturally generate reve-nue are just as much "signs and wonders" as healings, miracles, and deliverances. We are drawing divine resources from the same Holy Spirit—the indwelling Person and Presence of glory in the church. Oh, that the glory would characterize the people of God again! I know we use the word *glory*. I know we have Christian platitudes that exclaim "glory to God!" We have songs that declare, "*Show me Your glory!*" There is much discussion of glory, but I am concerned that we are witnessing little *demonstration* of glory compared to what the Day of Pentecost made available. When the church functions as the Ekklesia, operating in glory, we will witness a measurable shift and change in those high places of society that have been influenced by darkness. Ed Silvoso explains that "Jesus' intention is that the Ekklesia's proclamation of the Gospel of the Kingdom would confront the Gates of Hades now, in the present, until those gates collapse so that people, and eventually nations, are transformed."[2] The litmus test of an effective, glorious church will be the collapse of the gates of hell that are in operation over people, regions, and spheres of culture.

Arise and Shine!

Arise, shine, for your light has come, and the glory of the Lord has risen upon you. For behold, darkness shall cover the earth, and thick darkness the peoples; but the Lord will arise upon you, and his glory will be seen upon you. And nations shall come to your light, and kings to the brightness of your rising (Isaiah 60:1-3).

This portion of Scripture best outlines my theology on how end-time events will ultimately unfold. I believe that there will be both *deep darkness* and *great glory*. I believe that as history moves toward the conclusion of its present form, we will witness an increase of darkness and a simultaneous release of Holy Spirit glory. The glory we walk in, however, must be superior to the darkness trying to wreak havoc on humanity. If the glory being released by God's people is not superior to the thick darkness covering the earth, this indicates a trade has taken place. *We were made to encounter, carry, and release the glory of God.* What we walk in must have a tangible, measurable impact on the darkness. Some would argue that as the glory increases on the people of God, darkness will continue to destroy humanity with increased intensity — almost like the church is in some kind of glory "dome," insulated from the all-out assault of darkness, which is tearing the planet to shreds. This is a dualistic eschatology that even Jesus Himself does not embrace. I know this because He calls us to be *salt and light,* both of which have a measurable impact on the world around them (see Matt. 5:13-16).

Consider for a moment Jesus' very sobering commission for us to be *salt of the earth.* By the way, He did not say "salt of the church." Historically, God has been aiming His redemptive agenda at the whole of creation. Redeemed souls are of paramount importance, yes, but God is not stopping until the whole of created order is restored, healed, and brought into the glory we have received through redemption. How this will completely unfold, I am not entirely sure. What I do know is that those who are filled with the Spirit of God should be measurably seeing the Kingdom of God *within them* having influence in every sphere of society around them.

The Glory Must be Normal

We *need* Holy Ghost encounters and meetings now more than ever! Except we don't need "revival" meetings to be the exception; they should be the norm! The local church should be a place that people attend expecting an encounter with the Living God. In fact, it's those encounters that become catalysts that launch societal reformers into their assignments. This is exactly what happened to Moses in Exodus 3. It's easy to get excited about the "burning bush" scenario. The supernatural fire is awesome! The manifestation of the bush burning but not being consumed is miraculous! The spectacle caused Moses to "turn aside," but it was the Voice that spoke out of the fire that changed a shepherd into a societal reformer, national liberator, and a name that shaped history! Moses was a reformer, yes, but his reformation assignment was birthed through an encounter with the fire of God. This is what we have traded away, branding it as irrelevant, "spooky," controversial, and not necessary for this present generation. The truth is, we never graduate from needing a touch from the fire of God. We may think we are beyond it. Perhaps we are too sophisticated for "that kind of stuff," but I'm convinced that it's the fire-baptized who will always shape history. Reformation demands a church on fire.

We will never have societal reformation without sustained revival among Christians, and we will never experience sustained revival unless we reverse the trades that have prevented us from walking in the fullness of power the Bible promises is available. "Revival" has come and gone, ebbed and flowed since the Protestant Reformation. As a historian of revival, I absolutely cherish the great testimonies of the audacious individuals who contended with Heaven to see Bible promises become visible reality. Their stories remind me that such awakenings are possible in our day. And yet, I am dissatisfied with yet another "awakening" or "move of God" that history books identify with a start and stop date. I prophesy that the Spirit is raising up a company of people who will not tolerate a revival that "stops" but rather one that so alters Christian culture that *how* the local church operates will never be the same again. Instead of a "come and see" worship experience, the Lord is raising up a "go and transform" apostolic company. That's the church, or *Ekklesia*.

The ultimate goal is societal and cultural reformation — a world where history begins to be shaped by the impact and influence of the church. Although we have seen some measure of Christian impact, the last 100 years have, unfortunately, represented a season when the people of God have intentionally withdrawn from society in hopes of establishing their own spiritual subculture that was more interested in preparing for eternity than measurably impacting the "here and now." The devil has warped everything, as he trembles at the thought of an advancing Ekklesia.

He's threatened, sure, by our gathering together and worshiping, learning Scripture, giving money, and doing altar calls. Where we've been and what we've done *has had fruit!* Souls have been saved! Communities have been blessed! Foreign nations have been introduced to the love, compassion, and saving message of Jesus! Our worship services, community outreaches, and missions initiatives are to be celebrated, not condemned. Our programs are to be praised, not lambasted. Yes, be excellent! Yes, have quality musicians and vocalists! Yes, be a decent communicator if you are going to be the main teacher/senior pastor! Sure, it's fine to write books, utilize social media, and have an itinerant speaking schedule. But if all of these things *replace* the primary assignment, which is to accommodate the Holy Spirit and His manifestation, every "good" thing has instantly become a distraction. God can and does use all of this stuff, but more than anything, He desires His church to be a community that experiences His Presence, walks in His power, and advances His program (the Kingdom of God). As I said earlier, the devil is somewhat threatened by our present church system—but he is absolutely terrified by the prospect of the church becoming that advancing apostolic company that brings Kingdom transformation to everyone, everywhere.

For us to take our place as this community, we need to recognize the importance of the "here and now." In fact, I believe that our level of influence in the here and now will measurably impact our eternity, for our Lord is all about stewards who stand before His throne with results to show for their labor on earth. Remember, it is King Jesus who will say something like: *"Well done, good and faithful servant. You have been faithful over a little; I will set you over much. Enter into the joy of your master"* (Matt. 25:23). He is looking for those who did *something* with the life they were given. This life includes gifts, talents, abilities, and those spheres of influence we feel called to transform.

Knowing their ultimate, predetermined fate, the powers of darkness have cleverly lured an entire generation into a demonic trade. Their objective is to prevent the Ekklesia from *roaring*, for that is how the Lion of Judah will roar in the earth and destroy the works of the devil (see 1 John 3:8). Until the Second Coming of Jesus, I believe those called to release this "roar" of Jesus into the earth are God's people, which Paul describes as *His body*, declaring His decree in word *and* demonstration.

6

Open Up the Gates

SEVERAL YEARS AGO, I had a supernatural vision that profoundly impacted the way I live out my Christian life. It forever changed the way I understand and pray for Holy Spirit outpouring and became a key catalyst that motivated me to write this book.

A Supernatural Vision that Changed Everything

During a revival service in Orlando, Florida, I remember the worship leader, Lydia Stanley-Marrow, starting to sing a prophetic song. Over and over, she declared the lyrics: *Open up the gates, open up the doors.* As she was singing, it was as though a thick blanket of God's manifest Presence fell upon the entire congregation of Calvary Assembly. People were worshiping, crying, kneeling, and running forward to the altar—all responses that are historically characteristic of a dynamic visitation of God's Presence.

There was really no pastoral direction given as to what people *should* be doing; the Spirit of God was moving in power among the hungry worshipers. The main theme that seemed to be gripping those present was the need for revival.

As the worship intensified, I went up to the altar, not really knowing *why* I had walked up there. All I knew was that the Holy Spirit was undeniably moving in my heart. I knew He was working, but at the time I could not place exactly what He was doing. Then, I had what some might call a vision of the mind.[1] A picture flashed before my mind's eye that I was not at all looking for; it was given under the influence of the Holy Spirit.

Here is what I saw:

I saw the picture of big iron gates—the kind that you would see on the other end of a medieval drawbridge leading into a castle. Different from a standard door, the gates were fence-like in construction, with the bars being metallic in appearance. While a door would completely close off one side of the structure to the other, the gates left room for *restricted* entry. Even still, a human being, no matter how small in size, could not really squeeze through the bars of these gates. Basically, all that could comfortably pass through was wind, air, insects, and maybe small rodents.

As quickly as I saw the picture of these gates appear, I watched something very fascinating begin to take place. In the background, the congregation and the music team continued to declare, *open up the gates, open up the doors*. It was as though their spiritual hunger level directly impacted the gates' activity; as they sang, the gates began to rise up, to ascend. Even though I recognize that merely singing a worship song does not automatically presume that a person is hungry for God, songs do often give voice to a corporate level of spiritual desperation. This is exactly what was going on in this vision. The worshipers' hungry cry for revival and outpouring was being expressed in the form of this prophetic declaration. The more intensely they sang, the higher the gates lifted up.

Immediately, God granted me some clarity as to what all of this meant. My Master of Divinity from Regent University was a focused concentration in church history. The information that I gleaned over my years of study started to consume my thinking. During this vision, I was reminded that throughout the centuries, since the

Book of Acts, there has been a faithful remnant in the church who have pressed in to experience the fullness of the Kingdom. While we could discuss certain times and seasons in church history that may appear to have a dispensational element, I do not believe, biblically, we can make a solid case for a special "dispensation" of miracles or, more specifically, the manifest Presence of the Spirit. Quite the contrary—Jesus assured us that *He* would be with until the end of the age (see Matt. 28:20). How would Jesus *be* present with us in this manner? Through the Person of the Holy Spirit!

Some have mistakenly believed that revival—particularly a revival of the supernatural—was the byproduct of the early 1900s, with the Azusa Street Revival in Los Angeles and the birth of modern Pentecostalism. This is not true at all. The dynamic, supernatural manifestations of God's power, from divine healing to spiritual gifts, from the baptism of the Holy Spirit to the prophetic, have been prevalent all throughout church history.

From the desert fathers casting out demons in North Africa to St. Francis of Assisi walking in healing power, history is laden with examples of those who experienced what many people commonly call "revival." In many cases—particularly up until the 1600s and 1700s—these experiences were indeed limited to a few individuals and select small communities. Still, every man or woman who pressed in to experience the Spirit's fullness and then tasted of His power reminds me of God's faithfulness. Was it not the Lord Himself who extend this invitation: *"You will seek me and find me, when you seek me with all your heart. I will be found by you, declares the Lord"* (Jer. 29:13-14)?

God will always be found by the hungry, seeking heart. In considering history, it becomes evident that Heaven did not sovereignly issue some mandate to close its gates; sadly, the greater population of believers exchanged, or *traded,* their relentless pursuit of God for other things. Historically, church hierarchy and leadership, by and large, played a key role in determining the spiritual hunger level of the everyday people. Congregations would go only as far and as deep as the church leadership directed them. Sadly, the same is true in many cases today.

The Gate of Heaven

When the church was born at Pentecost, the *gates* were wide open. Nothing was restricting the Presence and power of Heaven from freely flowing into the earth *through* the people of God. It was as if the prophetic dream that Jacob had back in Genesis 28 came to pass through a Spirit-indwelt community of people:

> *And he dreamed, and behold, there was a ladder set up on the earth, and the top of it reached to heaven. And behold, the angels of God were ascending and descending on it! ...Then Jacob awoke from his sleep and said, "Surely the Lord is in this place, and I did not know it." And he was afraid and said, "How awesome is this place! This is none other than the house of God, and this is the gate of heaven"* (Genesis 28:12,16-17).

Notice the use of the word *gate*. At that moment in history, Jacob was identifying a "house of God" that was clearly not fashioned by human hands. This was before the Exodus tabernacle and Solomon's temple. It was as though Jacob was peering into the age that Jesus Himself would inaugurate. Consider how similar Jesus' language sounds to Jacob's: "*And he* [Jesus] *said to him* [Nathanael], *'Truly, truly, I say to you, you will see heaven opened, and the angels of God ascending and descending on the Son of Man'*" (John 1:51).

There is no question among the majority of believers as to whether or not Jesus operated in such demonstrations of supernatural power. Of course He did. However, when we start considering the church—the community of Spirit-birthed and Spirit-filled Christ followers—to be a fulfillment of Jacob's prophetic dream, things become uneasy. It makes sense for Jesus, because He was and is God; for everyday Christians, however, we are stretched by such a concept. Yet, this reality should not be that challenging for us to consider.

Jesus' redemptive work on the cross made it possible for us to be purified from sin and thus filled with the Holy Spirit. In other words, because we receive the atoning purification of Jesus' blood, we become cleansed of sin. This makes us fit to become what the apostle Paul calls the temple of God: *"Do you not know that you are God's temple and that God's Spirit dwells in you?"* (1 Cor. 3:16). Think of it for a moment. For the first time in a long time, there was a temple of God on earth that most closely resembled what Jacob saw in his dream. Granted, there is no specific language in Genesis 28 to suggest that Jacob saw people being the house of God. I don't wish to imply that at all. At the same time, the same dream does not make mention of a physical structure—church, temple, tabernacle, sanctuary, etc.

According to Genesis 28, the house of God is characterized by the supernatural activity of angels ascending and descending. Later in John 1, we see angels ascending and descending upon a person—Jesus. In that same chapter, John also described how *"the Word became flesh and dwelt among us"* (John 1:14). The word *dwelt* could best be translated as "tabernacled." Jesus was the firstfruits of a new tabernacle of God on the earth, one not fashioned by human beings of flesh and blood, but one handcrafted by God Himself. Jesus, the Son of God, made it possible for human beings to be forgiven of sin so that, on earth, they could become filled with the Spirit and thus, houses of God. *This is your inheritance!* This is the church that Jesus envisioned! This vision is incredible. And yet, there is more. There is action required of the house of God.

When giving marching orders for His church, Jesus instructed: *"And I will give you the keys of the kingdom of heaven, and whatever you bind on earth will be bound in heaven, and whatever you loose on earth will be loosed in heaven"* (Matt. 16:19 NKJV). The mandate for the church immemorial has been to forbid on earth that which is forbidden in Heaven, and likewise, release on earth that which is already released in Heaven. This is the essence of the Lord's Prayer, when Jesus instructs to pray like this: *"Your kingdom come. Your will be done on earth as it is in heaven"* (Matt. 6:10 NKJV). Could it be that angels are still ascending and descending upon Christ-followers today? In the same way they aided Jesus, Scripture makes it clear that these beings are supernaturally assisting believers today (see Heb. 1:14), descending upon us to release Heaven's resources on earth.

The Holy Spirit Brings Heaven to Earth

During the first three hundred years of church history, several accounts and writings make it clear that the believers expected supernatural assistance and empowerment. They moved in unusual boldness, even in the face of great persecution. These courageous pioneers of the Christian faith were continually ushering one world into another, bringing Heaven to earth, as every follower of Jesus Christ recognized that he or she was a qualified catalyst to carry and demonstrate God's power. In other words, all Christians clearly understood that they were anointed to continue the works of Jesus — works expressed in both righteous character and demonstrations of supernatural power.

Luke opens the book of Acts with the following introductory statement: *"In the first book, O Theophilus, I have dealt with all that Jesus began to do and teach, until the day when he was taken up"* (Acts 1:1-2). Previously, Luke's Gospel was an introduction of what Jesus *began* to do and teach. The truth is, the same Jesus continued to *do* and *teach* after He physically left the planet. His works and teaching would actually continue through His anointed Ekklesia, His body on earth. This would happen because of the Divine Advantage sent at Pentecost—the Holy Spirit. The same Spirit that anointed Jesus would inhabit redeemed hearts from that day until the consummation of the age. This promise is all inclusive, including you, me, and every other individual who has been transformed by God's amazing grace. Peter put it this way in his history-making sermon at Pentecost: *"For the promise is for you and for your children and for all who are far off, everyone whom the Lord our God calls to himself"* (Acts 2:39).

Pentecost made it possible for the works of Jesus to continue on earth, even after His physical departure. Perhaps this is why Jesus told the disciples *"it is to your advantage that I go away"* (John 16:7). I am sure that this statement brought some confusion to the disciples, as they surely wondered: "How could Jesus leaving us be to our advantage? God is right here walking and talking with us, and now God is telling us that it is better for us that He leaves? That doesn't make any sense!" Jesus explained that His departure would be to their benefit for a very clear reason—God would not leave planet Earth *without* God. Even though Jesus, God Incarnate, was leaving, God the Holy Spirit was coming. He was not about to leave His people as orphans.

Consider some of Jesus' final words to the disciples: *"for if I do not go away, the Helper will not come to you. But if I go, I will send him to you"* (John 16:7). The Holy Spirit is the One who made John 14:12 a possible reality for every disciple of Jesus throughout time immemorial:

> *Truly, truly, I say to you, whoever believes in me will also do the works that I do; and greater works than these will he do, because I am going to the Father. Whatever you ask in my name, this I will do, that the Father may be glorified in the Son. If you ask me anything in my name, I will do it* (John 14:12-14).

Using the language of open gates, Jesus was explaining that the *gates would be opened* to "whoever believes in Me." For too long,

Christianity has been aberrant when measured next to its original blueprint. Normal has become redefined, not by what Jesus clearly said in the Gospels or by the exploits the apostles performed in the book of Acts, or even the clear expression of the faith during the first few hundred years of church history. Rather, Christianity has become historically defined by the direction of the masses. It is unfortunate that church leadership, particularly in the Middle Ages, has long been susceptible to the desire of the people, in a quest for affluence rather than the agenda of Heaven. For us to open up the gates and start experiencing Holy Spirit outpouring as normative—not just some period of visitation or extended church gatherings—we must return to the standard given to us by Jesus Himself and demonstrated by the early church. For this return to happen, I believe there are trades we need to undo, and new trades that we need to make.

How Do We Get Back to Normal?

For right now, I want you to consider the fact that a supernatural lifestyle, where the power and Presence of God are made manifest in a regular manner, is not abnormal.

Jesus died so that the sins of mankind could be forgiven and we could one day spend eternity in Heaven. This is one side of the story, and a most important one. He also died to make the hearts of sinful humanity a fit dwelling place for His glory.

Until Jesus stepped into history and fulfilled God's redemptive assignment, the Spirit of God could not live inside a human being; He could only rest upon them for a time and a task. This was because mankind was still contaminated by the stain of sin. Jesus' atoning sacrifice at Calvary dealt with the sin barrier *eternally*. This is eternally worthy of extravagant, celebrative praise. At the same time, the barrier was not removed just so we could go to Heaven at death; it was removed so that we could actually live a resurrected life on earth. This is what sustained revival looks like: The church deciding to actually live the resurrected life that Jesus made avail-able. Revival *moments* are meant to launch reformation *movements*. God never meant the moments of revival to be sustained; they are sovereign, "suddenly" jump-start seasons for the church, purposed to adjust the operating system of how God's people do life and, ultimately, launch "sent ones" into the harvest field. Every period of revival confronts the people of God with a lost, forgotten, or neglected dimension of our inheritance in Christ that is meant to be normal in operation.

This might sound like a far-out "pipe dream" to some, even those who desire to see God's power manifest in the world today. The idea of the supernatural becoming the gold standard for Chris-tianity might sound outlandish, but consider the words of mission-ary, revivalist, and Pentecostal pioneer John G. Lake:

> We may never get one half or one quarter of the way toward the ideal. But never try to degrade God's purpose and bring it down to your level. But by the grace of God put the stan-dard up there where Jesus put it, and then get as near it as you can.[2]

Just because we are not walking in this reality yet, it does not mean it is off-limits and that we should cease our pursuit. Far from it. The ancient gates will open once again as the people of God step into their identity as those cleansed from sin, filled with the Spirit, and empowered to do the works of Jesus. Revival is not something new coming down from Heaven; it's the church becoming awak-ened to who she is and what she possesses as a spiritual inheri-tance. I present these words with great hope and expectation! I am confident the Lord wants to open up the gates, not because we are necessarily stepping into some sovereign moment, but because our divine discontentment is exceeding our comfortable Christianity. Spiritual hunger is pushing an entire generation into the Presence of God, stirring a contending cry within: "Lord, we desire to walk in *everything You made available!*" The cry, the hunger, the thirst are essential starting points — but there is a step further. Heaven is bending toward the earth, looking and listening for those who put action to their hunger. This action will demand sacrifice. It will demand a costly, continuous "Yes" to the manifestation of the Holy Spirit.

More than a temporary season of visitation or revival, we need a great awakening. We need to be awakened to the inheritance that Jesus gave us access to through the Holy Spirit. More than access, He has made a supernatural deposit into every single person who has become a New Creation through the redemptive work of Christ. Here is the challenge: Are we, collectively and individually, making withdrawals from the divine deposit that Jesus made at Pentecost? The problem is that, for a long while, much of the church has been operating in natural, human strength accomplishing limited results. Some loudly bash the institutional church for such faults. I, on the other hand, believe we need to extend much grace to the corporate body of Christ, while individually pressing into the fullness of God for our lives. A.W. Tozer explained that "what the church does is what the individuals do. How well or how sick the church is depends on how well or how sick individuals are."[3]

The only reason the collective church is functioning the way it has been is because of what has taken place over the years. While there is grace, there must also be honest confrontation. And although it's easy for us to point fingers at pastors, leaders, and everyone else, claiming them as responsible, I sense the Lord calling us to confess our responsibility in the closing of the gates. This is not meant to be a harsh criticism; it's actually intended to encouragingly awaken us to the truth that if we confront our collective issues in the church and own up to the trades we've made, *we* can reverse and undo them! It's time we stepped into the fullness of what Jesus made available, otherwise the Lamb is not receiving the full reward for His suffering.

Theologian and revival historian, Dr. Michael Brown, candidly notes:

I am absolutely convinced that the Church of today is not *fully* experiencing what Jesus died for and not yet becoming what He prayed for. There is something infinitely more and completely other than what we are walking in today. There is a power, a purity, an authority, an anointing, a glory that we have barely touched. The Lord is coming for a beautiful Bride. There is much preparation, restoration, and reformation still to take place.[4]

Even though these words may sting, they are needed reminders. They summon the church to settle for nothing less than the resurrection life Jesus made available. It's time for us to start living like we are really indwelt by God. When this happens, everything starts to shift. This is how men and women of old tasted the "powers of the age to come" and we branded it *revival* (see Heb. 6:5). Their spiritual eyes were awakened to what was available in the Holy Spirit and how His divine flow of power could be restored to the church. It's time for new voices to emerge that call this generation to great awakening.

Open Up the Gates!

Lord, raise up fiery evangelists like John and Charles Wesley, George Whitefield, Jonathan Edwards, and Charles Finney who preached Christ with such conviction and authority, that the power of God would touch people so dramatically they would drop to the ground under the glorious weight of the Gospel![5]

Holy Spirit, breathe upon a new generation who would be completely sold out to the Savior like St. Francis of

Assisi — a man who took Jesus' words so literally (notably concerning signs, wonders, and miracles) that there was no question as to whether or not the supernatural was available for his day. If Jesus said it was available, then St. Francis pursued it for the taking.[6]

God, stir up church leaders who would cling to the Scriptures like William Seymour — the catalyst of the Azusa Street Revival who passionately preached and unwaveringly stood upon the biblical truth of Spirit baptism, even though he had not personally experienced it.[7] *If the Bible says all believers can heal the sick, cast out demons, and walk in supernatural power, then the Word of God has the definitive word on the subject, regardless of what we have seen or not seen.*

Although the ancient gates have been shut over the centuries, faithful men and women have consistently emerged onto the stage of history who walked in the spirit of awakening. Just when it would seem as though the direction of Christianity had plummeted into an irreparable deluge of compromise, worldliness and religion, prophetic voices pierced the silence. These are the voices that thunder in Heaven, undoing trades and unlocking Holy Spirit outpouring!

Prophets emerged from the wilderness of obscurity, confronting the blasé of compromised Christianity with fiery summons to repentance and reformation. Throughout the ages, there have been rare Kingdom pioneers living amongst us. These were the few who became fed up with the status quo of Spirit-less spirituality and bulldozed through the red tape of religion, hungry to walk under an open Heaven while living on earth.

What is most exciting is that we are living in a time like none other. Though the Spirit-empowered remnant was small throughout history, particularly during the Dark/Middle Ages, its numbers have grown significantly. In this present hour, no longer is

God being pursued by an elite few, here and there. This is why the book you are reading is not designed to point you to some "Great Revival That Is Coming...*one day,* someday." I firmly believe that revival is upon us. Yes, we are on the brink of a tipping point— one, I prophesy, is already pouring out into the earth, for the Lord is responding to both the hunger and the action of His people. Yes, this hunger will increase, develop, and ultimately usher in great awakening throughout the church and reformation in the world. For now, though, I celebrate the fact that entire communities of people across the earth are pressing in to experience the fullness of God in their lives. What was previously accessed by only a handful of men and women throughout the centuries is now being experienced and enjoyed by the masses.

Truly, the ancient gates are opening. No longer will there be a limited quantity of divine resource released through the bars, but as the gates lift up, the world has yet to witness the majesty of God's supernatural power released through His anointed Ekklesia!

7

Getting Back to Normal

Restore us to yourself, O Lord, that we may be restored!
Renew our days as of old (Lamentations 5:21).

One day at three o'clock in the afternoon, Peter and John were on their way into the Temple for prayer meeting. At the same time there was a man crippled from birth being carried up. Every day he was set down at the Temple gate, the one named Beautiful, to beg from those going into the Temple. When he saw Peter and John about to enter the Temple, he asked for a handout. Peter, with John at his side, looked him straight in the eye and said, "Look here." He looked up, expecting to get something from them.

Peter said, "I don't have a nickel to my name, but what I do have, I give you: In the name of Jesus Christ of Nazareth, walk!" He grabbed him by the right hand and pulled him up. In an instant his feet and ankles became firm. He jumped to his feet and walked.

The man went into the Temple with them, walking back and forth, dancing and praising God. Everybody there saw him walking around and praising God. They recognized him as the one who sat begging at the Temple's Gate Beautiful and rubbed their eyes, astonished, scarcely believing what they were seeing.

The man threw his arms around Peter and John, ecstatic. All the people ran up to where they were at Solomon's Porch to see it for themselves (Acts 3:1-11 MSG).

Greater Than Silver or Gold

THIS STORY IS ONE expression of what *normal* Christianity looked like for the early church. The most profound, telling statement revealing the essence of faith comes from Peter, who said to the lame beggar: *"I have no silver and gold, but what I do have I give to you"* (Acts 3:6). What did Peter have to offer this man?

It was not a flashy church service that rivaled Broadway or Hollywood in production value.

It was not religious rhetoric or relevant spirituality that could have been mistaken for a pep talk.

It was not a program, event, or outreach.

None of these things are inherently bad. If flashy gatherings win lost people to Jesus, I celebrate! If religious rhetoric genuinely leads into to an encounter with God, wonderful! If our programs, events, and outreach efforts continue to evangelize the lost and disciple the found, keep them going strong. The problem is when we live disconnected from what we *truly* have to offer.

Peter and John walked in unusual supernatural authority, not because they were super-disciples, but because they lived aware of what—or *who*—they had to offer. These men were more aware of God's Presence within them than anything else. Everything in church life was secondary to accommodating the Presence of the Holy Spirit.

The journey toward unlocking revival is all about rediscovering our inheritance—one that is infinitely more valuable than the "silver and gold" that we try to offer through our natural efforts. Once again, we are reminded that as Spirit-filled sons and daughters of God, we are the wealthiest people in the universe.

Revival is *not* about trying to find our *lost inheritance,* as if somehow the people of God lost the Holy Spirit over the past two thousand years of recorded church history. He is still very much with us and inside of us! It is high time for us to open our eyes to the most precious gift we have ever been entrusted with. For Peter and John, there was no question as to who the most precious Person was to the early church community. The fruit of this revelation was a normal demonstration of supernatural power. This is what God is calling us back to.

You should not be content with a Christianity that is high in ideology but void in demonstration. This is a counterfeit spirituality that Jesus never presented. Consider it. The early church was not renowned for its programs; it was recognized for its power. This one demonstration of power in Acts 3 shifted the atmosphere over an entire region. This is not meant to be some nice Bible story that we read through and smile at because two super-anointed apostles healed a crippled beggar. This is a prophetic blueprint that summons the church throughout the ages to walk in the Holy Spirit power that Jesus made available.

Consider the implications of this one miracle:

> *And all the people saw him walking and praising God, and recognized him as the one who sat at the Beautiful Gate of the temple, asking for alms. And they were filled with wonder and amazement at what had happened to him* (Acts 3:9-10).

Note that *all the people* saw the previously lame man walking and praising God. This was not an isolated incident where only a few people got to witness this display of miracle-working power. Continuing on in verse 11, we see that *"while he* [the beggar] *clung to Peter and John, all the people, utterly astounded, ran together to them in the portico called Solomon's"* (Acts 3:11). Peter takes this opportunity to boldly preach the Gospel to those who were gathered and astounded by the lame man's supernatural healing.

> *And his name – by faith in his name – has made this man strong whom you see and know, and the faith that is through Jesus has given the man this perfect health in the presence of you all* (Acts 3:16)

Result? *"But many of those who had heard the word believed, and the number of the men came to about five thousand"* (Acts 4:4). This is nothing short of a stunning testimony! The lame beggar is supernaturally healed, which draws a large audience. Out of this audience, at least five thousand believe the Gospel and become Christ-followers. The following helps put everything into the appropriate perspective for me and makes this story relevant for generations to come.

> *Now when they saw the boldness of Peter and John, and perceived that they were uneducated, common men, they were astonished. And they recognized that they had been with Jesus* (Acts 4:13).

Peter and John were not special. They made this abundantly clear upon healing the beggar, explaining that it was the name of Jesus that brought supernatural strength to this lame man. These were uneducated, common men. What made them bold firebrands for the Kingdom of God? Peter and John recognized the priceless treasure that they received through inheritance – the Holy Spirit. They weren't asking for another Pentecost; they were stewarding the one they had already received.

How does God respond to good stewards? He entrusts them with more. Could it be that this is one of the reasons we see the unusual phenomena of Acts 4:23-31, where the believers pray and as a result, *"the place in which they were gathered together was shaken, and they were all filled with the Holy Spirit and continued to speak the word of God with* boldness" (Acts 4:31)? This verse is not suggesting that the believers received a Holy Spirit upgrade or that the first Pentecost was not sufficient. Quite the contrary. Acts 4 is an example of the indwelling Spirit coming to *rest upon* the disciples in a greater demonstration of power. This is the great pursuit of the Christian life. At conversion, the Holy Spirit comes to live inside of us. When we receive Spirit baptism, the Spirit within us comes to reveal Himself on the outside in greater demonstrations. With subsequent fillings with the Spirit, the disciples simply walked in greater expressions of power and effectiveness.

At the day's end, may our confession be the same as the apostle Peter's—silver and gold we don't have, but what we do have, we give. We freely give what we have freely received (see Matt. 10:8). Healing the sick, casting out demons, raising the dead, and walking in Kingdom authority flows through us with ease because we have become quick to recognize and draw from the spiritual inheritance we have received in the Holy Spirit.

Why introduce this chapter with Peter and John? These two men offer a prototype for what Christianity should look like, not just in the first century but from age to age until Jesus returns. Why does it seem like the power has been unplugged? Simple. By and large, the church traded supernatural power *for* silver and gold.

For now, we must approach the Scriptures with a new measure of vulnerability. We pray:

> *Lord, I am discontent reading about what I am **not** seeing in my own life. Thank You, Father, that there is no shame, guilt, or condemnation in this recognition. I don't come to You with my head hung low; I come as Your beloved son/daughter, hungry to be a good steward of the glorious inheritance You have given me.*

Open my eyes, Holy Spirit, to the priceless gift I have received in You. Make me aware of anything that I have allowed to quench Your unrestricted flow in my life. I repent, Lord. There is no silver, gold, or earthly currency that could ever remotely compare to Your Presence in my life.

The Early Church: Our Blueprint for Normal Christianity

True revival is *not* about getting some quick spiritual fix; revival is intended to restore Heaven's order to Jesus' church. For the first 300 years of church history, the community of faith was largely known for its resemblance to the church defined by Jesus and demonstrated in the Book of Acts.

Author, historian, and respected healing minister Francis MacNutt comments that "in the early apostolic Church...manifestations of the Presence of the Holy Spirit—tongues, joyfulness, prophetic words, visions—were regarded as normal."[1] In addition, when one reviews the works of the church fathers such as Irenaeus, Tertullian, and Origen, accounts of miracles, signs, wonders, healings, and exorcisms are consistently present in their writings.[2] The first disciples, and the disciples of these disciples, continued the supernatural ministry of Jesus, considering that to be the standard demonstration of the Christian faith.

These are the biblical models we are looking to revisit—to *revive*. Remember, revival is not pursuing some "new" thing; it is about restoring the primitive expression of supernatural Christianity that Jesus modeled.

When we honestly read the Gospel narratives, it is obvious that Jesus never envisioned a community of faith where the demonstration of supernatural power was optional. In fact, Jesus gave all of His followers — from generation to generation — the best picture of what normal Christianity should look like.

After examining the words of Jesus and reviewing the exploits recorded in the Book of Acts, I want to share four descriptions of what normal Christianity should look like.

Normal Christians are an advancing Kingdom Ekklesia that demolishes darkness and releases the power of Heaven on earth.

I will give you the keys of the kingdom of heaven; and whatever you bind on earth shall have been bound in heaven, and whatever you loose on earth shall have been loosed in heaven (Matthew 16:19 NASB).

Normal Christians are well acquainted with what is standard operating protocol in Heaven and enforce its legislation on earth. This is *not* some kind of dominion theology, where Christians believe that they are Heaven's hirelings, purposed to overthrow worldly governments and political arenas. In fact, such a thought process is the very counterfeit of what Jesus was really talking about here.

Time after time, Jesus corrected the disciples as they sought to approach the Kingdom of God from a dominionist perspective. While the disciples were hoping for a Messiah who brought political liberation to the Jewish people — and thus, overthrew the Roman government — Jesus did *not* teach or do this. If Jesus is our model, then to entertain any form of "dominion" theology is doing the exact *opposite* of what Jesus demonstrated.

Carefully review Jesus' words in Matthew 16:19. *Whatever you bind on earth shall have been bound in heaven.* This begs the question: What is bound, or forbidden in Heaven? These are the very things we are called to bind and forbid on earth. Jesus is the best example, giving us a physical demonstration of an Anointed Man who, through the power of the Spirit, bound the powers of darkness that were obviously prohibited in Heaven. This is most expressly seen in Jesus' functions as exorcist and healer. He bound demonic torment, affliction, disease, and in some cases the power of death.

Jesus did not simply bind darkness; He also loosed that which was already loosed in Heaven. He broke the enemy's power and in turn, released healing, deliverance, life, freedom, forgiveness, peace, and wholeness — the currency of the Kingdom of Heaven.

Normal Christians are a charismatic community that operates in signs, wonders, and miracles.

Truly, truly, I say to you, whoever believes in me will also do the works that I do (John 14:12a).

Respected Pentecostal historian Dr. Vinson Synan notes that "the church of the New Testament was indeed a charismatic one."[3] Jesus' invitation is very clear — the lifestyle of supernatural works and the promise of greater works is reserved for *whoever believes.* The expression of Christianity demonstrated with power was not exclusive to the apostles or the early church. Rather, such a miracle lifestyle is available to *whoever* believes in Jesus! Why does it seem like the frequency of miracles was more normative among the early church than it is today? They adhered to a simple, undiluted Gospel. Cessation theory had not crept in, corrupting theology. The church had not yet become strange bedfellows with the state. Any concept of a "nominal" believer or "casual" Christian was alien. In fact, most church historians agree that "the institutionalization of the early church was accompanied by the demise of the charismatic gifts."[4] For the early church, normal meant power!

Before the loss of power, the early faith community was *not* charismatic in terms of a denomination; it was charismatic in its demonstration. Contrary to belief, the word *charismatic* is not a twentieth century invention that is limited to describing a more expressive and flamboyant flavor of Christianity. To be charismatic is to minister in the grace gifts of the Holy Spirit. Charismatic comes from the Greek word for grace—*charis*. To be charismatic is to be one who operates under the supernatural, empowering influence of God's grace.

What made the early church such a powerful community? They recognized that the same grace that broke their bondage to sin and made their hearts alive to God *also* empowered them to bring a physical demonstration of the Kingdom *on earth as it is in Heaven*. It was not a stretch for them to believe that every single believer was anointed to perform signs and wonders in Jesus' name. This was simply normal to them.

Normal Christians are a spiritually hungry people who press in to access greater works and extraordinary miracles.

> *...and greater works than these will he do, because I am going to the Father* (John 14:12b).

> *And God was doing extraordinary miracles by the hands of Paul, so that even handkerchiefs or aprons that had touched his skin were carried away to the sick, and their diseases left them and the evil spirits came out of them* (Acts 19:11-12).

Is it possible for us to do greater works than Jesus? This seems like a shocking prospect, because Jesus was God. How is it possible that human beings could do *greater* miracles than God Himself?

Consider this. Jesus was, is, and forever will be God; that is an undisputable, theological standard that was vehemently fought for in church history. Our problem is perspective. Whether Jesus was performing the miracles in the Gospels or the Spirit of God is performing the miracles *through us* today, God is still the wonder worker. Jesus Himself attributed the miracle ministry to the Pres-ence of the Holy Spirit, acknowledging that "*if it is by the Spirit of*

God that I drive out demons, then the kingdom of God has come upon you" (Matt. 12:28). Jesus healed and delivered, thus advancing the Kingdom of God through the anointing of the Spirit that was upon Him.

Henry Blackaby, a prophetic voice and the author of the classic *Experiencing God*, describes the unique relationship between the Holy Spirit and Jesus:

> When Jesus took on human flesh, He chose to live under the limitations that come with a physical body. That doesn't mean He ceased to be divine, but He willingly set aside His rights as God and lived as a human. And being limited by His physical condition, He was forced to rely upon the Holy Spirit as His source of wisdom and power...the Holy Spirit who came upon Jesus is exactly the same Holy Spirit given to you and me.[5]

If we have truly received the same Holy Spirit that empowered Jesus—and Scripture says we have—we can confidently pursue the John 14:12 promise of greater works. This is Jesus' personal invitation. The God who anointed Elisha to perform miracles is the same God who empowered Jesus to do the miraculous; this same God is inside of you today through the Holy Spirit. No matter which way we look at it, God is the one performing the miracles and God is the one who ultimately receives the glory.

The apostle Paul is a powerful example of an anointed person who began to see the *greater* works come to pass in his life and ministry. If miracles were not astonishing enough, Luke assigned the descriptive "extraordinary" to the miracles that Paul was experiencing in Acts 19:11-12. Consider the contrast for a moment. In the Gospels, people touched Jesus' clothes (hem of His garment) and received their healing; with Paul, people took the sweatbands and handkerchiefs that he wore during everyday life, brought them to the sick and demonized, and they were healed.

Was it because Paul was some kind of super apostle? Was it because Paul had somehow surpassed Jesus in anointing? "No" to both. Paul was a human being, like you or I, who was saturated in the Presence of the God whose world has no sickness, disease, and torment. Paul was not even placing an emphasis on the miracles; he simply lived to experientially know the Miracle Maker. That was his primary aim above all else, as expressed in Philippians 3:8: "*Indeed, I count everything as loss because of the surpassing worth of knowing Christ Jesus my Lord.*" Truly, this scripture describes the life that is the prime candidate to experience greater works and extraordinary miracles.

Normal Christians are a people with a vision to see entire cities repent and regions transformed by the power of God.

There are two scriptures that illustrate this point, one from the Old Testament and one from the Book of Acts.

Old Testament: The City of Nineveh

The word reached the king of Nineveh, and he arose from his throne, removed his robe, covered himself with sackcloth, and sat in ashes. And he issued a proclamation and published through Nineveh, "By the decree of the king and his nobles: Let neither man nor beast, herd nor flock, taste anything. Let them not feed or drink water, but let man and beast be covered with sackcloth, and let them call out mightily to God. Let everyone turn from his evil way and from the violence that is in his hands. Who knows? God may turn and relent and turn from his fierce anger, so that we may not perish." When God saw what they did, how they turned from their evil way, God relented of the disaster that he had said he would do to them, and he did not do it (Jonah 3:6-10).

Why use this Old Testament illustration to describe what normal New Testament Christianity looks like? If God could supernaturally transform the heathen, wicked city of Nineveh under the Old Covenant, how much more could God do today? Lift up your eyes and heighten your expectation of what the Spirit can do. This passage calls us upward in vision to entertain the idea that God could actually transform an entire city or region.

New Testament: City of Samaria

> *Philip went down to the city of Samaria and proclaimed to them the Christ. And the crowds with one accord paid attention to what was being said by Philip, when they heard him and saw the signs that he did. For unclean spirits, crying out with a loud voice, came out of many who had them, and many who were paralyzed or lame were healed. So there was much joy in that city* (Acts 8:5-8).

This is the New Testament counterpart to Jonah 3. One of the most striking aspects of this account for me is verse 8. Such would suggest that a significant portion of the city of Samaria was experiencing supernatural joy. It is an easy verse to skip past, as it is but a fleeting comment. Could it be, though, that because of the mighty demonstration of God's power through healing and exorcism, Samaria became a transformed city?

We must believe this is possible for today. Perhaps the notion of transformed cities is so distant from modern church culture because of our neglect of the very elements that brought the Kingdom of God to Samaria to begin with — the normative expression of healing and deliverance among the saints of God.

It's Time to See
Cities, Regions, and Nations Opened!

Could it be that once we get back to the Bible's definition of normal, we will begin to see entire cities come to Jesus? I prophesy that it's the supernatural church that will break open cities for the Kingdom of God. For many churches have struggled with winning their cities to Jesus. They've toiled and labored, implementing every strategy that they could get their hands on. Their intentions are pure, yes, but there is a greater, more effortless way to see the multitudes transformed. I see megachurches with multiple campuses confounded by the grim reality that their regions have not been shaken by the Gospel. In the spirit, I see these pastors and leaders discussing, consulting, considering, all basically wanting to know, *Why?! Why aren't we seeing greater breakthrough? More souls being saved? And perhaps most measurably, why are our cities and regions in the horrible conditions they are in, even when there are major church buildings all around?*

Our efforts will only take us so far. The Spirit of God is visiting people in this season, absolutely wrecking them for anything less than a holy visitation of His Presence. I see divine "messes" hitting churches—notable churches! Big churches! Churches with a good reputation! And yet, the reason some of these churches have a good reputation is because the leaders actually value and prize integrity. It's easy to take cheap shots sometimes at megachurches and influential leaders, but the reality is that many of these places and people are experiencing great results because they are good stewards. Yet, in all of the success, the Lord is stirring the waters. From pulpit to pew, from pastor to parishioner, I see a collective cry for *more* breaking something open in a region. Churches will become regional influencers to the degree that they are an open gate of Holy Spirit outpouring!

If God the Father gave Christ the Son *nations* as His inheritance (see Ps. 2:7-8), I must ask—what's a *city* to God? What's *your* city to God? It does not matter how dark it seems, or how strong a grip territorial spirits have over it. You might even think you are living in one of the immoral, depraved, heathen communities on the planet. Doesn't matter. Let's dare to believe that the God who brought the entire city of Nineveh to repentance and released supernatural joy throughout the city of Samaria can do the same things today.

Our Road Back to Normal

I simply presented only four descriptions of what normal Christianity looks like, as defined by Jesus and as demonstrated by the early church. Please do not allow my thoughts on the subject to be your definitive stance on the matter. Dive into the Gospels and come out wonderfully rearranged. Commit yourself to being challenged by what you read in the Book of Acts, allowing the Holy Spirit to expand your imagination.

To restore the church to its intended role as God's vehicle for supernatural restoration on earth, we must honestly confront our present condition. Where we are, by and large, is not what God has for us. These words are not meant to condemn; they are intended to incite hunger. *There is more!*

How do we get back to normal and start experiencing the supernatural Christian life God has made available to us?

Repent

When repentance is presented in the same context as revival, there often seems to be an emphasis placed on weeping and wailing over personal sin. Many preach that in order to experience revival, we need to first deal with these sins. This is true, as the eyes of the Lord are searching the earth for a people who treasure His *Presence* more than the sinful pollution being propagated in the world.

Does God use imperfect people who struggle with sin to do mighty exploits for Him? History proves the answer to be a resounding "Yes!" Yet, as imperfect people start pressing into God's Presence, they start to recognize the supernatural exploits that are their inheritance to walk in. As we come face to face with our true inheritance in Christ, sin loses its allure.

In order for the church as a whole to get back to normal, there is a very specific corporate sin that we need to acknowledge and repent of — *our redefinition of Christianity*. In future chapters, we are going to explore this in much greater depth, as I believe one of the greatest sins we need to repent for is the sin of trading away God's glory.

Many people and churches have created a god in their own image. We have traded the God of Scripture for a deity of convenience who does what we want, when we want it, and never challenges our theology. This is not Yahweh; it's "my way" with a spiritual bent. To begin our journey back to normal, we must confront this one sin that, just maybe, has distracted the church right out of her supernatural birthright. I guarantee you, when you sincerely search the Bible for God's definition of the Christian life, you will quickly discover it is supernatural through and through.

Return

Often, repentance is birthed as we honestly return to the pages of Scripture, looking for solutions to a Christianity in crisis. The same living words that convict us are also those that instruct us, faithfully leading us back to normal. The Word of God is our ultimate standard for what Christianity should look like throughout time immemorial. It does not matter what the latest church growth strategies say, polls indicate, or popular pastors are experimenting with in their local congregations. While such things certainly have their appropriate place, they should always be in subservience to the unrestricted move of the Holy Spirit.

While there are certain things that change with the times, the very fundamentals of the faith must remain consistent. Sadly, the very works that Jesus did and anointed us to do are labeled as archaic, ancient, and even irrelevant by some believers. Even those who belong to so-called Charismatic or Pentecostal denominations have been caught downplaying the supernatural while choosing a more "mainstream" and socially acceptable faith blend. Wherever you fall on the spectrum, the Holy Spirit is inviting you to return to His standard. Come back to normal!

The problem we face with returning to this "new normal" is that it has been so long since the supernatural has been normal that, at first glance, it seems abnormal. The more you allow the Scriptures to pierce your heart, revealing God's standard for the Christian life, the more God's vision of normal will become your great pursuit, regardless of what others think.

Review

As you seek to return to normal, I invite you to review the mighty works of God throughout history—and then consider the miraculous deeds He has performed in your own life. This is your history with God. This generation needs an accessible starting point for building a history with God that is grounded in the miraculous and supernatural. I pray this book is one among many that helps lead us back to this place.

The purpose of this book is to set before you historical examples of men, women, and entire movements who pressed in to experience the supernatural "normal" they saw in the Bible.

Oftentimes, when we read about the spiritual pioneers who went before us, there tends to be an "off limits" air about their stories. In other words, we think it is okay to celebrate their incredible Kingdom exploits, but we should not *expect* such special works in our own lives today. After all, *they were unique. Such works were special and reserved for apostles, heroes, revivalists, evangelists, and spiritual leaders.* The message of this book is simple: Anything that the revivalists of old did, you can do too.

Do not believe the "off limits" lie. As you read these testimonies, claim them as your own inheritance. Regardless of whether the people lived a thousand years ago or are living today, their inheritance in Christ is also your inheritance. Every grace and gift they pressed in to receive is also available to you.

Just as Evan Roberts saw the spiritual landscape of the nation of Wales transformed during the Welsh Revival, you can see *your region* impacted.

In the same manner that William Seymour pressed in to experience the baptism of the Spirit, you too can experience new realms in God as you believe His promises — no matter what you are presently experiencing.

Your mouth can carry the Gospel of fire like Wesley, Whitefield, and Jonathan Edwards.

You can contend with Heaven to see a region shaken by the Presence of God like two 80-plus-year-old sisters did just preceding the Hebrides Revival of 1949.

Are you ready to receive your supernatural inheritance and open up the gates of God's power in your life? Remember: *Revival is birthed when we believe that the church has received all access to all promises.*

Revival is not the church waiting around for God to move if He so wills; it's recognizing that God has already made the ultimate move *toward earth* at Pentecost, and now it's up to us, Jesus' body on earth, to align with what He is doing. As we operate in sync with what He is doing — when we move as He moves and speak what He says — the Holy Spirit will roar out of a people who carry the glory!

8

I Hear the Roar
of the Holy Spirit

THIS THING CALLED "REVIVAL" is both sovereign and "steward-able." God breaks in through powerful, dynamic "suddenly" movements. And yet, somewhere behind the scenes, there is a person, or company of people, preparing themselves for these suddenlies of God.

Arthur Wallis, in his classic work *In the Day of Thy Power*, describes revival as having two key foundations: "the sovereignty of God and the preparedness of man."

I sense that we are in a season of preparation for another sovereign suddenly—a climatic "suddenly" that will ignite a revival/awakening/move of the Spirit that will not have start and end dates; it will be a provocative, un-ignorable outpouring that demands a response—reception or rejection. Those who reject it can continue on with "business as usual," while those who meet God with a "Yes" (even if the "Yes" comes with hesitation, trembling, and all-out fear), will be stepping into a prophetic moment in the unfolding of divine timing: *"restoring all the things about which God spoke by the mouth of his holy prophets long ago"* (Acts 3:21).

A Supernatural Vision
of Desperation in Prayer

Recently, the Holy Spirit allowed me to see a brief vision. I saw the image of an influential pastor in his office. Didn't know who he was specifically, I just knew that this person led a recognized, popular, and successful church.

I see this pastor figure sitting in a darkened office with the window shades/blinds closed. He is leaning over his desk, crying out from a deep guttural place in his spirit. You cannot fake this cry; it's the cry of the barren womb. It's the cry of a Hannah who doesn't care about reputation; she just wants a son (see 1 Sam. 1:1-20). The author of Proverbs describes the barren womb as one of the four things that never are satisfied—they never say "enough" (see Prov. 30:16).

Immediately, I remembered John Kilpatrick, the pastor during the historic Brownsville Revival (1995-2000). In the days leading up to the revival, July 15, 1995, Kilpatrick was a desperate man. Before revival broke out, Kilpatrick was enjoying a measure of success. He had a TV ministry. He had the respect and love of the congregation. The church was prospering on all fronts. I know specifics were different back in the 1990s, but ultimately, Kilpatrick was enjoying what many leaders are walking in today. And yet, he was gripped by a poverty that no numbers, respect, or media exposure could fill. It was the poverty of a hungry spirit that knew there was so much more than he was presently experiencing. This compelled Kilpatrick to drive over to the church sanctuary in the middle of the night, lay down prostrate over the front pew, and cry out from the depths of his anguished, thirsty soul: "Oh God, there's got to be more! I need You, Lord!" I know it's not cool to consider ourselves an impoverished people, but the cry of a poor spirit is considered by Jesus to be a blessing (see Matt. 5:3).

Back in my vision, I sensed this nameless, faceless, influential pastor represented a generation of leaders who are burnt out with the same old, same old when it comes to doing church and ministry. They've done everything in the books and yet are still absolutely desperate for something supernatural—for God to rend the heavens and break in with His power. I see the hunger of John Kilpatrick being represented in the cry of a new generation of millennial church leaders. They are tired of the gimmicks; they want God. *But how?*

I believe a price has to be paid. To experience a true move of God, it demands a people who are willing to say a costly and consistent "Yes" to the Holy Spirit's movement and manifestation. We must be willing to say, "Holy Spirit, I want You—on Your terms, not mine. I want Your Presence more than my preference." History clearly shows the results of this kind of hunger.

The Presence of the Spirit
Is Brooding Over the Church

At the same time, while pastors and leaders are crying out in the secret place for a fresh touch of the Spirit, I see entire congregations being visited by the hovering Presence of the Spirit. What does this look like?

Look at Genesis 1 and notice how the Holy Spirit hovered over the waters at Creation (see Gen. 1:1-2). He was hovering, brooding. Nothing explosive happened until a decree was made from the Father.

Right now, in the church, I believe we are seeing evidence of the Spirit brooding as we witness an increased intensity in praise and worship, interest in prayer, and fervency for outreach and service. These are signs that the Holy Spirit is moving among us. And yet, the brooding Presence and the explosive Presence are two different dimensions. Everyday people are growing dissatisfied with religion and disinterested in trendy, cool Christianity. Regardless of people's theological upbringing or denominational backgrounds, I sense that a strong population in the body of Christ, particularly young people, want to see God actually do what Isaiah 64:1 cries out for: *rend the heavens and come down.*

Yet, this is where the spiritually hungry pastors and church leaders factor into the equation. Like in Genesis 1, the Spirit is waiting for an announcement. He was waiting for the Father to say "light be!" In our case, the Spirit is not going to just barge into our churches and disrupt everything; that would prove disastrous, especially if the pastors and leaders didn't want anything to do with "that Holy Spirit stuff." Rather, He is looking for a few radical friends who are willing to lay everything down—namely their reputations—to see God move in His fullness and thus see cities, regions, and even nations transformed by the Gospel of the Kingdom. What will this look like? People in the earth bringing the cries of their heart into agreement with the decree of the Father in Heaven. You see, the same Father who decreed *light be* at Creation also made a decree concerning the move of the Holy Spirit. Simply stated, He said: "*I will pour out my Spirit on all flesh*" (Acts 2:17). When we give voice to this decree of outpouring in our hearts, with our mouths, and through our actions, I believe we position ourselves for that combustive explosion of the Spirit.

I am not content with a theology of Holy Spirit outpouring and open heavens without seeing the manifestation. I want to see what it looks like to see churches, families, cities, and regions experience the blessing of a torn-open heaven (see Isa. 64:1). I want to see the resources of one world flow into this world through an Ekklesia that serves as the legislating, governing body of Christ in the earth, exercising authority in the spiritual airways.

I prophesy that the hovering of the Spirit will escalate into obvious and marked "holy moments." These are definable moments in the midst of our services and gatherings when the atmosphere is simply electric with God. Everyone recognizes it. In fact, to go on with business as usual would just feel completely wrong, like one was shutting down what God wanted to do in that moment.

It will be in these "valleys of decision" where pastors and leaders will have the opportunity to "go for it" and say "Yes" to what the Spirit wants to do. Or, sadly, they will also have the ability to move on with the program, completely shutting down the potential for landscape-changing revival. Even those who legitimately cried out for the move of God, interestingly enough, have the potential to say "No" to it.

The Idol of Reputation
Is Restraining the Move of God

In studying the history of significant moves of God, both past and present, I've noticed a recurring common denominator. Those whom God used as either catalysts to help ignite revival or stewards to help sustain it made a decision to completely surrender their reputation.

There is no place for the exaltation of personal reputation if we want to see a move of God. If we really want to experience the outpouring of the Holy Spirit and every blessing that accompanies it, we need to truly follow the model of the Suffering Servant and be willing to make ourselves of *no reputation* (see Phil. 2:7 NKJV). Not some reputation—no reputation. If there is a trace of the love of reputation in us, I believe it can hinder us from stepping into the fullness of what God wants to release into the earth. He's looking for those who are all in, completely yielded. Not perfect—yielded.

I'm convinced that one of the key restraining agents for the move of God is the idol of reputation. It's an idol because when we are motivated to preserve and guard our personal reputation, any prayer we pray for "revival" will have unseen, unheard strings attached. God can move—just as long as He doesn't do anything that messes up my_____ (fill in the blank). Life. Church. Ministry. Public persona. After all, "I've got a good thing going here." That attitude must die if we are to break through the self-imposed ceiling of "ministry" and begin seeing God manifest in our midst.

A Divine Synergy that Will Produce a Revival Explosion

We've seen what happens when leaders say that uncomfortable but glorious "Yes" to the holy moments of God. History notes these amazing lightning strikes of the Spirit, where regions and generations are touched by outpouring. I sense we are stepping into a season when lightning strikes of God will not be exclusive to one church but, rather, a collective of churches throughout cities and regions. I believe it was author and minister Tim Sheets who spoke of a day coming when people would have access to a center Holy Spirit outpouring within a 15-minute drive. Let it be, Lord! Any church, really, that says "Yes" to the move of the Spirit. And these explosive lightning strikes of God will be the result of two things coming into collision—the secret-place cry of the pastors and leaders combined with the desperation of the people who attend church week after week.

Yes, I prophesy the lightning strikes of the Spirit are coming to local churches. It's the local church, not the revival center, where everyday people come, week after week, for community, service, and spiritual development.

A Vision for Revival and Reformation

The Lord gave me a significant word in 2017 about the marriage of revival and reformation. It's easy see the burning bush encounter of Exodus 3 and get caught up in the overt "revival" symbolism. We see the fire of God, an unusual manifestation of God's Presence, and encounter the holiness, awe, and fear of the Lord. I love all of these things, and yet if revival becomes our driving focus I believe the very thing we wish to see transform the church will only go so far. God wants to come "down" so He can come out. In other words, He wants to move powerfully in our midst and encounter us so that, like Moses, we experience His fire and also hear His voice. And when that voice speaks from the fire, it commissions us to become societal reformers, like it did Moses in Exodus 3 and even the prophet Isaiah (see Isa. 6).

I prophesy that in this season, as the church opens its doors to the unrestrained move of the Spirit, there are going to be dynamic and dramatic encounters that people have in the Presence of God. The people who have these encounters with the fire of God are the 98 percent of everyday people who attend church week after week who have no aspirations to be pulpit preachers or international ministers. They have career ambitions. They have trade skills. They have passions, talents, and desires that make them uniquely qualified to occupy certain spheres of influence.

The Lord is passionately pursuing everyday people, for He wants to invade everyday places with extraordinary power. This assignment is not exclusive to "revival people." Everyday, normal people called to medicine, government, education, politics, and media. People who work 9 to 5, Monday to Friday, for the Lord wants His Presence in the places where the people go.

The goal is not to create a separate supernatural revival culture where the move of the Spirit becomes exclusive to special events, conferences, revival hubs, and arenas outside of the local church. These are absolutely necessary as outlets that pour into the church, but I sense the objective of the Lord in this hour is a Holy Spirit reformation in the local church that produces cultural revolution.

What Will Happen in the Day of His Power?

Every revival in history seems to be the result of a few people becoming so hungry for God that they wanted Him more than oxygen. Those who have such hunger will not be denied. — Rick Joyner

Pastors and leaders are crying out for more of God in the secret place. Congregations and local church communities are increasing in corporate hunger for the Holy Spirit's movement and manifestation. God is hovering over local churches, noticeably charging the spiritual climate.

Next, the church will be faced with a decision: say yes to the holy moments the Spirit is extending — which demand a dead reputation and a complete yielding to the move of God — or say no and continue with business as usual, all the while living dissatisfied because we are unwilling to slay our reputation so that Jesus can rise in our midst in Holy Spirit power.

For those who take the ultimate glorious plunge with a "Yes," I see local churches radically shifting. A new reputation will be established. These local venues will become known in their communities — not because of their personalities, programs, or production value, but because of the Presence of a Person moving powerfully in their midst.

People won't come because of some celebrity speaker or dynamic personality; they will come because word got out that a living God is moving among those people. I see a normalization of the gifts of the Spirit, including healing, prophecy, deliverance and other demonstrations of power. And yet, I don't see those becoming focal points; they will be seamless byproducts of God moving in the midst of His people. More than anything, I see the days ahead being marked by glory. Presence. Fire. Awe. Fear and trembling before a holy God. Unusual manifestations. Weight. Yes, even provocative miracles — signs and wonders that provoke responses from entire cities and regions because they cannot be ignored or avoided. I see the desperate, the seeker, the hungry, and the thirsty coming and being touched dramatically by the fire of God.

So what will we do? Will we say yes to the Holy Spirit and no to our reputations? It may be a painful exchange at first, but the testimony of every revival leader, both alive today or chronicled in the pages of history, is ample proof that what we lay down is nothing compared to what we pick up. If seeing God move in this generation means we lay down what people think about us, so be it! *We want God!*

Part Two

The Process of Restoring the Glory

In Israel, following a sovereign encounter with the Holy Spirit, the Lord released a prophetic blueprint based on how David handled transporting the Ark of the Covenant that, we believe, is a summons on how to accommodate the Presence of God. We are not waiting for the Holy Spirit to come down from Heaven; Heaven is waiting for a people who are willing to lay down their lives and agendas to prioritize God's Presence and accommodate the move of the Spirit. As we do this, we will begin to see sudden and dramatic Holy Spirit outpouring. God will truly have a resting place in and among His people. This is so that a broken and sin-stained world can have a glory-filled community in its midst who constantly remind people and places that redemption is available.

9

Serving the Presence

THIS SECTION WILL BE delivered in a series of smaller bite-sized chapters, so you can process and meditate on each one of these steps.

It was my encounter with the Holy Spirit in Israel that birthed the following section, as I believe the Lord was biblically revealing the steps to serving His Presence and accommodating His glory.

An encouraging word of caution, though: Anytime you have a dynamic, overwhelming encounter with the Holy Spirit, some kind of heavenly deposit is taking place. Perhaps this is why our physical bodies respond the way they do with shaking, laughing, weeping, or other physical phenomena. I figure if God is opening us up and putting something inside of us, we are going to respond — *some way!*

Serving the Presence of God

During our Israel trip, one passage I could not escape from was First Chronicles 16:37: "*David arranged for Asaph and his fellow Levites to serve regularly before the Ark of the Lord's Covenant, doing whatever needed to be done each day*" (NLT).

The last phrase stood out to me: Asaph and the fellow Levites served before the Ark of the Covenant, doing whatever needed to be done each day. Their occupation was to serve the Presence of the Lord. I believe this is a prophetic summons to us today, in an age of self-gratification that places mankind at the center of the universe. Sadly, this perspective has even crept into the community of believers. We sometimes think that the walk of faith is all about us getting whatever we want, need, or desire from God. I am so grateful we serve a good Father who heals, delivers, and provides. I wholeheartedly believe that Jesus made it possible for us to live a John 10:10 *abundant life*, where we flourish and walk in victory, testifying to *His* victory. However, we need to reacquaint ourselves with a painful but exceedingly rewarding process that David went through in order to discover how to experience an abiding habitation of the glory of God. This is what we want. I want us to be a people like Asaph and the Levites who serve God's Presence instead of placing demands or expectations on God to serve us. We don't have the luxury of telling the Lord how we want Him to move or how we would prefer for Him to show up. We want Him on His terms, even if He comes in ways that are unfamiliar to us. Revival history is wave after wave of God's Presence colliding with people in fresh ways that, at first, brought tremendous controversy. Dr. Michael Brown has said you can have controversy without revival, but you cannot have revival without controversy. I am not suggesting we mindlessly welcome all manifestations or phenomena that people claim to be the works of the Spirit. We must be Bereans who carefully search the Scriptures, recognizing the nature and character of God in the movement (see Acts 17:11).

> Pentecost came with the sound of a mighty rushing wind, a violent blast from heaven! Heaven has not exhausted its blasts, but our danger is we are getting frightened of them.
> —Smith Wigglesworth

Just remember, though, that the Day of Pentecost was not universally received. People needed to make a decision to either serve the outpouring of the Spirit or reject what God was doing. After all, these phenomena of mighty rushing winds, divided tongues of fire, and people speaking in different languages were new and unusual. The responses to this event were varied. In Acts 2:6, we see some were *"bewildered."* In verse 7, others were *"amazed and astonished."*

Verse 12 continues with those who were *"amazed and perplexed,"* asking one another, *"What does this mean?"* Finally, there were the mockers who completely rejected what was going on and claimed *"They are filled with new wine,"* accusing the tongue-talkers of being under the influence of alcohol (see Acts 2:13).

I prophesy, though, that just as God has in the past, He is once again raising up bold, theologically grounded "Peter voices" who proclaim, *"this is that"* (Acts 2:16 KJV)! He gives explanation to the manifestation of the Spirit and provides a biblical context for what was taking place. If we are ultimately unable to do this, we have reason to be suspicious of the phenomena that people are claiming are "of God."

What did Peter announce? He restated the prophecy found in the Book of Joel, in which God Himself gave the ultimate end-time prophetic word: *"And in the last days it shall be, God declares, that I will pour out my Spirit on all flesh, and your sons and your daughters shall prophesy, and your young men shall see visions, and your old men shall dream dreams"* (Acts 2:17).

What is God's ultimate objective? *All flesh*. Not all church. Not all Charismatic or Pentecostal followers of Jesus. His goal is to fill the planet with His glory. How will He do this? Through a people filled with glory, carrying and transferring this powerful Presence into every sphere of society.

So I must ask, why aren't we seeing this?

10

Rivers of Glory, Not Trickles

YOU'RE READING THIS BOOK because you are tired of the ebbs and flows. Can we be really honest here? You're tired of spiritual hype. You're tired of hearing about how "it's coming, it's coming!" and when you look in earnest for the manifestation of this glory, you don't really see anything. Or if you do, it's only a trickle. A taste. I know the following observation contradicts and challenges our current state, but the good news is that Jesus did not die so that we could simply enjoy a "trickle" of His Presence moving in and through us. He didn't envision a trickle; He saw a torrent.

Jesus prophesied of a day when, following His death, resurrection, and ascension, a people would arise in the earth who would carry *rivers* within them and release this healing river to the nations.

> *On the last day of the feast, the great day, Jesus stood up and cried out, "If anyone thirsts, let him come to me and drink. Whoever believes in me, as the Scripture has said, 'Out of his heart will flow rivers of living water.'" Now this he said about the Spirit, whom those who believed in him were to receive, for as yet the Spirit had not been given, because Jesus was not yet glorified* (John 7:37-39).

Ana and I both love the stunning prophetic picture that Ezekiel 47 is, pointing to a day when the River of God would flow out of the temple and bring healing to the nations. In verses 1-5, Ezekiel shares his vision of becoming progressively overwhelmed by a stream that was flowing from beneath the door of the Temple. We watch the water continuing to rise until the river became *"too deep to walk across. It was deep enough to swim in, but too deep to walk through"* (Ezek. 47:5 NLT). He was consumed by the river. Oh, let this be a picture of where we are headed, a people who are so saturated with God that they seamlessly swim in His Presence, flowing with the current of the Spirit. In order for us to carry the River of God's Presence to the nations, we need to first be a filled people. I want to encourage you, one filling is not enough. That's not meant to be a negative, condescending statement. Oh no! Perhaps the reason you feel dry and thirsty even right now is that you have believed it's only legal to get filled once, either at salvation or through an initial baptism in the Spirit.

Maybe your theology believes that you are filled completely with the Holy Spirit at the time of salvation. This is true; you don't need another Holy Spirit. However, you need to experience the power and the Presence of the One who is within you. We were not filled with a concept or theology; we were filled with a Person. So, I say to you friend, yes you have the Holy Spirit. Don't let anyone convince you otherwise! The real question is, how much of the Holy Spirit are you personally experiencing? This is why people press in for what we call "the baptism of the Spirit." This is not God coming into you again; if anything, it's God inside of you coming out with power! It's the Spirit who lives within you resting upon you.

And I would encourage my Pentecostal and Charismatic friends who teach the "baptism of the Spirit" that there is so much more than one touch, one filling, one experience, one encounter, and one altar experience. Oh, let those first encounters always be precious and treasured. But remember, the apostles were baptized with the Spirit in Acts 2 at Pentecost and filled again in Acts 4. Paul makes it clear that the Christian life is a continual process of being "filled" with the Spirit. *"Don't be drunk with wine, because that will ruin your life. Instead, be filled with the Holy Spirit"* (Eph. 5:18 NLT). The Greek word for *filled* implies a continuous, ongoing filling. The English doesn't come out quite right, but it would be like saying "Be ever continually be *being* filled with the Spirit." This tells me there is always more! The River can always rise higher.

However, this River is unto something. We are not simply pursuing the greater glory so we can have greater experiences with God, more intense encounters, more dramatic manifestations of the Spirit's Presence, and more sold-out conferences or events. Greater glory is a mandatory requirement for the people of God because the level of glory that emanates from us must be superior to the level of darkness that's present in the earth. If we are to be the salt of the earth and light of the world, as Jesus said, then what's within us must be stronger than what's having influence in the earth. Remember, salt and light are called to have a measurable impact on the world around them (see Matt. 5:13-16).

In Isaiah 60:1-3, we see this powerful picture of what God envisions for us and the world:

> *Arise, shine, for your light has come, and the glory of the Lord has risen upon you. For behold, darkness shall cover the earth, and thick darkness the peoples; but the Lord will arise upon you, and his glory will be seen upon you. And nations shall come to your light, and kings to the brightness of your rising.*

Yes, there is darkness covering the earth and thick darkness covering the people. To ignore this reality, we would be living in denial. At the same time, we must understand that *we* carry the glory of God. It's within us and we are called to transfer it to every broken, unredeemed, sin-stained, fall-infected part of the earth, from seeing fallen human beings reconciled to God all the way down to the very soil of the earth being healed. The River of God is not coming down from Heaven; it's coming out of us, a people filled with the Holy Spirit who have made themselves completely yielded and surrendered to

God's movement. What's all of this heading toward? *Nations* and *kings* seeing something upon God's people and responding to it. That "something" is the glory — that manifested Presence of God within you that grants you access to the mysteries of creation. Every solution to every problem can be found in the glory. Every strategy can be discovered in the glory. I prophesy that a day is coming when the glory of God will manifest with such intensity that the prophetic unction and operation of the church will go to a new dimension. I prophesy that in that realm, scientists will discover cures for incurable diseases. I prophesy that educators will be granted access to divine downloads of new methods to train up the next generation. I prophesy there will be an acceleration of wealth-creation ideas and inventions, not just for the sake of making money, but so that wealth would translate into Kingdom impact.

This shouldn't sound like "pie in the sky." Pay careful attention to how Paul describes the Holy Spirit, as I believe we experience the "glory" when we, individually and corporately, begin to see the Spirit within become the Spirit *upon* in greater measures. When He rests upon us, there is no limit to what He can say, do, or reveal. After all:

> *The Spirit searches everything, even the depths of God. For who knows a person's thoughts except the spirit of that person, which is in him? So also no one comprehends the thoughts of God except the Spirit of God. Now we have received not the spirit of the world, but the Spirit who is from God, that we might understand the things freely given us by God* (1 Corinthians 2:10-12).

I love how *The Passion Translation* phrases it, as I believe it's faithful to the original text:

> *This is why the Scriptures say: Things never discovered or heard of before, things beyond our ability to imagine — these*

*are the many things God has in store for all his lovers. But
God now unveils these profound realities to us by the Spirit*
(1 Corinthians 2:9-10 TPT).

The great objective of God for planet Earth is a world filled with
His glory. *"But as truly as I live, all the earth shall be filled with the glory
of the Lord"* (Num. 14:21 KJV). When we read these portions of Scripture, I hope this idea becomes less of a spiritual pipe dream and
more of an available reality.

How will this happen? It begins with us dramatically shifting
both our personal and corporate paradigm concerning the Presence
of the Holy Spirit. Rather than Him serving our needs, it's time for
us to serve His. And that leads us into what the Holy Spirit revealed
to me at that little desk in Israel out of First Chronicles 13–16.

11

Consult the Lord First

David consulted with all his officials, including the generals and captains of his army. Then he addressed the entire assembly of Israel as follows: "If you approve and if it is the will of the Lord our God, let us send messages to all the Israelites throughout the land, including the priests and Levites in their towns and pasturelands. Let us invite them to come and join us. It is time to bring back the Ark of our God, for we neglected it during the reign of Saul" (1 Chronicles 13:1-3 NLT).

I WANT TO EXPERIENCE the glory of God in my life. I am sure you do too! For pastors and leaders reading, I have no doubt you want to experience the glory of God in your local churches and gatherings as well. For us to enter into this realm where we can access the greater glory of God, we need to change who we consult concerning the handling of God's Presence. David did not initially consult the Scriptures (he should have), nor did he seem to consult the Lord directly on how to carry the Ark of the Covenant. Rather, he consulted with his *human* officials, who represent mankind and natural strategy. The flesh. What makes sense, feels good, and is logical. What promises the most immediate payoff. This is human nature. God understands it. However, we need to rise above the need to please people and, rather, seek to please God.

Revival is not locked up in Heaven waiting for the loudest cries of intercession to release it; revival is a very present, very accessible reality that is simply waiting for the "Yes" of a yielded life. Who are we giving our lives to serve? Do we wish to please man or please God? If we want to please man, we will continually consult people. Some of these people may be spiritually minded and listening to the Holy Spirit; but there is a good chance that many of them will not be. If we want to experience the manifestation of God's glory, we need to simply do what God says concerning the proper handling of His holy Presence. More of this will make sense as we explore the story further.

Repackaging the Glory
(on a New Cart)

They placed the Ark of God on a new cart and brought it from Abinadab's house. Uzzah and Ahio were guiding the cart. David and all Israel were celebrating before God with all their might, singing songs and playing all kinds of musical instruments — lyres, harps, tambourines, cymbals, and trumpets (1 Chronicles 13:7-8 NLT).

I understand the need to be relevant and communicate ancient truths in modern language. That makes sense. I'm grateful for many of our reputable modern translations of the Bible, which help us connect with the original Greek and Hebrew texts.

However, there is a form of relevance that can actually hinder us from experiencing God in our lives. This is when we mistakenly believe that we need to "repackage the Holy Spirit." I've heard this more and more, where people claim, "We don't need any of that Holy Spirit stuff anymore," referring to the manifestations and signs of the Spirit's movement in our midst. I am sure much of this is a knee-jerk reaction to the imbalances, controversies, and downright goofy stuff that has taken place in the name of the Holy Spirit. Pastor Robert Morris, senior leader of Gateway Church in Southlake, Texas, provides such amazing context for this in his outstanding book *The God I Never Knew*.

> I am convinced that one of Satan's primary strategies for keeping people from experiencing all the amazing help and benefits that come from a relationship with the Holy Spirit is to convince us that doing so will make us weird — really weird. Of course, Satan has a lot of help in reinforcing that lie. The world has its share of truly eccentric people, and some of them are "Spirit-filled" Christians. But here's a news flash: they were weird before they were filled with the Spirit.[1]

Joking aside, we must recognize our absolute dependence upon the Holy Spirit and His movement in our midst. And yes, if He wants to show up in unusual ways that produce certain manifestations or responses from the people He is touching, *let it be.*

Wesley Duewel has written one of the most outstanding books on revival called *Revival Fire*. These are all non-Charismatic/Pentecostal outpourings of the Spirit, and yet we see the unusual physical evidences of God touching people in all of them. He observed rightly: "Many people fear revival because of the unusual manifestations. There is nothing to be feared. If occasionally someone is too unrestrained or overexpressive of his sorrow over sin or his joy at Christ's forgiveness and God's overwhelming presence, this can be understood and accepted. People are accustomed to unrestrained exuberance at sports events or upon seeing loved ones after a long absence."[2] If we can be excited about natural, worldly things, how much more should we respond to the move of the Spirit?

I am convinced we are not seeing a greater manifestation of God's glory because many places or people who have roots in the move of the Spirit — classical Pentecostalism — have traded the glory for "*a new cart*," just like we read about in these verses. What's startling is that as we are going after something "new" in the church world today, we are 100 percent following the model we see in these passages. We're singing and dancing, playing our music and delivering spiritual lip-service, but there is an absence of true glory. Why? God is moving contrary to our comfort levels.

> "There are always some who are desirous of revival until it comes and then they bitterly oppose it because it has not come in the way they anticipated." — Arthur Wallis

12

For the Glory to Come, Fear Has to Go

Ana has a powerful word below explaining why so many people exchange the glory for a "new cart" that is comfortable and controllable—fear. I believe this section carries a real anointing to help break off the spirit of fear that's preventing you from stepping into new realms of God's glory.

"No Fear!"

PERHAPS I HAVE JUST dated myself by titling this section "NO FEAR!" as I remember when a clothing company with that logo was super popular back in my adolescent years. Fear is something we all can struggle with. Fear also looks different depending on what season of life we are in and what we are walking through.

I remember my daughter's first day of school. As I held her at the door and gave a hug goodbye, I remember her hesitation at first with making new friends. Fear was gripping her in that moment. Quickly, she got over that fear and went to color with another little girl. At that point, I could get over my fear as well, as her parent at leaving her for what seemed like eternity, but in retrospect it was only a few hours. Now you might be well past that stage of life with little ones at home, or perhaps you have never had children, but fear at times can come against us all.

Fear and the Greater Glory

Larry jumping in for a minute!

Fear often creeps at the door of the new. I'd propose to you that as we are moving toward entering a new era of increased glory, one of the "Goliaths" we will need to stand victoriously against is fear. This is why what Ana is sharing is essential. When we enter into the "greater" glory, by default, greater is a realm we have never seen, tasted, experienced, or navigated. *Greater* is uncharted territory for the body of Christ. We claim to want greater. I know I do! And yet, "greater" challenges us, because to operate in greater demonstrations of His glory, we cannot return to a framework or operating system that worked nicely in the past—as anointed or effective as it was. This is why, according to Martyn Lloyd-Jones, "When the next revival comes, it will come as a surprise to everybody and especially to those who have been trying to organize it."[1] We cannot organize or coordinate what we've not yet seen.

Greater demands pioneers. *Greater* is for the Abrahams, who follow God even though they don't know where they are going—they go off the map (see Heb. 11:8). *Greater* demands those with a prophetic ear to Heaven, utterly dependent upon the direction of the Holy Spirit, moment by moment. *Greater* demands those who read, love, and search the Scriptures, as the disciples did in the Book of Acts. As they experienced demonstrations of God or shifts in times and seasons that challenged them, they referred to the Scriptures to give them a framework. It's the Bible, ultimately, that tells us this is that which was prophesied (see Acts 2:16). *Greater* is amazing, but it's also demanding. And we cannot be a people who carry fear into greater glory.

Back to Ana.

Proverbs 29:25 in TPT says, *"Fear and intimidation is a trap that holds you back. But when you place your confidence in the Lord, you will be seated in the high place."* And in the NASB it translates: *"The fear of man brings a snare, but he who trusts in the Lord will be exalted."*

I use both these translations because it is important to view that fear, whether it be in general or fear of man's opinion, does one thing — *it holds us back.* Fear restrains and restricts. Fear keeps us from unlocking all of the blessings that God has in plan for us. Fear is actually the opposite of faith. Jesus as our model and example was "seated in the high place" and He always operated out of a place of faith, doing what He heard the Father tell Him to do (see John 5:19).

Faith is the currency of Heaven. When you operate by faith, Heaven responds. Faith is not a reaction to what you're dealing with; faith draws from the resources of another realm, Heaven, to equip you to have victory over what you're confronting in the here and now. So, do you want to move in the currency of Heaven today? Then fear has got to go!

The glory of God requires all fear to go or be burnt away, because *"perfect love casts out fear"* (1 John 4:18). In the glory of God, there is only wonderful and perfect love.

Many of us operate out of fear without even realizing it. We work hard or perform trying to get things just perfect, for love. This is an inadequate view of love, and actually is coming from a place of fear. The mind says: "If I don't have it just right...."

Maybe we like control and having things a certain way. Unfortunately, the world doesn't work with our controlling ways most of the time (take it from a mother of a toddler boy!), and it can throw us for a loop. Relationships go through tension—this isn't the way it's supposed to be. Life is sometimes just messy. What we do with the mess and how we manage our emotions through the mess is a good indicator of the intimate space we are creating with the Lord daily, as He helps us through it all. But control, at its core, has a root of fear. The fear is, if things feel out of my control then the outcome won't be the best. When this is the case, fear is actually what is leading our lives—not faith, not trust, and not resting in God. Recognize that fear produces control, as this is a key stronghold we need to break in stepping into new levels of God's glory.

As we move into greater realms of God's glory and Presence, we come into right understanding of how His beautiful love works. It's unconditional and generously poured out on us all. We are clothed in His love, head to toe, and so all fear melts away.

Do something with me if you would. *Take a moment now and have a heart check with the Lord. After you read this, I want you to imagine yourself being clothed with the love of the Father being put on you physically, from head to toe. Now as you sit there and imagine that blanket of love wrapped around you, ask the Father—is there any place that I have been agreeing with fear today in my life? If He shows you something, I want you to lay it down and say, "God, I break my agreement with fear over this, and I choose faith and love instead."*

Corporate Fear and Control Has to *Go* for the Glory to *Come*

Why address fear? Simple. Fear, which manifests in control, prevents people and communities from experiencing the *greater* glory of God. *Greater* points to dimensions of something we have not yet seen or experienced, right? Greater sounds good, but really it runs against fear. Every great move of God since Pentecost (and really, even the Day of Pentecost) was met with controversy, skepticism, criticism, and mockery. When we enter into greater realms of His glory and Presence, it challenges our control. The greater glory of God we experience, the less control we have. The less control we have, the more submitted and surrendered we are to *Him*.

John Arnott, founder of Catch the Fire Toronto, said this: "Self-control is for you, not the Holy Spirit." The fruit of self-control is all about us submitting to the Spirit, saying "Yes" to Him and "No" to our sinful desires and flesh (see Gal. 5:22-23). Operating in self-control, however, is not controlling the Holy Spirit.

As leaders, we have to conscientiously be aware that when a move of God's Spirit hits, it doesn't always look organized and that's okay. *Decently and in order* is not God adapting to what we're comfortable with; it's simply God doing what He wants and us partnering with Him.

There are so many moments when I have sat through services where my pastor was speaking on one subject and then Holy Spirit interrupted him, giving a different direction for the meeting. In the moment, it feels out of place, but actually it opens something up in the spiritual realm, and God's movement breaks out. Why? We're adapting to God's order instead of trying to make Him adjust to ours. I am so grateful for pastors and leaders who are willing to move wherever the Holy Spirit is directing.

We have to be ever aware of listening to God's direction and being willing to move and adjust however He wants to go. This might mean laying down our own agendas for a meeting or our daily schedule and saying, "God, have Your way even if I look silly as the leader, if it costs me my pride, if it looks messy and unorganized at first, if I am not even able to lead in the moment because I am so undone by the manifest Presence of God resting upon me. God, if You want to do something that is so different and I don't have experience yet in this new territory...*God I am willing!*"

Our willingness to move where Holy Spirit is wanting to move, and our yielding to His control, will directly influence the measure of glory we are able to see, sustain, and walk in.

We want to end this chapter encouraging you about fear:

- Just because you feel fear doesn't mean you need to respond to it.

- Just because the spirit of fear comes against you, and you sense it looming and making an offer to you, does not mean you need to partner with it.

- We break any guilt or shame you have experienced for "feeling fear." All believers, even those with seemingly the most faith, will feel fear. You don't graduate from feeling fear. The enemy would love you to think, however, that because you feel it you've partnered with it. That's a lie!

- We pray that even when fear comes against you, you would follow Jesus' model—you would only say and do what He is telling you to do. We declare that fear is not a dictator over your life!

- Finally, we pray that you would submit wholly and completely to the Holy Spirit—without fear. Let Him be in control. He is totally good and trustworthy!

13

Touching the Glory

But when they arrived at the threshing floor of Nacon, the oxen stumbled, and Uzzah reached out his hand to steady the Ark (1 Chronicles 13:9 NLT).

THE MOVE OF GOD is a sacred and holy thing; we have no right to touch it or steady it. Rather, we need to take our cues from the Holy Spirit, submitting to His every step. The degree to which we embrace this protocol will be the degree that we see the greater glory flowing out of the people of God.

I believe the Lord is raising up a community that has confronted its powerlessness, is absolutely dissatisfied in its present state, and is willing to do whatever it takes to operate as a glorious bride that Jesus will be returning for (see Eph. 5:27). Paul states that the Lord is seeking a *glorious church*. This strongly suggests that the community Jesus is returning for is expected to be operating in glory!

We will see revival, outpouring, and awakening only as we take our hands off what God is doing. This is not a call to be sloppy and just let "anything go" in the name of the "move of God." Surely not. Paul wrote to the Corinthian church specifying that their meetings must be conducted "decently and in order" (see 1 Cor. 14:40). However, Heaven's idea of "decently and in order" is often quite different from ours. We need to take our hands off what the Spirit is doing, while responsibly pastoring, overseeing, and navigating the goings-on in these gatherings. If people are behaving in the flesh, trying to manufacture an experience, let's try to lovingly discipline and pastor them into maturity. If someone is showing signs of demonic possession or oppression, great. Yes, great! The manifestation of God's glory will make demons very uncomfortable, as it will be like Jesus is standing right there in front of them.

As the glory intensifies in your life, don't find it a strange thing for the demonic influences around you to manifest in response to you. You're just stepping into a new dimension of spiritual warfare. Jesus would simply walk into regions and territories, and the demons would manifest. In Luke 8:28, we see this example where as soon as the demonized man *"saw Jesus, he shrieked and fell down in front of him. Then he screamed, 'Why are you interfering with me, Jesus, Son of the Most High God? Please, I beg you, don't torture me!'"* (NLT).

They weren't challenging Him; far from it. His very Presence in those places was confronting their assumed jurisdiction.

I prophesy over you that as you begin to see the glory of God move in and upon you in greater measures, like Jesus, you will step into environments and provoke the demon powers in those places. Fear not! Demons commonly asked Jesus what to do. They were waiting for Him to tell them where to go. I declare to you right now that in your job, in your industry, in your family get-togethers, in your schools, in the places you go where God grants you spiritual jurisdiction, you have a voice of authority. You tell the demons where to go! No, I am not recommending you just go up to some mountain in some city and challenge the demonic principalities over that area. That's foolishness. I am telling you that because of Christ in you, the glory of God moving through you, you have authority in the places you are assigned to tell those spirits what to do: *Go!*

Again, this is one evidence of what happens when we put no restrictions on God's Presence moving through us individually, or through us corporately.

Touching the Glory Is Lethal

Then the Lord's anger was aroused against Uzzah, and he struck him dead because he had laid his hand on the Ark. So Uzzah died there in the presence of God (1 Chronicles 13:10 NLT).

When we "touch" God's Presence by trying to restrict His movement or making Him accommodate our terms, we are killing the only real source of life that we have as believers. It's possible to experience some measure of results without the glory in our midst. But for how long? How long until we are absolutely exhausted trying to do things our own way without leaning upon His empowering Presence?

Just as it was with Uzzah, so it will be today. To "touch" God's Presence means a death to the possibility of dynamic Holy Spirit movement in our midst. The good news is that there is always an open door back to God's way. This is called *repentance*. When we become increasingly aware of how dead our methods are compared to the life and vitality of the Spirit in our midst, we will be more inclined to confront our error, repent, and turn back to God. After all, repentance is not just feeling bad about our sins.

Godly sorrow produces repentance, yes (see 2 Cor. 7:10). There is an appropriate grief to feel over committing sin and disobeying God. But repentance is two-dimensional. Many don't experience the blessing of repentance because they linger too long in grief. We turn away from our sins and dead works *so that* we can turn toward God. The author of Hebrews calls this an elementary doctrine of Christ—repentance from dead works and faith toward God (see Heb. 6:1). Repentance is both *from* and *toward*. We are moving away from self-focus to God focus. We are moving away from a desire to have God do everything the way *we* want and instead are prioritizing what *He* wants. True repentance never leaves one imprisoned behind bars of failure, condemned by their sin. Rather, repentance moves us past our sin and toward a future filled with God.

People of God, it's time for us to re-embrace the gift of repentance, starting with repenting for two thousand years of often trying to follow Jesus on our own terms. It's only when we get on *His page* that we jump into *His move.*

14

The Glory and
the Fear of the Lord

David was now afraid of God, and he asked, "How can I ever bring the Ark of God back into my care?" (1 Chronicles 13:12 NLT)

AFTER BEING ANGRY over what happened to Uzzah, David was struck by the fear of the Lord. The way I see it, both the Presence and absence of God's glory produce holy fear. When God does *not* seem to be present in our midst, this should produce a fear. *What is incompatible with His Presence?* That should be the question we ask; otherwise, we begin to dive into ungodly introspection that seeks out every sin or transgression we've committed since potty-training (thanks Kyle Winkler for this language) or back to several generations. In other words, when there is no measurable trace of God's Presence upon our lives or in our gatherings, rather than feeling guilt, shame, or condemnation, we should ask, "God, what in my life (my church) is not hosting Your Presence? What might be incompatible with the Holy Spirit? Reveal it, Lord, so I can make more room for the Spirit's Presence upon me." Don't fall into the devil's trap of trying to convince you that God has left you. Beloved, God has not left you. If you are born again and have made Jesus your Messiah and Lord, you have a promise straight from the mouth of God Himself: *"I will never leave you nor forsake you"* (Heb. 13:5). When Jesus gave the Great Commission, He gave the assurance of His abiding Presence: *"never forget that I am with you every day, even to the completion of this age"* (Matt. 28:20 TPT). God is with you, period. However, if you are not experiencing His Presence resting upon you, begin to engage the Holy Spirit in honest, open conversation with the questions I mentioned earlier. His absence should produce a godly fear, which should ultimately compel us to repent and make room for Him in whatever area(s) of our lives have not been yielded to His Lordship.

> Only when we are captured by an overwhelming sense of awe and reverence in the presence of God, will we begin to worship God in spirit and in truth. — Alistair Begg

I also want to announce that the manifestation of His glory produces holy fear as well. Perhaps the most striking prophetic dream I have heard in recent years comes from Carol Arnott, co-founder of Toronto Airport Christian Fellowship (now Catch the Fire) with her husband, John. John and Carol are most recognized for leading and stewarding a global outpouring of the Holy Spirit that commenced in January of 1994, often called *The Toronto Blessing*. While this revival was known for contagious joy, the Father's love, and holy laughter, the Arnotts lived in a very delicate balance of celebrating the kindness of God while also recognizing His holiness. In Carol's dream, a visible cloud of God's glory appeared at the front of the church. There was an altar call following this powerful manifestation of glory: "Run to the altar or run for your lives." The quest for a greater manifestation of God's glory will always come accompanied by an increased measure of awe, wonder, and holy trembling. To simply want "more glory" so we can walk in more miracles, power, and Kingdom demonstration is missing the point. We desire more glory so that *more God* can be made visible to a planet that desperately needs redemption. They need to see a real God in action. I'm convinced that when the church trembles again before God, the world will listen to what the church has to say.

Things did not end well for Uzzah because he touched the Ark, trying to steady it. David was offended and angered over what happened but then was filled with fear. This fear of the Lord provoked the *right* question in him: *How can I bring the Ark of the Covenant back into my care?* I believe he was sincerely seeking a protocol from the Lord on how to accommodate His Presence.

What happened? "*Instead, he took it* [the Ark] *to the house of Obed-edom of Gath. The Ark of God remained there in Obed-edom's house for three months, and the Lord blessed the household of Obed-edom and everything he owned*" (1 Chron. 13:13-14 NLT). Pausing here for a moment, I love that David did not assume he knew what to do next.

More and more, I prophesy that as we experience a greater manifestation of God's glory in our midst, the more we are going to look at each other, puzzled, asking: "What do we do next?" As God is moving, I encourage you, don't assume that your response to His movement should be what it was yesterday, or two weeks ago, or six years ago. God is not a formula. Yes, He does respond to protocol, but even the protocol must be motivated by a heart filled with awe. We follow protocol because we recognize the King is worthy, not because we are plugging in some formula to get whatever we want, need, or desire from God and then move on to the next thing. David learned from the deadly mistake with Uzzah that he could not just carry God's Presence any old way; he had to adapt to God's protocol in order to move the Ark back into his care. While David figured this out, Obed-edom was certainly not complaining. This is where the Ark remained for three months. As a result, this man's household was radically and richly blessed! God's Presence must be accommodated a certain way.

Consider this powerful word that the Lord gave to Ana about holiness coming back to the church and how it's essential to host His glory.

Ana

Holiness Returns

The holiness of God needs to return to the church. He is so accessible, and He reaches out to us in our broken, imperfect state. But that's just it. We are imperfect without Him. Let us not forget just how much we do need Jesus and can't live without Him.

He is pure. The day that I encountered the throne room, I just remember somewhere I heard my own voice, crying out, "Holy, Holy, *holy!*" In Israel, Larry and I both had the opportunity to listen to stories from a wonderful saint of God who had travelled and ministered with the late Ruth Ward Heflin. This amazing woman observed, "When you experience God in ways that you can't explain, the only thing you can do is cry *holy*."

This was a sacred moment for me. Truth be told, as I saw the glory and light and felt the power of God go through me in such a powerful way, the fear of the Lord came over me. In that moment, I just longed to be close to Him and more like Him.

Encounters with His glory and Presence create a reaction of the fear of the Lord and a purification. Imagine a kiln where fine pottery is placed inside for the glazing process. As the heat increases and the air pressure increases, the purification process occurs and the most beautiful colors are released. When the purification process is complete, the potter takes the pieces of pottery out of the kiln and gets to stare in amazement at what colors came to life. That's the story of our lives. Purification and repentance aren't comfortable or easy, but they are such beautiful processes. As our fleshly ways are burnt away in His Presence, we can radiate Him all the more and truly step into the way we were created to be.

I love intimacy with God, and often preach on it as I know He is always after our hearts. But He is a holy God. The deeper and more intimate our relationship is, the more we desire to become more like Him. Repentance and the turning away from sin must be our response to encountering His glory.

The message of repentance has been watered down a bit in church as it's not very popular. Often in church history, we see eras when one subject was perhaps over-emphasized, and now we have a culture that doesn't want to go there anymore. Yet God is blowing dust off old wells, and repentance is necessary. He chooses us in our sinful nature and loves us all the same, but He wants us to walk out a lifestyle that is worthy of having His glory rest upon us.

> *You must prove your repentance by a changed life* (Matthew 3:8 TPT).

Our Inheritance: A Changed Life

A changed life is our inheritance. Isn't that the truth! One touch of His glory, one encounter with Him and you are forever changed. Things that used to be important sometimes no longer are. Your perspective on life itself is altered. Your purpose is rewritten as your heart learns to match the heartbeat of the Father. Your identity becomes grounded and knit into the love of the Father.

When I think about the holiness of God, that old worship song comes to mind that's based off of Psalm 95:6: "Come, let us worship and bow down. Let us kneel before the Lord, our God, our Maker."

I enter into His Presence, knowing my place is at His feet worshiping Him. This is my response to holiness. He is great, and I am so little. Have you ever thought of the fact that He allows us to be in His Presence? He allows us to enter in and encounter Him. He allows us to climb up on His lap as His children and draw close. He is God. We, though, have authority and we are heirs as His sons and daughters. Isn't that incredible! As we go low and surrender our lives fully, He gives us an inheritance that is beyond anything we could ever fathom. Jesus gives us access to Heaven!

I find myself in a season right now when Jesus is very close. He is so lovingly drawing near to me daily, and I'm so grateful—often in the midst of change and challenge. Daily we take walks together in the early part of the morning. As I put my hand in His, we walk together and chat heart to heart. I find myself falling for Him all the more. I'm so in love with Jesus. How can we not be when we remember the cross and what He bore for us? Being in His Presence creates a deeper measure of love for Him. And when the busyness of life gets to us and we are not feeling His Presence, we ache to be with Him. Like the Shulamite saying, "*Have you seen him whom my soul loves?*" in Song of Solomon 3:3, we long to be with Him.

I remember when I first met my husband. We would spend hours together talking in coffee shops. Each day I would wake up, excited and thinking about the next time we could spend time together. That's *love!* I pray right now, as you read this, love for Jesus will be reawakened and grow more deeply in your heart. Our response to His Presence is always falling more in love with Him. It's not religious works that produce a holy life—far from it. It's beholding Him, experiencing His love, and loving Him in return that changes everything!

15

Ask God:
"What Do You Want?"

David now built several buildings for himself in the City of David. He also prepared a place for the Ark of God and set up a special tent for it. Then he commanded, "No one except the Levites may carry the Ark of God. The Lord has chosen them to carry the Ark of the Lord and to serve him forever" (1 Chronicles 15:1-2 NLT).

WE PICK UP THE STORY with David returning to God's biblical protocol for carrying His glory. I have to believe David did some serious research, seeking what God's specifications were for transporting the Ark of the Covenant. This is where he most likely came upon Deuteronomy 10:8, which states: *"At that time the Lord set apart the tribe of Levi to carry the Ark of the Lord's Covenant, and to stand before the Lord as his ministers, and to pronounce blessings in his name. These are their duties to this day"* (NLT). The Ark of the Covenant was never meant to be transported in something man-made but, rather, carried on the shoulders of priests.

Perhaps you are wondering *why* there is an absence of glory in the land. Fair evaluation. When so much has been promised and yet we are often witnessing the opposition, we have to ask, *what's going on?* I have to believe this is how historical revivals were birthed. A man, a woman, a church community—someone—rose up and was so provoked by the fact that God promised so much and they were experiencing so little that they leveraged this frustration, turned it into intercession, and contended with Heaven *until* they received a divine strategy or download. I cannot say for certain, based on what's clearly revealed in Scripture, that David did this. But why wouldn't he? He was angered over Uzzah's death. He desperately wanted to provide the Ark of the Covenant a resting place. David was a man of the Presence, a man after God's own heart, a worshiper. I have to believe that David was deeply provoked to search God out for a divine solution for hosting His Presence. In his quest, he discovered what was written concerning the protocol of carrying the Ark of the Covenant and commanded that those regulations be adhered to. Remember, we set our hearts to accommodate what God wants, not satisfy our personal preferences.

Prepare a Place for His Glory

Then David summoned all Israel to Jerusalem to bring the Ark of the Lord to the place he had prepared for it (1 Chronicles 15:3 NLT).

We prepare a place for God by seeking what He likes, accommodating what He wants, and adjusting everything to make room for His Presence.

We never graduate from that desperation, hunger, and thirst. As time goes by, things get more sophisticated. We discover new and exciting relevant methods of communicating truth — connecting people with the Gospel message. Many of these methods are positive, but sadly many have replaced the glory of God. We've intentionally *traded* the glory of God for a "new cart" of our own making, something that's manageable, controllable, comfortable, and culturally relevant. Something that makes a whole lot more sense than the undignified sights and sounds of revival. I mean, that stuff is just messy. We assume people do not want to see people weeping at the altar, lying prostrate on the ground, laughing uncontrollably as they are touched by joy, trembling as the Spirit of God touches them, or falling down under the power of God. We never graduate from being in dire need of the powerful Presence of God. This is what happened to John Kilpatrick; he was a man in dire need of a fresh touch from God.

Here's the question of the hour: how much do we want Him? We can cry out in private, yes, but are we willing to take risks in public? We can ask for "more of God" in the secret place, but are we willing to lay down our reputation in order to see God move? This is what it means to prepare a place for God. It has nothing to do with building a church sanctuary or establishing some kind of ministry; it has everything to do with the posture of our heart toward the move of the Holy Spirit. This is not exclusive for megachurch pastors or ministry leaders. All of us need to make a key decision: what is the glory worth? Do I want to continue with everything same ole, same ole, or am I willing to seek God with all of my heart, just as David did, and listen for His instructions on how to host His Presence?

16

Redeeming the Supernatural Bloodline of Christianity through Trading

Because you Levites did not carry the Ark the first time, the anger of the Lord our God burst out against us. We failed to ask God how to move it properly (1 Chronicles 15:13 NLT).

AS ANA MENTIONED in an earlier chapter, we are exploring a subject that, sadly, is not talked about too much these days—repentance. Taking it a step further, we are exploring this concept of *identificational repentance*. This is an intercessory act where we repent on behalf of others.

As someone who has given much of my academic career to studying revival history, I have learned that over the centuries the supernatural bloodline of Christianity was traded for political affluence, cultural acceptance, and now postmodern relevance. In other words, we have intentionally laid down the supernatural dynamics of our faith in exchange for a "spirituality" or religion that people could more easily wrap their natural minds around. We considered the supernatural, the gifts of the Spirit, the prophetic, the manifestation of God's Presence and power to be too controversial—too out there. Because *we* deemed the supernatural elements of our faith too extreme, we exchanged them for something more palatable. The following chapter focuses exclusively on this subject, as I believe the Lord is raising up *this era* to repent on behalf of past generations who laid down the move of the Spirit and, in turn, experienced "glory shortages" in the eras they lived in.

> As the Church grew into its new status, many of its leaders learned to rely more on the power of possessions and political force and less on spiritual power. —Francis MacNutt, *The Nearly Perfect Crime*

In preparation for this section, I sensed the Lord tell me to study "the trade of Constantine." As I sought the Lord further on this, I was led on a prophetic assignment to go back through the bloodline of Christianity and identify what trades were made that resulted in the church being stripped of its power. We need to pause here, in the process of restoring the glory, and focus on a topic that is not often discussed in the modern church—identificational repentance. We are repenting for our neglect with the glory of God, yes, but we are also taking an intercessory position and repenting on behalf of those in the past, those in the present, entire movements and communities who have rejected the Spirit of God because they traded the glory for other things.

Defining Trading in the Spirit

First, let's explore what trading looks like. I've heard a few prayer and intercession leaders start using this language of *trading* in the spirit. To me, it makes sense when we understand the process of spiritual exchange. Trading is not a demonic activity; what makes the process of trading pure or evil is the heart attitude that motivates the trade. The truth is, the practice of trading is all throughout Scripture, but perhaps one of the most evident places is in Ezekiel 28. It's here we are introduced to a figure who gives us insight on how Satan himself operated when he existed as the archangel Lucifer. Even though it's directed at the King of Tyre, many theologians agree that these descriptive scriptures pull back the veil and give us clarity on how Lucifer became Satan.

Consider all that the archangel Lucifer had access to:

> *You were the anointed cherub who covers; I established you; you were on the holy mountain of God; you walked back and forth in the midst of fiery stones. You were perfect in your ways from the day you were created, till iniquity was found in you. By the abundance of your trading you became filled with violence within, and you sinned* (Ezekiel 28:14-16 NKJV).

What brought about the iniquity of Lucifer? Pride. We don't see this in Ezekiel's account, but we do see the source of pride revealed in Isaiah 14. Pride influenced Lucifer's trading and, as a result, we clearly see that he was willing to trade his position of high service to God Almighty for the worship of him*self*. He was the first being in recorded history to *trade* the glory.

Right here, we see what contaminated and thus influenced Lucifer's trade:

> *For you have said in your heart: "I will ascend into heaven, I will exalt my throne above the stars of God; I will also sit on the mount of the congregation on the farthest sides of the north; I will ascend above the heights of the clouds, I will be like the Most High." Yet you shall be brought down to Sheol, to the lowest depths of the Pit* (Isaiah 14:13-15 NKJV).

How is this act of trading relevant to us today—specifically when it comes to the subject of revival and outpouring of the Spirit?

Even though it *seems* like we are operating our churches and governing our ministries from a place of purity, it's very possible that we or others before us have made trades that have restricted the flow of the Spirit's Presence and power. How is this possible?

Lucifer traded worship of God for his own reputation. He traded service to God because he wanted his way—he wanted to be worshiped and served instead of God. I know many of us wouldn't dare compare ourselves to Lucifer, but what motivated his trade has motivated our spiritual trading for these last two thousand years of church history. *Pride.* We want what we think is right. We have a human concept of what the demonstration of God's "glory" looks like and we are willing to trade Bible-glory for the glory of man. We might not like to call it that, but the pursuit of an expression of glory that is in disagreement with God's definition is idolatry. Religious systems can perpetuate this idolatry, even when good-intentioned, well-meaning people are propagating them.

Furthermore, we don't want people to think less of us or negatively of us. We want a good reputation. We want to be thought of highly. We want followers, friends, and fans. We want a place of prominence. Sound familiar? I believe all of us are constantly being invited onto a "demonic trading floor," where we exchange what God wants for what we want. This is something all of us have to deal with on a regular basis.

Specifically, however, I believe the church needs to openly and honestly confront this issue of trading. For many, we have traded away the sacred anointing of the Spirit for something that would maintain our status and likability. This is where trades need to be reversed and undone.

I've said it multiple times: Programs are not bad. Lights and production value can be excellent in the context of the local church! Have a nice building. Go out of your way to pursue the finest children's programs. Because we follow Jesus, we should be a people committed to excellence. Having big churches is a wonderful thing, because—in theory—bigger attendance should mean bigger opportunity for impact. All of these things are not bad; they are very good.

They are great! At the same time, good things and even great things can become expressions of downright spiritual rebellion *if* they are the result of a trade. In other words, if we make a conscious decision to trade the glory of God and the outpouring of the Spirit for methodologies, strategies, and programs that replace the Holy Spirit with the ways of man *so that* we can get more people and have a bigger ministry and a stellar reputation, we are guilty of trading and need to repent. Plain and simple.

I'm convinced the reason we are not seeing the full manifestation of glory in and through the church today has everything to do with trades that have been made in the spirit over the last two thousand years. But the good news is that glory, power, and influence beyond what we have ever seen are right on the other side of wholehearted repentance and a people who give themselves fully to God.

17

What Have These Trades Produced?

I would like to lay it down as a principle that there is a great value in the reading of Church history and a study of the past, and nothing, surely, is more important for us at this present time than to read the history of the past and to discover its message.
—Martyn Lloyd-Jones[1]

ALTHOUGH THERE ARE glaring contemporary issues we need to confront, church history gives us a context of why we are dealing with what we are dealing with today in terms of trading away the glory for something more acceptable and appealing. This is not new. For generations, Satan has sought to lure the wealthiest people in the universe (the Spirit-filled Ekklesia) onto a trading floor where we traded away our Holy Spirit inheritance for the "bowl of stew" he was offering.

The early church was a supernatural community. Miracles were not the exception; they were normative.

Christ-followers believed that when they prayed, the Holy Spirit would show up with powerful manifestations. Healing was part of everyday life. Deliverance was not confined to a back room somewhere or exclusively administered by a "man of the cloth." The gifts of the Spirit were not believed to have ceased, nor were they reserved for a few top-tier ministerial leaders. Vineyard Church leader John Wimber's old adage perfectly applied to how the early church engaged the supernatural: "Everyone gets to play."

In the early years of water baptism, there was an expectation that when someone was baptized in water, he or she would come up out of the waters of repentance and be endowed with the baptism of the Holy Spirit. Church father Tertullian wrote of this:

> You blessed ones, for whom the grace of God is waiting, when you come up from the most sacred bath of the new birth, when you spread out your hands...ask your Father, ask your Lord, for the special gift of his inheritance, the distribution of the charisms.[2]

It was normal for recently converted Christians to speak in tongues, prophesy, and operate in other gifts of the Holy Spirit following their immersion into the baptismal waters. Again, this was because of the *expectation* attached to the expression of the Christian life. There was no powerless alternative of the faith available for these early disciples to consider. Miracles were not "take it or leave it"; they were normative.

So why did things change? Some theologians erroneously believe that, in God's sovereignty, He decided to pull the plug on such miraculous demonstrations of power. This has come to be formally known as cessation theory. Although many of these highly educated and respectable theologians can try to deliver eloquent arguments in an effort to support this view, eloquence cannot compensate for the ultimate lack of solid biblical foundation. There is no solid scriptural ground for the cessation argument to stand on. To study this topic in greater depth, I strongly recommend Jon Ruthven's exceptional exposition *On the Cessation of the Charismata*.[3] In short, it's illogical to believe that upon the canonization of Scripture, the Spirit of God ceased being a Person who moves in power and somehow became a concept to be understood intellectually. He is both — a Person to encounter and a Person to know!

Is there another story — perhaps darker and more insidious than most of the church would like to acknowledge? I believe there is. It is one hallmarked by fear, compromise, and downright rejection of the very mission Jesus gave His church to fulfill from Pentecost to the end of the age. This resulted in spiritual trading that has had a disastrous impact on the whole of Christianity.

Trading for the Latter and Greater Glory

The good news is God is raising up a generation that is destined to undo these trades and see the glory restored. And I prophesy that we would see a new level of glory manifestation in accordance with Haggai 2:9 — "*The latter glory of this house shall be greater than the former, says the Lord of hosts. And in this place I will give peace, declares the Lord of hosts.*"

God is a restorer. He specializes in restoring things to a position that exceeds their original design! Although we have been in a season when we have had to deal with the ramifications of past trading in the spirit, I see the Lord raising up a people who bring Haggai 2 into full view for a generation.

Perhaps one of the most prophetic, timely, and applicable pronouncements of Haggai to a contemporary generation is "the importance of worshiping God in the ways God *himself* ordains."[4] In other words, God has an order that He is looking for His people to operate in agreement with. Problems come when we assume we have a superior order or blueprint to God and trade away His ways for the ways of man.

Back to Haggai. Briefly, the reason the Temple was in a state of ruin was due to the spiritual trading of the people of Israel. They traded Jehovah God for idol worship. The result was "Ichabod" — the removal of the glory from their midst. In the historical context of the prophet Haggai, Solomon's temple had been rebuilt. Sadly, the new temple lacked the glory of the former temple, thus causing sadness among the people. *"Does anyone remember this house – this Temple – in its former splendor? How, in comparison, does it look to you now? It must seem like nothing at all!"* (Hag. 2:3 NLT).

Likewise, I know there are many who remember the move of God in its former splendor, just as the people of Israel remembered the glory of Solomon's temple. Consider this fascinating observation on the Haggai text by one of the princes of preachers, Charles Spurgeon:

> The older folks remarked that this was a very small affair compared with the temple of Solomon, of which their fathers had told them; in fact, their rising building was nothing at all, and not worthy to be called a temple. The prophet describes the feeling in the verse which precedes our text. "Who is left among you that saw this house in her first glory? and how do ye see it now? is it not in your eyes in comparison of it as nothing?" Feeling that their work would be very poor and insignificant, the people had little heart to go on. Being discouraged by the humiliating contrast, they began to be slack; and as they were quite willing to accept any excuse, and here was an excuse ready made for them, they would soon have been at a standstill had not the prophet met the wiles of the arch-enemy with another word from the Lord.[5]

Hold that thought. Many reading these words most likely attended some of the world-changing revivals of the 1990s — Toronto, Brownsville, Smithton. Perhaps some can even remember the "former" glory of the Charismatic Movement of the 1960s, or the Latter Rain Revival of the late 1940s, or perhaps the emergence of the tent revivalists and healing evangelists. If you had spoken to former generations, they would have likely remembered the glories of the Hebrides Revival in 1949, or the Azusa Street Revival of 1906, or the Welsh Revival of 1904. The point is there will always be a revival remnant on the earth whose eyes have seen the former glory. This creates a dissatisfaction in their hearts for anything that doesn't compare to this.

What did Spurgeon note? In Haggai's day, there was a generation who knew of the glory (Solomon's Temple) and this new thing (the new temple) they were building actually produced discouragement because it wasn't what the Temple used to be. It's fascinating that, historically, those who could actually recall the glory of Solomon's temple were in their 70s and older.

This goes to show that we can build all we want; in order for something to be effective, it needs to be filled with glory. "*Unless the Lord builds the house, those who build it labor in vain*" (Ps. 127:1). The people who had tasted of the previous glory were discouraged by what they were confronted with in the present.

God's next move, as history has clearly demonstrated, will likely look different than it has in the past (although there are always certain repeated characteristics and manifestations of Holy Spirit outpouring). I am not talking about a generation that "camps out" on the former glory days of a past revival, refusing to move into the future. I am simply using the illustration of Haggai's day to say this: There has historically been a remnant on the earth who had heard of, or seen, the previous glory. This burns in their hearts. When Christianity moves in a different direction, trading this glory for affluence or acceptance, the generation that tasted a demonstration of glory will react. This is not because they are rejecting a new thing of God. Hardly! Don't confuse a new thing of the Spirit with an attempted innovation of man. What's being propagated is not a new expression of glory; it's a shallow shadow of what once was because, instead of glory, it is a mixture of man's attempts and good intentions.

Here is my concern: often, the revivals of the past seem to exceed the overall spiritual climate of our present. Revival and awakening don't exist to linger forever. We're not supposed to have extended church meetings indefinitely, and then when they end we claim the revival is over. I'm guessing many revivals have ceased because we misinterpreted the season change. God uses sustained, nightly gatherings and meetings for His purposes, but we would be naïve to think that God would continue indefinitely in this fashion. Sustained meetings impact believers, yes, but they do not reform nations. We often want to have more meetings when God wants to have more nations. We want prayer lines; God wants intercessors who shape history in and out of the prayer closet.

We should be like the people of Haggai's day when we consider the lack of sustained Presence and power in our present reality. Let's be intentional about celebrating where God *is* moving—because He most certainly is! However, let's not become content with Him moving "here and there" when His target is all flesh, all nations, all the earth.

There was indeed a former glory. As in the days of Solomon's temple, throughout church history, we have tasted measures of glory. This glory transformed cities and impacted nations. This glory marked individuals and ignited revolutionaries. We remember the glory, we memorialize the glory, and we long for it. These are all legitimate approaches to the former glory. What ultimately caused the glory to withdraw? Our trades. How can we step into what Haggai prophesied as the *"latter glory"*? Undoing past trades.

God never made a sovereign decision to close Heaven's gates, preventing His people from experiencing a sustained abiding of His glory and power. Could it be that throughout history the supernatural power of God has been available all along and the very people who had been made inheritors of this heavenly gift traded it for the "silver and gold" that the world offered?

Perhaps one of the most striking scenes from history that depicts what was lost on a demonic trade is a conversation between St. Thomas Aquinas and Pope Innocent II.

Entering the presence of Innocent II, before whom a large sum of money was spread out, the Pope observed, "You see, the Church is no longer in that age in which she said, 'Silver and gold have I none.'" — "True, holy father," replied Aquinas; "neither can she any longer say to the lame, 'Rise up and walk.'"[6]

This is exactly the story that history tells us. It's vital for us to recognize what happened in church history so we can identify *where* and *how* trades were made. That way, we can repent for the past and step into a future destined for *greater glory!* Personally, I'll take the lame walking in Jesus' name over any sum of money, affluence, or positive reputation the devil wants to "offer."

18

What Unplugged
the Power?

FOR THE FIRST 325 YEARS of church history, the standard operating procedure for the church was supernatural. In fact, Augustine notes that it was in fact miracles that were primarily responsible for reproducing the Christian faith: "Christianity must have reproduced itself by means of miracles for the greatest miracle of all would have been the extraordinary extension of this religion apart from any miracles."[1]

Miracles and supernatural phenomena are by no means side items in the halls of church history; they are key landmarks. Randy Clark explains that "we tend to look at the today's moves of the Holy Spirit through the tiny peephole of the present, instead of through the telescopic lens of history. Our history is a wonderful story of how God has moved among His people throughout the entire Church Age."[2] History is an important reference point for us, especially when we start to experience the full measure of Holy Spirit power being released in and through our lives today. For many people, the manifestations of revival can be troubling because we often live cut off and detached from the Spirit's history of divine, unusual intervention.

We would do well to heed the words of Dr. A.T. Schofield when it comes to responding to the outpouring of God's Spirit in our day:

One thing to be borne in the mind is that since the days of Pentecost there is no record of the sudden and direct work of the Spirit of God upon the souls of men that has not been accompanied by events more or less abnormal. It is, indeed, on consideration, only natural that it should be so. We cannot expect an abnormal inrush of Divine light and power, so profoundly affecting the emotions and changing the lives of men, without remarkable results. As well expect a hurricane, an earthquake, or a flood, to leave nothing abnormal in its course, as to expect a true Revival that is not accompanied by events quite out of our ordinary experience.[3]

To sum it up, when God collides with human flesh, *something* is going to happen. It is by sheer grace that we are not consumed and left for dead, as the Old Covenant priests would have been had they entered behind the veil unworthily.

Shifts that Disconnect the Power

There was also a disconnect from the supernatural because the Christian worldview was being steadily detached from a more *warfare model* of theological expression and replaced with a strongly predestination-influenced blueprint system. This means that the early church recognized it was in dire need of supernatural power to violently advance the Kingdom of God into areas where darkness had taken hold. Randy Clark explains it this way:

Prior to Augustine and for a few hundred years after him, the predominant understanding of life was the warfare worldview — that forces of evil were at war against Christ and His Church. This warfare caused the sickness and demonic bondages people experienced. Within this worldview, believers were to fight against sickness, disease, and demonic oppression through the power of the Holy Spirit.[4]

The church's warfare paradigm saw the existence of demons and demonic forces as trying to restrain the onward march of Heaven on earth. In the warfare paradigm—which I believe was biblical and represented the model of Jesus—sickness, torment, and oppression were *not* seen as gifts from God. The works of the devil *are not* sent to sanctify God's people or increase their level of holiness. Yes, God can turn bad around for His good. He can work through sickness and demonic oppression, but He is not the One to cause or provoke these things. On the contrary, the early church viewed these as enemies that tried to thwart the advancement of God's Kingdom. This explains why healing, deliverance, miracles, and other supernatural phenomena were so normative in the early church. Their theological perspective influenced their supernatural expectation. Because their perspective was one of being an offensive army aimed at destroying the works of the devil, they saw supernatural power as a desperate need, not an "add on" option.

Francis MacNutt notes the prevalence of this supernatural activity in the early church:

Spirit baptism, together with healing and exorcism, flourished in those early years following Pentecost. From those ancient times, long before the printing press, we have only a few records of how the poor, uneducated, ordinary Christians lived, but we have enough to know that they expected to be filled with and led by the Spirit.[5]

What happened that so quenched the Spirit's fire and caused the majority of believers to cease expecting His empowerment in their lives? Many historians mark the conversion of Emperor Constantine as the beginning of the end for the prevalence of supernatural ministry among the early church. This is where, I believe, a trade took place in the spirit realm that would set the course of Christianity for the coming generations. Until this point, Christians met in homes to worship. Church buildings and centralized worship gatherings were not instituted yet.

In the context of these house churches, participation in the liturgy was communal. Once again, there was an open door for the ordinary, everyday people to operate in the gifts of the Spirit. This is exactly why the apostle Paul wrote First Corinthians 12 and 14. These were instructions for those who were meeting in these particular contexts on how to create a safe and orderly environment where spiritual gifts could flow. Contrary to what many teach today, Paul's definition of "decently and in order" was not a total absence of spiritual gifts. Rather, he urged the Corinthian believers to "*earnestly desire the spiritual gifts*" (1 Cor. 14:1).

Familiar leaders and church fathers such as Origen, Justin Martyr, Tertullian, and others recognized the Presence of God's supernatural power among the people. Even Irenaeus spoke of supernatural resurrections and those being raised from the dead![6] As you begin to read some of their personal experiences with the miraculous, you will quickly discover that the spiritual pioneers—figures who literally shaped the very faith we embrace today as orthodox Christianity—were people of the Spirit. Though this community was continually under the threat of persecution, with many giving their lives for the Gospel through martyrdom, they "continued to proclaim the Kingdom of God and to show demonstrations of God's power."[7]

The power of God started to get unplugged just around the fourth century.

- Miracles became the exception, not the normal.

- Supernatural demonstrations were reserved for the "holy" elite.

- Charismatic gifts were not for everybody; they either signified demon possession or sainthood.

- Baptism was treated as a rite and ritual, not a monumental spiritual occasion for a supernatural impartation.

Next, I want us to specifically review the trade of Constantine's era, which is what provoked this entire section.

19

The Trade of Constantine's Era

AS CHRISTIANITY INCREASED in popularity — following Emperor Constantine's conversion and the overall institutionalization of the church — there seemed to be a progression toward a very inclusive faith. Baptism was no longer for adult believers who made a wholehearted commitment to follow Jesus, even in the face of death. Now, infants were being "baptized." Baptism became more of a symbolic ritual, where the expectation of the miraculous that was once associated with it was all but lost.

More and more nominal Christians started to join the newly forming churches, while the more devoted believers — many of whom operated in the miraculous — became hermits and monks, forced to retire from society and live out in the deserts like recluses. This includes the monastic desert fathers of North Africa, such as Antony and Pachomius, who were renowned for moving in unusual signs and wonders such as healing, discerning of spirits, and exorcism.

I'm not interested in simply providing a history lesson for you. I believe that the Lord is calling for a people who actually cleanse the ancestral bloodline of the church, repenting on behalf of trades that were made centuries ago. You might not agree with this theological perspective (identificational repentance), but the fact remains: we are still facing the same issues that the church did under the reign of Constantine.

While many historians would celebrate Constantine's impact on the mainline acceptance of Christianity, there are those who would claim that his widespread propagation of the faith was actually cat-alytic to it becoming supernaturally impotent. On one hand, I have to celebrate the fact that Emperor Constantine seemed intent not only on evangelizing souls but transforming the whole of society through the influence of Christianity. On the other hand, the church became state-run and political in nature. Constantine and those who followed him became increasingly involved in the affairs of the church, exercising governance that previously belonged to spiritu-ally qualified apostolic leaders.

It's sad, but true. A community that was formerly persecuted ended up, in some situations, becoming the *persecutors*. Even though Constantine was not completely heavy-handed on forcing his faith on others, the influence of his reign would impact other leaders down the line to pronounce exclusive edicts, basically threatening those who did not practice Christianity.

Using the language of this book, I believe Constantine, and those of his era, entered a demonic trade. This goes to show you that someone who has the best intentions (and we really cannot evaluate his ultimate intentions) can be lured to trade God's glory for self-ish gain. While there were multitudes who genuinely turned to the Christian faith during this era, many were coercively forced into the church because of the state-initiated persecution that was aimed at non-Christians.

It then became possible for the community of true believers to include and ultimately be influenced by non-believers who were trying to save their necks. After all, if you are given the option of Christianity or death, you find a way to make Christianity work *on your terms*. There you have it. I believe this ancient trade actually introduced something into the bloodline of Christianity that needs to be revoked and renounced — a faith on man's terms, not God's.

Those who were pagans continued to live as pagans — only they existed in a duplicitous lifestyle, with one foot in Christianity and one foot continuing in their idolatrous, false religion. Could it be that where we *were* back then is where we *are* again? If we don't deal with trades that were made in the past, I am convinced we will continue to repeat them. This is why it's vital for us to understand the bloodline of the church and identify where specifically it was infected.

John Chrysostom, who was the Archbishop of Constantinople, observed that the church of his day was "no different from the theater or enterprises in the marketplace."[1] Chrysostom's comments on the state of the church are definitely worth considering, as he seeks to account for the lack of power and diminishment of the spiritual gifts. He wrote, "The present church is like a woman who has fallen from her former prosperous days. In many respects she retains only the symbols of that ancient prosperity. She displays, in fact, the repositories and the caskets of her gold ornaments, but she is, in fact, deprived of wealth. The present church represents such a woman...only the tokens of the charisms (gifts of the spirit) remain of those ancient times."[2]

What was the response to the formalized, state-run church? The monastic community. I do not believe the Lord ever willed for His people to pursue a monastic or ascetic lifestyle, per se. There might be exceptions to the rule; I surely can't judge. But in its historical context, I believe monasticism was the only response, in that era, to a church that was becoming increasingly institutionalized and thus, powerless. Church historian Eddie Hyatt explains that "following Constantine's ascent to power, most supernatural phenomena are recorded either by monastics or by those who venerated the monastic lifestyle."[3]

Perhaps the greatest trade that took place under Constantine's rule was exchanging the organic, advancing, apostolic community of the Ekklesia for something that was location- and building-oriented. Hyatt continues to describe how "Constantine also initiated the building of facilities to accommodate the religious gatherings of Christians. Prior to this, believers had met primarily in homes.

Constantine, however, erected buildings in which the church was to meet. *These he modeled after the architecture of the civic auditoriums of the day.*"⁴ Are buildings bad? No. The problem is that, progressively, the model of Church initiated by Jesus was being replaced with something that more and more resembled the world. Even the setup of these buildings made the realities of First Corinthians 14 challenging to non-existent, thus discouraging the participation of everyday believers in the liturgy. More and more, we see how the move of the Spirit was traded for something more theatrical in nature.

Following Constantine's death, his sons continued to protect and promote the advancement of the Christian church. Unfortunately, as mentioned earlier, future leaders would arise, like emperor Theodosius I, and declare Christianity as the state religion. Sounds good on paper. In practice, it was deadly for those who did not ascribe to the Christian faith, and furthermore it promoted all forms of spiritual mixture in the context of the church. Hyatt gives a picture for what happened: "As a result (of the threat of persecution for non-Christians) hordes of unconverted pagans filled the churches, bringing with them heathen ideas and practices."⁵

We absolutely want "godless pagan heathens" in our church gatherings! They are the ones who need to have a power encounter with the Risen Christ. The only hope for these people is an environment where they can be introduced to Jesus through the power of the Holy Spirit. If, however, they are introduced to a welcoming, casual, cool, relevant, and non-threatening version of "Christianity," where there is no mention of Jesus' blood, no confrontation with sin, no proclamation of the resurrection, and no demonstration of the Spirit, it's possible for the demonized to continue in their delusion and, even further, begin to infect communities of faith with these ideologies. After all, if our primary objective is to make people comfortable and not offend them, then it's possible for us to modify our practices to accommodate those who *don't* even know the Lord. This can be a sure sign that we are moving into dangerous territory.

It's not possible to receive Jesus Christ on our terms. Likewise, we don't get the Holy Spirit on our terms. Any expression of Christianity that is subject to the terms of mankind is false and aberrant. Those who claimed Christ in the days of Constantine and his successors but really were secular or even pagan in heart were propagating a false religion.

More and more, the gifts and power of the Spirit were being claimed as exclusive or unique to the top religious leaders. Sacramentalism became a key emphasis, with baptism and the Lord's Supper being two sacraments possessing power to actually impart spiritual gifts. Adding further layers to the exclusivity, it was only the bishops who had authority to administer these sacraments. If an un-ordained person attempted to perform them, they would be seen as illegitimate.

Hyatt's final thoughts on this trade: "These developments had devastating ramifications for the ministry of the Holy Spirit through the people of God. The gifts that once had flowed spontaneously among the whole congregation were now bound to the ecclesiastical office and transmitted by a sacramental act."[6]

One of the reasons why the Protestant Reformation did not place emphasis on a restoration of Holy Spirit gifts or manifestations was because those who claimed to practice them were also encouraging people to visit shrines for miracles, endorsing the selling of indulgences, etc.

The liturgy, which was once participatory, spontaneous, and Spirit-led, became structured to the point where there was no breathing room for the supernatural. Jack Hayford and David Moore explain that the "growing emphasis on formalized leadership coupled with the development of creeds in answer to theological disputes created inevitable tension between the church's institutional nature and its charismatic character."[7]

Following the declension of supernatural manifestation in the church, the main point of emphasis was the deity and humanity of

Christ, while the ministry of the Holy Spirit was not given much focus. Structurally, the church system did not accommodate the Spirit's empowering Presence. Though some would argue that the move toward a more formalized and organized church protocol was protective in nature, it ultimately proved to be the wrong move.

A trade took place that contaminated the bloodline of the Christian church—the glory of God was exchanged for delusions of grandeur. Although God has always had men and women throughout the ages who pressed in for the power of the age to come, historically they were a minority. The Holy Spirit never left the planet, nor did His supernatural power ever cease operating. It has always continued, but it has flowed to the degree that those on earth function as gates for it to flow *through*.

Let us repent on behalf of our forefathers who thought the move of the Spirit to be a "common thing," worth exchanging for worldly affluence. Let's repent on behalf of more recent generations who were willing to lay down the move of the Spirit for increased popularity or acceptance among the spiritual elite. All of us have surely struggled with these things. After all, we have self-image to be mindful of and a reputation to maintain. We'd all do well to follow the example of Jesus, who made Himself of *"no reputation"* (see Phil. 2:7 NKJV).

I see church-wide repentance breaking out in the days ahead—repentance that will attract sudden outbreaks of overwhelming, uncontainable glory. I see cries and groanings of travail gripping people both in the secret place and in the public meeting. No longer will we run from the sounds of hunger and desperation, anguish and thirst. They are beautiful to the Lord's ears, as they represent the failure of our mortal human words to communicate how deeply we need Him.

20

What Hinders the
Spirit's Flow in Our Midst Today?

I HAVE IDENTIFIED four things that significantly hinder the move of the Holy Spirit in our lives and churches today. These are based on what I observed in how the early church leadership responded to the supernatural.

Institutionalism

When the church decides to place the main emphasis on its identity as a business or organization, this is often when the supernatural is exchanged for a more formal and palatable version of the Christian faith. In truth, there is a business side to church matters that needs to be handled with excellence. While I do not deny the need for this, I also call the body of Christ to ultimately consider what is more important in the grand scheme of things: Becoming a well-respected organization, or being supernaturally functional as a Spirit-filled community that boldly releases the Kingdom of God? We always need to keep the words of Jesus in the front of our minds when we consider the fundamental purpose of the church: "*I will give you the keys of the kingdom of heaven; and whatever you bind on earth shall have been bound in heaven, and whatever you loose on earth shall have been loosed in heaven*" (Matthew 16:19 NASB). Jesus did not give the church a business strategy; rather, He gave it keys to binding the powers of hell and unlocking the culture of Heaven. All institutional and business aspects of the church should be committed to stewarding the supernatural advancement of God's Kingdom through the community of a local church.

Formalism

As we observe in church history, institutionalism gave birth to a rigid formalism. Gone were the days of spontaneous house church meetings. Now, it was all about the liturgy. The meeting place was often exalted above the Holy Spirit who, above all, chose to make human hearts His dwelling place and sanctuary. Spontaneity was replaced with religious protocol, which progressively became more and more inflexible. We see the results of this in the Dark Ages, where the church had moved so far away from its supernatural assignment that it resulted in selling tickets out of a fictitious purgatory (which were called indulgences). Amazing how salvation and heavenly assurance—priceless gifts of God—could now be purchased with natural currency. Often we look at the Dark Ages and wonder how things got that bad. Just as Rome was not built in a day, the declination of the Christian faith was the result of many years where the collective voice of church leadership said "No" to the free-flowing move of the Spirit and "Yes" to a political and acceptable aberration of the faith. Are we moving in this direction again today? Yes, but in a much more subtle and perhaps even more insidious way.

Worldly Compromise

This is when the church tries to become like the world that it hopes to "bring in." In the most blatant examples, we see churches and entire denominations laying down time-honored biblical values to accommodate immoral trends in society. We also see examples of this when churches attempt to integrate secular culture into their liturgies in order to gain worldly appeal. This is compromise. You know what this says? *Holy Spirit, You are not enough; I need to use the strategies and tactics of the world in order to bring people into the church.* When we reach that point, it is a surefire sign that we need to break some significant strongholds in our thinking, as both individuals and in our church communities.

My question is, when we use the world to draw people into the church, *how do we keep them?* How do we disciple and train them? What are people even being discipled into? What glimpse of "normal Christianity" are we giving them? Even though this issue of worldly compromise tends to rear its head among the younger, next-gen congregations, it is sadly starting to infiltrate the Charismatic-Pentecostal community as well. I notice a trend where the "sons and daughters" of the Charismatic movement of the 1960s, by and large, are forming denominations, movements, fellowships, and churches that "believe" in the supernatural but restrict its practice. Some of these neo-Charismatic churches look, sound, and function no differently than the churches that have no paradigm at all for the move of the Spirit. Many have embraced this approach because they want to give the Holy Spirit a "soft introduction." In many cases, this is done to please longtime believers who have historically been uncomfortable with more demonstrative and unusual expressions of the supernatural.

In the same way that we should *not* manufacture the supernatural, we cannot tone down the Spirit's movement in our midst. Remember, the Bible uses extreme language to describe Him. Nowhere does Scripture tell us He is like a "gentleman." While He is pictured like a dove when He alights upon Jesus at His baptism, He also comes like a mighty sound, fire, and a rushing wind (see Matt. 3:16; Acts 2:1-4).

Exchanging the Presence of God for Popularity with People

Truth be told, the world does not want the world repackaged in the church. People who do not know God come to church—whether it is a stained-glass cathedral or a modern megachurch auditorium—because they are looking for answers. Perhaps the great question they are seeking answers to is: *God, are You really out there? Are You really real?* For those who remain committed to a supernatural expression of the faith, they have the upper hand in pure evangelism. The goal is not to ultimately accommodate the people who come to your church; your goal is to host the Presence of the Great Evangelist, the Holy Spirit. John Kilpatrick, pastor of the Brownsville and Bay Revivals, considered himself to be a "custodian of the Lord's Presence." The very heart of ministry is to reach out to people, absolutely. We want to help people answer the fundamental questions of life. However, our words ultimately cannot satisfy. Our programs won't do it. Our buildings, as nice as they appear, cannot usher people into life-altering encounters with God. Everything that we do must be directed toward accommodating the work of the Holy Spirit. It is He who is jealously pursuing the hearts of mankind. I heard someone once say, "I consider us a seeker-sensitive church; however, we acknowledge the Seeker to be the Holy Spirit." Everything changes when we build church around the preferences of the Spirit of God rather than our imagined ideas of what people "in the world" really want. I'll tell you what they want—what they *need*—God. We do the people who are legitimately searching for God a grievous disservice when we exchange the Holy Spirit for something "hip, cool, modern, and relevant." Think about it—if an unbeliever is earnestly looking for God and we deny them an encounter with the Holy Spirit because of the perceived importance of our flashy programs or because we don't want to "scare them off," we are denying this person the very thing their heart longs for. God the Father is in Heaven and God the Son is seated at His right hand. This means that the often misunderstood Holy Spirit is the very Person of the Trinity that the God-starved world is searching for. Let's not deprive them of encounter any longer! Dr. Vinson Synan described the early church's exchange of power for popularity and acceptance this way:

After gaining acceptance and power, however, the church began to experience less and less of the miraculous power of the primitive church and turned more and more to ritualistic and sacramental expressions of the faith.[1]

Keys to Unlocking the River of God's Presence in Your Life and Church Community

This book is specifically written for individual Christians who are desperate to see a restoration of the greater glory in their personal lives. Additionally, I am writing to pastors and church leaders, as you are being extended the most glorious invitation imaginable. God has chosen *you* to learn how to pastor the move of His Spirit. I know there is some tension when it comes to churches that have experienced great outpourings of the Holy Spirit, as some believe that once a church community has had a mighty visitation of God, it is difficult to actually sustain the outpouring in the context of a single local church. You know what? That is absolutely correct. The move of God was never meant just to revive our personal lives and even our individual local churches. Maybe the church has not witnessed true, sustained revival to the level that Heaven desires because we remain narrow in our focus. Perhaps we are often so self-focused that we haven't asked bigger questions like, "How can my church become a source of life and refreshing to other believers and pastors in this region…without trying to recruit them?" We need to learn from what has *not* worked in order to embrace Heaven's blueprint for what *does* work. This comes through trial, error, risk, and much grace. These words are not intended to be a rebuke; they are, I pray, a divine confrontation with some of the deceptive ideologies we have bought into over the years.

So many people just want to *break free*. Congregations want a deeper spiritual experience, while church leaders genuinely do want to press into the fullness of what God has available. What prevents all of this from happening? We keep doing what we have always been doing, intimidated about stepping out into unfamiliar, uncharted waters. This is exactly what happened with the early church in its formative centuries. It entered into an institutionalized formalism and simply embraced this as the new binding protocol on how to "do church." We must constantly ask ourselves the probing question, *What is Heaven's protocol? For my life? For my family? For my business? For my church?*

In conclusion, I want to give you four quick keys that will help you unlock Heaven's supernatural power in your life and community.

1. Pursue God's Presence Above Protocol

Pastor Bill Johnson has remarked, many times, that often in the church world today we gather around a sermon; Israel, however, camped around the Presence of God. We will deal with the balance of Word and Spirit in the following point. For now, it is absolutely vital that we make accommodating the Holy Spirit's Presence our chief end in life and ministry. When the early church drifted away from its supernatural roots, one of the driving forces was the emphasis on protocol. Order is necessary. Liturgy is not a bad word, for every church has its own unique expression of liturgy (even Charismatic ones). In the midst of this, we need to actually live with our protocols in a constant state of flexibility. Let's have a plan, but also be sensitive to the Holy Spirit's leading. In fact, I believe God wants us to get to the point where we delightfully exchange our plans and protocols for His. Right now, it is more often a wrestling match (and who are we to think that we are even capable of winning that one?). Hold to protocol lightly, whether it is in your personal life or church liturgy. The Spirit wants to increasingly tune our ears to hear His voice. As we respond to His promptings, we will experience the supernatural.

2. Don't Uphold the Word Above the Spirit (or Vice Versa)

Bill Johnson's statement is not saying that we need to exchange the preaching of the Word for the Spirit. He is not saying that we don't need sermons, good teaching, and increased biblical literacy. We need these things desperately. However, there must be a merger between the Holy Spirit and the Holy Scriptures. For too long, there has been an unbiblical dividing line between the two. Fundamentalist evangelicals have claimed to be people of the Book, while Charismatics and Pentecostals proudly describe themselves as "people of the Spirit." Can't we be both? Shouldn't we be both? There is no famine for teaching in the world today. We have Christian books, Christian conferences, Christian television, Christian seminars, and every other form of Christian media imaginable. We have every possible kind of Bible translation you could think of. And yet, why isn't the world completely transformed? The Word was never meant to function apart from the Spirit. The Spirit is the One who shows us that everything in the Word is available for us today.

3. Embrace the Risk of Hosting the Holy Spirit and Adapt to God's Blueprints

To shift from a protocol-driven life or church community to one yielded to the Holy Spirit demands risk. Whether the Spirit gently prompts you personally to pray for someone, giving you a word of knowledge or prophetic utterance about that person or, if He invites you as a church leader to exchange your sermon for an extended time of worship, prayer and ministry, it is going to take courage. At the same time, who does our allegiance belong to? Who is completely deserving of our trust? God. For some, trusting the Father and trusting Jesus is one thing, but they cannot graduate into trusting the Holy Spirit. This is because they have erroneously bought into the lie that the Spirit is somehow less than or substandard to the Father and Son. He is not some cosmic force;

He is the eternally good God Almighty and is completely worthy of our unreserved trust.

4. Create a Culture of Humility and Hunger, Where Everyone Gets to Operate in the Gifts of the Spirit

As we continue in our journey, we will notice that the declination of the supernatural throughout church history took place when the common, everyday people were no longer taught on how to move in the gifts of the Spirit. Signs and wonders became reserved for the saintly, holy, and unattainable. Even though there have been some normal, everyday believers who pressed in to experience the fullness of God throughout the centuries, the larger population of Christians was taught that the supernatural was off-limits to "common people." This deception can be propagated in the church, as some believe that only church leaders and alleged spiritual giants can flow in God's supernatural power. This is a lie. Paul reminded the Corinthians (and is reminding us today):

> For consider your calling, brothers: not many of you were wise according to worldly standards, not many were powerful, not many were of noble birth. But God chose what is foolish in the world to shame the wise; God chose what is weak in the world to shame the strong; God chose what is low and despised in the world, even things that are not, to bring to nothing things that are, so that no human being might boast in the presence of God (1 Corinthians 1:26-29).

I conclude where we began, with John Wimber's announcement of all access to God's supernatural power: "Everyone gets to play." From the moment a person makes the transition from being lost to becoming a believer, that individual is able to move in the miraculous power of God. It has nothing to do with that person; it has everything to do with the Person who came to live within them—the Holy Spirit.

Even though the church made some unfortunate trades in its formative centuries, the Spirit of God was not withdrawn from the earth. Even though church leadership chose to "close the gates" through key decisions that prohibited the supernatural, there has always been a faithful remnant who still pressed in. Trades are reversible! Yes, we repent, but next, and perhaps most importantly, is that we turn from our ways and turn toward God's. We return to His protocol and instructions!

21

Follow God's
Presence Protocol

So the priests and the Levites purified themselves in order to bring the Ark of the Lord, the God of Israel, to Jerusalem. Then the Levites carried the Ark of God on their shoulders with its carrying poles, just as the Lord had instructed Moses (1 Chronicles 15:14-15 NLT).

"IT'S TIME TO BUILD GOD A HOUSE!" No, it's not a temple or tabernacle. And yes, *we* are the New Covenant house of God. But it's time for the *house* of God to make Him more comfortable living in His house. It's time for us to prayerfully consider every "room" in our lives and ask the Spirit of God to shine His light of conviction on areas that do not accommodate His Presence.

Perhaps the greatest illustration I've ever heard on this subject matter came from Pastor Bill Johnson in the context of his teaching and book on *Hosting the Presence*. He asks the question, "How would you move and function if you had a dove on your shoulder?" The common answer is "carefully." Good answer, but not the most correct one. Bill reminds us that the appropriate answer is, "We take every step with the dove in mind." This is the evidence of a yielded life. A life that is presented to God as a living sacrifice is not evidenced through words and rhetoric. It's not about how spiritual we make ourselves sound or how holy we project ourselves to be. It goes far deeper. A yielded life is exemplified by the one who prioritizes God in every step they take.

David clearly instructed the Levites to carry the Ark of God according to the instructions given to Moses. These instructions were given to him by God, which tells me that God has a preferred way for His Presence to be handled, carried, and stewarded. Our top priority should be accommodating God's protocol for transporting His Presence. And His Presence will not be carried or moved by one with an agenda contrary to His own. It will not be compatible with an "Uzzah" spirit, who assumes that man has the right to touch or tamper with what God is doing,

The bottom line is that the King's protocol demands obedience and adherence. It's not motivated by a religious spirit. "I *have* to do this in order to have God's approval." No. Rather, it's motivated by the question: "God, how do You want me to carry Your Presence? What are You doing and how do I adapt and adjust to Your movement?" We don't want to move out ahead of God, nor do we want to be moving behind Him. We want to be moving in sync with Him, and the only way to do this is to remain, moment by moment, in tune with what the Holy Spirit is saying.

Summon the Musicians and Worshipers, Not the Entertainers

David also ordered the Levite leaders to appoint a choir of Levites who were singers and musicians to sing joyful songs to the accompaniment of harps, lyres, and cymbals (1 Chronicles 15:16 NLT).

Singers and songwriters are on assignment to both accommodate and *announce* the move of the Ark. Why? It seems that the Ark of the Covenant moves with musical accompaniment. Translating this to our day and age, I believe the move of the Spirit is also announced and accompanied by the sound of our songs.

I prophesy that the Lord is raising up a new breed of psalmist, musician, songwriter, and worship leader whose primary ministry is unto the Lord, not to the people. The people will ultimately be benefitted, yes, because as these minstrels first connect with the Lord they will capture both the sights and sounds of God's world and be given instructions on how to translate them into this one. We don't need more songs, we don't need more albums, we don't need more performances, we don't need more music in church. None of these things are bad, per se, unless of course they are the result of trading Presence for performance. If we have decided to exchange the Ark of the Covenant for music that simply entertains or even connects with people emotionally, then we are settling for something far beneath what God has envisioned.

Here is what I envision, and I want to offer this as a prophetic word for musicians, songwriters, singers, and worship leaders (although it's vital for all believers to have this information so we know what God is doing right now).

Your first assignment is responding to the summons into the "counsel room" of Heaven, not the songwriters' table. I know right now it's very popular for songwriters to gather and collaborate on writing anthems of praise and worship for the church. This is beautiful, as I love the collaborative nature of this. But this is not where the sounds will be birthed. Sounds from Heaven are birthed in the counsel of the Lord. This is a realm exclusive to the friends of God but accessible to anyone who would step into that role. Specifically, for songwriters, the counsel of the Lord is open for those who want to simply see and hear the sights and sounds of Heaven.

If we don't capture the new sounds from Heaven but continue simply writing songs as usual, I predict the body of Christ will trade the new songs for old ones. Why? We will continue to go back to where there was anointing. We will continue to look back in history for a song or sound that was prophetically announcing what God was doing and how He was moving. Remember, our songs should both announce and accompany the move of His Presence.

Guard the Ark

Berekiah and Elkanah were chosen to guard the Ark (1 Chronicles 15:23 NLT).

This was very interesting language: "*guard the Ark.*" In context, these were uniquely chosen individuals who would literally guard the Ark of the Covenant. That was their function. Priority number one was to guard or protect that which carried the Presence of God. What if that assignment was restored to the contemporary church?

Pastor John Kilpatrick has referred to himself as simply a "custodian of the Presence of God." This assignment is not exclusive to pastors and leaders. Every one of us should make the Holy Spirit's comfort in our lives our top priority. It would be easy for me to write about how we should do this in the context of our church services and gatherings — absolutely.

But let's make it more personal, shall we? Both Ana and I are convinced that the key to accessing the Greater Glory is nothing short of becoming a living sacrifice before the Lord, wholly yielded and completely surrendered. What does this life practically look like?

Holy Spirit, does this conversation make You comfortable?

Holy Spirit, is what I am thinking right now something that *You* would think?

Holy Spirit, is the decision I am excited about making pleasing and exciting to You?

Stop right there. No, I am not advocating some kind of hyper spirituality where we ask the Lord about what kind of toothpaste to purchase. (Although, if that floats your boat, go ahead; I am sure He has some great recommendations!) You know what I am saying, though. But when it comes to how we do everyday life, if we really want to walk in greater measures of anointing and experience increased demonstrations of God's glory, we simply need to pursue a life that is compatible with the Holy Spirit.

When we are saved, our spirits are regenerated. They are transformed. That is the part of us that becomes what Paul defines as a "new creation" (see 2 Cor. 5:17). This is our invisible inmost being, the part of us that transitions into eternity with God in Heaven or eternity separate from God in hell. We know, though, that when our spirits are saved our souls (typically believed to be comprised of our mind, will, and emotions) are not immediately saved, but Scripture says they are being saved. *"Therefore put away all filthiness and rampant wickedness and receive with meekness the implanted word, which is able to save your souls"* (James 1:21). Our physical bodies will become supernaturally transformed when the Lord returns and we receive what the Bible calls a "glorified body" (see 1 Cor. 15:35-58).

You might be asking, "Larry, what does any of this have to do with guarding the Presence of God?" Even though our spirit is saved immediately upon receiving Jesus as Lord and Savior, our soul — mind, will, and emotions — is progressively saved as we walk the earth in relationship with the Holy Spirit. This is what theologians typically call "sanctification." Many believers run away from this language because it often involves talk of "holiness," and in the past holiness has been inappropriately tied with legalism, lists of dos and donts, and hypocrisy. Let's put all of that behind us.

Do you want to know how to guard the Presence of God in your life and actually see His glory rest upon you in an increasing measure? Live asking this question: *Holy Spirit, does this make You comfortable?* Is that thought, attitude, or action compatible with the Holy Spirit? Is it something He would say, do, or think? I am not at all advocating some hyper sin-awareness, where we are always looking over our proverbial shoulder, wondering if we have done something that God is "not pleased with." Sin is a big deal and we need to deal with it in a much bolder way in our present society; at the same time, God has not called us to be hyper sin-conscious but, rather, Spirit-conscious. I so appreciate John Piper's explanation of sin, comparing it to the glory and Presence of God:

> What is sin? It is the glory of God not honored. The holiness of God not reverenced. The greatness of God not admired. The power of God not praised. The truth of God not sought. The wisdom of God not esteemed. The beauty of God not treasured. The goodness of God not savored. The faithfulness of God not trusted. The commandments of God not obeyed. The justice of God not respected. The wrath of God not feared. The grace of God not cherished. The presence of God not prized. The person of God not loved. That is sin.

This is not a call to become hyper sin-focused; let's become a people who are increasingly Holy Spirit-focused! This simply means we live increasingly aware of the Person who lives inside of us. We give our lives to guarding His comfort. I believe that as we do this, we will witness an increased measure of glory resting upon the people of God.

One time I asked God about heroes like Smith Wigglesworth, John G. Lake, and Kathryn Kuhlman. I wanted to know the "secret sauce" to their breakthrough ministries. For one, God is not into giving out "steps" because we would be quick to rely on steps to an outcome rather than a relationship with a Person. Second, God reminded me of each person's shortcomings and weaknesses. It's easy to deify those who have walked in greater measures of glory than we have seen or tasted; we put such people on a pedestal. They deserve special honor and recognition, yes, but the Lord was quick to remind me that those three names (and countless others) walked in greater realms of glory because they gave their imperfect lives to making the Holy Spirit comfortable. Wow. They were all guardians of the Presence. And it doesn't take long to research their lives and see how each of these heroes placed a supreme value on the Presence of the Holy Spirit.

John G. Lake lived with a strong awareness of the reality of "Christ in you."

> We are awakening to that marvelous truth, that Christ is not in the heavens only, nor the atmosphere only, but Christ is in you.

Consider what Lake said concerning the presence of unholiness in our lives:

> Beloved, if any unholiness exists in the nature, it is not there by the consent of the Spirit of God. If unholiness is in your life it is because your soul is giving consent to it, and you are retaining it. Let it go. Cast it out and let God have His way in your life.

More than anything, we desire to make our lives *resting places* for this wonderful person called the Holy Spirit. Aimee Semple McPherson, the pioneering founder of the Foursquare denomination and a dynamic communicator whom even the entertainment community went to for inspiration, captured it in this observation of her assignment:

> What is my task? First of all, my task is to be pleasing to Christ. To be empty of self and be filled with Himself. To be filled with the Holy Spirit; to be led by the Holy Spirit.

Study the quotes from faith heroes who seemed to live with unusual anointing and power. You'll quickly discover that the secret was in surrender to the Spirit.

Much of Christianity has lived satisfied with the Spirit living within them when there are unexplored realms of glory waiting to be released by a people who allow the Spirit to rest *upon* them. For this to happen, it requires that we become guardians of His Presence in our lives.

22

Let Go of
Human Dignity

Then David and the elders of Israel and the generals of the army went to the house of Obed-edom to bring the Ark of the Lord's Covenant up to Jerusalem with a great celebration. And because God was clearly helping the Levites as they carried the Ark of the Lord's Covenant, they sacrificed seven bulls and seven rams.

David was dressed in a robe of fine linen, as were all the Levites who carried the Ark, and also the singers, and Kenaniah the choir leader. David was also wearing a priestly garment. So all Israel brought up the Ark of the Lord's Covenant with shouts of joy, the blowing of rams' horns and trumpets, the crashing of cymbals, and loud playing on harps and lyres.

But as the Ark of the Lord's Covenant entered the City of David, Michal, the daughter of Saul, looked down from her window. When she saw King David skipping about and laughing with joy, she was filled with contempt for him (1 Chronicles 15:25-29 NLT).

RETURNING TO THE ORIGINAL outpouring that took place on the Day of Pentecost, we see many different responses to the Holy Spirit's movement—perplexed, confused, amazed, and mocking, to name a few that are listed in the biblical account.

To position ourselves for the greater glory, we need to be willing to become increasingly undignified.

Throughout revival history, long before the Azusa Street Pentecostal outpouring of 1906, we have witnessed "manifestations" or signs of the Holy Spirit touching people—swooning (slain in the spirit, falling under the power), shaking, trembling, laughing, trances, weeping (travail), running, etc. When God comes into collision with human vessels, something is bound to happen.

At this point, I want to prophesy where I believe all of this is headed. I was watching a youth gathering at a ministry called The Ramp in Hamilton, Alabama. This is one of the most significant youth ministries on the planet, as the senior leader and founder, Karen Wheaton, is intent on seeing the young people have a real encounter with a real God. During this gathering, the young people in attendance began to groan in travail. They started to cry out, as there was a real spiritual birthing taking place. They were praying, like Hannah in the Old Testament, crying out for God to break through in their lives. These sounds are not pretty; they are not trendy. In the natural, it would seem that allowing these sounds in our gatherings would be off-putting. But I am convinced that these sounds are signs of life. Birthing rooms are not pretty places, but they are chambers where life comes forth.

I prophesy we are entering a season when the groan will not be containable. And yes, the children will lead us. I believe many pastors and leaders across the earth are sincerely seeking the Lord for strategies to see their cities transformed *and* young people come to the Lord.

This will sound strange, but I believe it's timeless—the growth is in the groan. The groan of travail is the sound of something birthing in the spirit. This is not exclusive to the weekly prayer meeting or even the intercessors' group; I see megachurches with thousands of people being caught up in a spirit of travail. I see the worship actually opening up realms of intercession and prayer as the people finally hit the ceiling of where the song can take them. In other words, they have sung the lyrics continually but they are absolutely exhausted singing about realities they have not personally seen or tasted. I see the songs becoming catalysts for groans and cries of travail. I see God falling on these groups. I see God falling on *you* as you are reading this because revival starts with you. It begins with you saying, "God, I want to taste and see what I am singing...what I am reading."

God is ready. For some reason, I get the phrase "on the edge of His seat." God is ready now. The Holy Spirit has already been poured out. Where are the ready ones? Where are the yielded and surrendered? Where are those who are willing to become as David was, undignified and foolish unto the Lord?

And yes, this display of crying, weeping, wailing, falling, laughing, and any other kind of "undignified" manifestation will certainly receive scorn and mockery. David's own wife was filled with contempt for him. But we cannot shut down what God is doing because there are the skeptics and mockers. Case in point, they didn't shut down the Day of Pentecost because there were those accusing the 120 of being drunk on new wine. They endured the persecution and mockery because what they received in return, the Holy Spirit, infinitely outweighed any criticism they received. The same is true for us today!

The Lord revealed some amazing insights about the dance of David to Ana in the following segment.

Ana

Go Low!

When God moves, we are absolutely stripped of our own flesh and are humbled. David danced wildly before the Lord as the Israelites brought the Ark of God into the city. It says in Second Samuel

6:14 that David danced with *"all his might"* in a linen ephod. Now I, being of curious nature, one time looked up what exactly would be a linen ephod and let me just save you the search—there wasn't a whole lot going on there as far as covering!

So, there was King David, dancing with all his might and joy, rejoicing in the Lord in front of his whole kingdom practically in his underwear! Let that sink in for a second. We have heard this story so many times that we can often overlook the significance of why God would allow this scene to be included in His Word for us later to ponder over.

David has been called "a man after God's own heart"! Although he made many mistakes, he is still foundational in the genealogy of Jesus.

Yielding

There comes a place where all our pride is laid down for the glory of God. Like David we become unrestrained. When we worship without caring what it looks like or the response of others watching, it is a sweet incense unto the Lord. "All of Me for all of you," He has said to me so many times, reminding me over and over again to 100 percent yield to Him and give Him everything.

There is no *pride* in Heaven! Do you think we will care what we look like when we sit before the King of Kings one day? Nope. Our very response will be "Holy, Holy, Holy!" Then why do we sometimes struggle with our pride now? "What if I look silly, God? What if it just seems so out of the box that people may not understand when You are moving on me? What if I am totally misunderstood and people might slander me?"

All of these questions I wrestled with personally as the Presence of God would hit me in waves and I could barely walk. I think specifically of my baptism at the Jordan River. It was truly humiliating as I had to lean on my brothers to carry me around or slide me down the hallway to my hotel room. For days, God's Presence was resting on me in such a heavy measure that I struggled to walk normally. I know that is hard to understand, but all of my pride was being burnt away. Here I was, one of the ministry leaders on that trip to Jerusalem, and I would hear people on the trip walk down the hallway saying, "Ah, there goes that drunk Ana again!" There are times when people didn't even realize that I could still hear their comments, even though I was pinned to the floor by an angel and couldn't get up under that weighty Presence of the Lord, and yet I would hear them.

Moving with the *Move* of God

Acts 2:12-13 says: "*And they all continued in amazement and great perplexity, saying to one another, 'What does this mean?' But others were mocking and saying, 'They are full of sweet wine'*" (NASB). Some other translations even say: "They're drunk!"

When the day of Pentecost came, it says that there was noise in Heaven that broke out like rushing wind, and tongues of fire fell on the group that was there. The group was filled with the Holy Spirit and were speaking to each other in different languages — tongues. People who were watching had reactions of bewilderment, amazement, astonishment, perplexity, and mocking.

To this day, when there is a move of the Holy Spirit that falls, those reactions still are a tendency. I've personally watched and been in revival environments where God moves in a sudden, dramatic way, and some things that occur are just unexplainable. There is always the opportunity to react in offense or criticism, jump in the river of the move of the Lord, or sit on the sidelines and simply watch in amazement.

As we look back over Pentecost and what occurred for that group of people, one thing is strikingly clear: they were not in control, and God was 100 percent! This idea or notion is scary to some of us because, quite frankly, we like being in control. Let me tell you, as a homeschool mother of two children, and also director of healing rooms, as well as having my own ministry, I like to be in control of my life, schedule, and timing of things. When unexplainable happenings hit my life, the enemy can really use them to try and send me off my rocker and steal my peace. And yet in those moments, the Lord whispers in my ear, "I am in control. Would you trust Me?" The safest place we can be in is trusting God and giving Him leadership of our lives, knowing that He wants and has what's best for us in store. So, we are not in control; we never were, and that's a good thing!

So can we just take a moment and lay our pride, our fear, our control issues, our platforms, and even our own expectations aside and say, "*God, have Your way in me!*" God wants to bring a new level of freedom to each of us.

When I got baptized in the Jordan and had that wild dose of God zapping me for days, the more I yielded to whatever God was doing, the more He could and would use me in power to touch others around us. The connection was there. The more connected I was in that place of deep intimacy with the Lord, being completely yielded to however He wanted to move, the more I witnessed Him using me to move in signs and wonders. We often want the platform, but perhaps not the sacrifice of our own will. It's God's will, not my own anymore. I had to get to the place where I just didn't even care what it looked like anymore. I just wanted more of Him and none of me, and for that reason He could use me. *He can and wants to use you too. He wants to move with, in, and through you!*

Part Three

The Prophetic Invitation

Revival is personal; reformation is corporate. The outpouring of the Spirit was never meant to ebb and flow. We see this, though, throughout church history. We witness periods of great Holy Spirit power and outpouring, while others seem to be spiritual "dark ages." In order for us to sustain the outpouring of the Spirit, we need to adhere to God's prophetic blueprint. Both Joel 2 and Acts 2 speak of "all flesh" experiencing this outpouring of glory. For this to happen, those who carry the outpouring need to venture beyond the four walls of the church and Christian culture and intentionally influence every sphere, place, and cultural mindset that has been impacted by sin. Those who carry glory need to run toward, not away from, these areas of darkness, for this is the only way the powers of darkness will be challenged and contested. Until carriers of Holy Spirit glory actually show up in government, entertainment, sports, business, politics, media, science, and education, the prevailing demonic strongholds operating in those places will remain and increase.

23

Israel, the Glory,
and the Coming Great Move of God

They are Israelites, and to them belong the adoption, the glory, the covenants, the giving of the law, the worship, and the promises (Romans 9:4).

THE GLORY OF GOD *is the inheritance of Israel.* It was to the Jewish people that the Lord first revealed His glory — His wonderful manifest Presence. This is obvious throughout the entirety of the Old Testament narrative, as God sought a place of habitation among His people. With Abraham, Isaac, and Jacob, we witnessed powerful but sporadic visitations of divine Presence. Enter Moses, and the very heartbeat of the Lord is laid bare: He desires a place of habitation among His chosen. Thus, God Himself provides Moses instructions to build a tabernacle, a dwelling place that makes it possible for the glory of God to dwell among mankind. Of course, this was at a very limited measure compared to what would become available in the New Covenant. But we would do well to pay attention to *how* God manifested Himself in the Old Testament, as I do not believe Scripture makes a case for God changing the manifestation of His glory. The manifestation of Presence can certainly change, yes, and appear however God sovereignly wills, but throughout the Old Covenant we see the following accompanying manifestations of divine Presence: angels, clouds, pillars of fire, and smoke. We see, perhaps, the most profound manifestation of glory unveiled to Moses while on Mount Sinai, during the exchange where Moses asks God, "Please, show me Your glory!" (see Exod. 33:18). Israel, the Jewish people, and the Old Covenant specifically are vital to us understanding, experiencing, and releasing the greater glory of God into the earth.

On the cusp of every move of God, however, there are invariably false doctrines that arise, which aim to dismantle what Heaven is releasing into the earth. One such doctrine is replacement theology, which basically teaches that there are no unfulfilled promises left exclusively for Israel, and that the Gentile church has replaced Israel and the Jewish people. While we as Gentiles are "grafted in" spiritually, God is not finished with His covenant people. To the degree that we neglect Heaven's agenda for Israel and the Jewish community, we are actually prolonging outpouring and the second coming of King Jesus.

The good news is that God *will* get what He wants: *the whole earth filled with His glory* (see Num. 14:21). However, Scripture does seem to present a possibility for *hastening* the plans and purposes of God in the earth—namely, the second coming of Messiah Jesus (see 2 Pet. 3:12). My question is, *how can we effectively participate in hastening the Lord's coming?* Perhaps the greatest way would be partnering with the Holy Spirit's movement in Israel and among the Jewish people.

Speeding Up the Coming of the Lord

Master expository preacher Dr. Adrian Rogers explains it this way: "We are causing the day to come more quickly today when we fulfill the conditions without which the day of the Lord will not come." Pause and think about that observation. There are certain biblical conditions that must be fulfilled in order for the day of the Lord to come. This book is not an eschatological study of unfolding end-times events; I don't have the theological authority to write on such matters. That said, I do believe that in conjunction with the

Lord's return to the earth, we will witness a significant national turning of Israel to Messiah Jesus, which will be accompanied by a powerful demonstration of signs, wonders, and miracles.

Greek scholar Dr. Marvin Vincent explains more thoroughly: "that day being no date inexorably fixed, but one the arrival of which it is free to the church to hasten on by faith and prayer. See Matt 24:14: The gospel shall be preached in the whole world, 'and *then* shall the end come.' Compare the words of Peter in Acts 3:19, 'Repent and be converted...*that so* there may come seasons of refreshing.'"[1]

Note the two elements that Dr. Vincent listed — faith and prayer. Faith and prayer are meant to produce measurable results, not theological rhetoric. Everything Scripture says is allowable and available should be manifesting in our lives. This is especially true for the unique plan of God for the Jewish people and nation of Israel. I know that as a modern church, particularly in other nations, it's easy for us to get caught up in using prayer and faith for our own national conditions and personal circumstances. While this makes sense, there is a missing paradigm that, when embraced, will fling wide the ancient gates and open the doors for the King of glory to come in (see Ps. 24). Are we using our faith to believe for God's plans to come to pass in Israel? Are we praying proactively for the peace of Jerusalem, national turning of the Jewish people, and historic outpouring of the Holy Spirit among God's elect? If not, let's get praying!

When Jesus returns to the earth, He will be evaluating many things; after all, He is returning for a return on His investment(s). On the basis of the Luke 18, I believe Jesus will be evaluating what we actually *did* with faith and prayer. *"When the Son of Man comes, will he find faith on earth?"* (Luke 18:8). He is not looking for how many books we wrote on the subject, sermons we preached about it, or times we encouraged people to "pray" or "have more faith." Jesus is looking for measurable results produced by faith and prayer. This is right on the tail end of the *Parable of the Persistent Widow*, the account of a woman who contended for justice in the face of an adversary who was against her and a judge who was unjust. The point is she persisted relentlessly and she received justice.

Could it be the coming of the Lord could in fact be linked to our faith and prayer? This chapter, however, is not primarily about the power of prayer or how to use your faith. I believe we need to specifically apply faith and prayer for the move of God among the Jewish people and the place of Israel in God's cosmic plan. In the same way we pray earnestly, intensely, and persistently for our own needs, I want to encourage you to do the same concerning Israel. Shortly, we are going to review a portion of Scripture the Lord highlighted to me about how to pray specifically for Israel. As we mine the depths of these passages, I believe the Spirit is going to give us prayer strategies for every other area of our lives; the key is understanding "to the Jew first."

To the Jew First — *Why?*

For I am not ashamed of the gospel, because it is the power of God that brings salvation to everyone who believes: first to the Jew, then to the Gentile (Romans 1:16 NIV).

This almost feels like a "new" message sometimes, particularly to the younger generation. I'm convinced, however, this is the most overlooked key to accessing the greater glory of God and seeing this generation witness the "same works and even greater works" that Jesus promised in John 14:12. What happens when we start seeing "*the Jew first*" again?

First, we must understand that the Jewish people and Israel still have a very unique place in God's plan for humanity. In the last days, Scripture makes it clear there will be a great turning of Jewish people to the Messiah.

In a message presented by author and preacher John Piper he comments on Romans 11, explaining, "Not only is salvation for Israel *only* through the Deliverer, Jesus Christ, but this salvation for Israel also is *certainly* coming…the salvation of Israel is not just a possibility but a certainty. God has given the promise, and God has called Israel for his own, and Paul says in verse 29, 'The gifts and the calling of God are irrevocable.'"[2]

> *I want you to understand this mystery, dear brothers and sisters, so that you will not feel proud about yourselves. Some of the people of Israel have hard hearts, but this will last only until the full number of Gentiles comes to Christ. And so all Israel will be saved. As the Scriptures say,*
>
> *"The one who rescues will come from Jerusalem, and he will turn Israel away from ungodliness. And this is my covenant with them, that I will take away their sins."*
>
> *Many of the people of Israel are now enemies of the Good News, and this benefits you Gentiles. Yet they are still the people he loves because he chose their ancestors Abraham, Isaac, and Jacob. For God's gifts and his call can never be withdrawn* (Romans 11:25-29 NLT).

Second, we need to recognize there has been much false teaching on the unique place of the Jewish people and Israel in God's unfolding plan for humanity. *Replacement theology* has polluted the body of Christ, convincing us there are no unfulfilled prophecies or promises awaiting fulfillment for the Jewish people. This is false teaching. However, the worst response we could offer to confront false doctrine or erroneous teaching is complete disengagement from the discussion. Usually, when there is false teaching concerning a certain subject, this is an invitation for us to press in deeper to discover the biblical truth of what the enemy is trying to pervert or pollute. Such is the case with Israel's unique place in the unfolding of God's agenda in the earth.

Although the language might change from generation to generation, the enemy's objective is still the same—downplay the prophetic role that Israel and the Jewish people play in the advancement of God's Kingdom on earth or, worse, completely write them out of the equation all together. This can often turn into anti-Semitism. For more information on the history of anti-Semitism and the church, read Dr. Michael Brown's hard-hitting book, *Our Hands Are Stained with Blood.* Scripture is filled with unfulfilled promises and prophecies concerning Israel and God's chosen people, the Jews. Yes, as Gentiles we are wonderfully grafted in to these promises and blessings, but at the same time, we will never replace the uniqueness of God's dealings with the nation of Israel and this precious covenant people.

Romans 9 presents God's plan for Israel in no uncertain terms. This book is *not* an apologetic against the dangers of replacement theology. Rather, I want to present a case for how our dealing with Israel and the Jews is absolutely integral to see the *greater glory* of God released throughout the earth. I'd go out on a limb and say that we will not witness the fullness of the manifestation of His glory, power, and Presence into the earth *apart* from participating in God's covenant place for His people and Israel. Why?

The Jew Seeks a Sign...and We've Focused on Wisdom

In First Corinthians, Paul describes what methods of evangelism are effective in certain people groups.

> *For Jews demand signs and Greeks seek wisdom, but we preach Christ crucified, a stumbling block to Jews and folly to Gentiles, but to those who are called, both Jews and Greeks, Christ the power of God and the wisdom of God.*

> *For the foolishness of God is wiser than men, and the weak-*
> *ness of God is stronger than men* (1 Corinthians 1:22-25).

Signs and wonders speak specifically to the Jewish community, while wisdom does often win over the Greek (or Gentiles). Of
course, signs, wonders, and miracles are effective in ministering to
anyone, Jew or Gentile, but in this particular context, Paul points
out the importance of signs in reaching the Jew.

Some might say, "Larry, did you read the rest of the passage? It's
not signs and wonders that win people, Jew or Gentile; it's preaching Christ crucified!" Consider Paul's further evaluation, that Christ
is *"the power of God and the wisdom of God"* (v. 24). Then, right in
the beginning of chapter 2, Paul clarifies that he is not simply presenting information through eloquence and well-orated rhetoric. He
boldly states:

> *And I, when I came to you, brothers, did not come pro-*
> *claiming to you the testimony of God with lofty speech or*
> *wisdom. For I decided to know nothing among you except*
> *Jesus Christ and him crucified. And I was with you in*
> *weakness and in fear and much trembling, and my speech*
> *and my message were not in plausible words of wisdom,*
> *but in demonstration of the Spirit and of power, so that*
> *your faith might not rest in the wisdom of men but in the*
> *power of God* (1 Corinthians 2:1-5).

As the Gospel is preached with miraculous signs following,
and the "Jew seeks a sign," I believe we will witness the greatest
outpouring of the Spirit among the Jewish people and in the land
of Israel. If there will be a national turning of the Jewish people to
Messiah Jesus, it stands that this will be accompanied by a powerful demonstration of signs and wonders. The Old Testament contains many prophecies that have yet to be fulfilled concerning God's

chosen people and nation. Our assignment? We make these unful-filled promises and prophecies part of our prayer lives.

> *And I will pour out on the house of David and the inhab-itants of Jerusalem a spirit of grace and pleas for mercy, so that, when they look on me, on him whom they have pierced, they shall mourn for him, as one mourns for an only child, and weep* (Zechariah 12:10).

For Israel to recognize "him whom they have pierced," a "spirit" needs to be poured out upon the Jewish people. I believe it is the Holy Spirit who will administer the supernatural "grace and pleas for mercy," making it possible for Israel to receive the redemptive work of Messiah.

> *Who has heard such a thing? Who has seen such things? Shall a land be born in one day? Shall a nation be brought forth in one moment? For as soon as Zion was in labor she brought forth her children* (Isaiah 66:8).

While this Scripture, I believe, points to Israel and the Jewish people first, it reminds us that as we move toward the culmination of the age, it is possible for nations to be birthed into the Kingdom in a day. This does not assume theocracies where religious rule abso-lutely governs the nations, nor does it guarantee every single indi-vidual in the nation will be a follower of Messiah Jesus. But as Jesus Himself discussed a division between "sheep and goat" nations, I do believe as we step more and more into this outpouring of greater glory, the fruit of this outpouring could be entire nations birthed into the Kingdom of God with supernatural acceleration (see Matt. 25:31-46).

Much of modern evangelism has focused on winning people with wisdom, namely through apologetics. While this field of study is vital for raising up mature believers who can defend their faith, biblically, the only way into the Kingdom of God is through a power encounter with the risen Messiah. Jesus must become *real* to us. Yes, He can do this through "wisdom," as I know of many people who have been converted through this means. Even still, wisdom and information will take you only so far; at some point, the heart must bow to the supernatural work of the Holy Spirit.

We will explore more of the practicals on how to engage this assignment in the next chapter. For right now, it's vital for us to recognize that Israel and the Jewish people have a vital place in the unfolding of God's plan in the earth. I believe they will step into a "fullness" as the Gentiles operate in signs and wonders, provoke the Jews to jealousy, and in turn they will rediscover a lost inheritance. After all, *"to them belong...the glory"* (Rom. 9:4). Everything we learn about the substance of God's glory we discover in the Old Covenant. Until Jesus, that glory was reserved, restricted, and restrained. It was kept in a box, behind a veil, and in tents and temples. Now, God has broken out!

24

Relentless Prayer

A supernatural blueprint for contending for Israel's salvation, global glory outpouring, and answered prayer.

FOR THIS CHAPTER, I want us to study Isaiah 62 from the English Standard Version of the Bible. The blueprint here is integral, as I believe we are given a strategy on how to pray with breakthrough results.

> *For Zion's sake I will not keep silent, and for Jerusalem's sake I will not be quiet, until her righteousness goes forth as brightness, and her salvation as a burning torch. The nations shall see your righteousness, and all the kings your glory, and you shall be called by a new name that the mouth of the Lord will give. You shall be a crown of beauty in the hand of the Lord, and a royal diadem in the hand of your God. You shall no more be termed Forsaken, and your land shall no more be termed Desolate, but you shall be called My Delight Is in Her, and your land Married; for the Lord delights in you, and your land shall be married. For as a young man marries a young woman, so shall your sons marry you, and as the bridegroom rejoices over the bride, so shall your God rejoice over you.*

> *On your walls, O Jerusalem, I have set watchmen; all the*
> *day and all the night they shall never be silent. You who*
> *put the Lord in remembrance, take no rest, and give him no*
> *rest until he establishes Jerusalem and makes it a praise in*
> *the earth* (Isaiah 62:1-7).

I am convinced this is a blueprint for the kind of prayer and intercession that unlocks the greater glory of God. Pray and prophesy this portion of Scripture, not simply over Israel, but also over the nations of the earth. On a macro level, we are praying this way for nations; on an everyday level, we are using this as a blueprint to pray and contend for *every promise* God has said "Yes and Amen" to in Christ to be fulfilled (see 2 Cor. 1:20).

Nearly every verse has significance and assignment for us to participate in.

Pray Until…

> *For Zion's sake I will not keep silent, and for Jerusalem's*
> *sake I will not be quiet, until her righteousness goes forth*
> *as brightness, and her salvation as a burning torch.*

First and foremost, we are praying for the physical Zion—Jerusalem. In our modern culture, we have gotten used to an inappropriate way of reading and interpreting Scripture—we start with what the Bible says to *me* instead of what the Bible was saying to the people in its historical context. Yes, it has inspiration, application, and prophetic relevance to us in whatever point of history we are living in, but let's first consider the immediate context.

Let's lift up relentless persevering prayer for Israel, Jerusalem, and the Jewish people. This is a post of intercession all believers are called to. Pray that she would shine as a burning torch to the nations.

Second, I believe this Scripture shows us *how to pray* for God's will. For the context of this book, we are talking about praying for outpouring and greater glory. This is God's will according to Joel 2 and Acts 2: *all flesh* experiencing the outpouring of the Spirit. So, how long do we pray for these things? The time period is right there — *until*. Pray until. We pray until Jerusalem's righteousness goes forth as brightness. We pray until the earth is filled with His glory and all flesh experience Holy Spirit outpouring. And we pray *until* that which God said in His word comes to pass in our lives or in the lives of those we are praying for.

Pray for a glory demonstration that's visible to nations and kings.

The nations shall see your righteousness, and all the kings your glory, and you shall be called by a new name that the mouth of the Lord will give. You shall be a crown of beauty in the hand of the Lord, and a royal diadem in the hand of your God.

To the Jew first, we are praying that Israel would be filled with such divine Presence that nations would see her righteousness and the kings of the earth would behold her glory. In other words, we are not just praying for Israel for the sake of Israel; in the same way, we are not just praying for Holy Spirit outpouring just so the church can be refreshed. We pray into this great objective of God because, like Him, we need to see nationally. We need to recognize that the demonstration of glory and outpouring of the Spirit will provoke the nations. They *will* see the movement of God in Israel. They *will* behold His glory in our nations, churches, and households. It will be such a provocative demonstration of glory that no one will be blind to it. They will either turn toward God or continue to harden their hearts against Him. Let's pray for a great turning!

Pray according to the names
that God has given Israel, nations, and people.

You shall no more be termed Forsaken, and your land shall no more be termed Desolate, but you shall be called My Delight Is in Her, and your land Married; for the Lord delights in you, and your land shall be married. For as a young man marries a young woman, so shall your sons marry you, and as the bridegroom rejoices over the bride, so shall your God rejoice over you.

As you pray for Israel, don't pray according to what's going wrong in the nation or among the people. Don't pray reactionary, "Oh God, help!" prayers. I know it's tempting, especially when we feel like things are moving further and further away from God's ordained plan of salvation and reconciliation. It appears that way in the natural. But we are not called to pray according to what we see; we are called to pray according to what God says. We pray according to what *God has called* the land. When you pray for Israel, call her "the Delight of God." Prophesy that she is married to her Maker through Yeshua. Declare that this is the land the Lord delights in. This is not an invitation to pretend away the problems going on in the Middle East and simply embrace some "pray the positive" perspective; no, it's much deeper than that. In the midst of darkness, and in the midst of nations or people going in seriously different directions than God's assigned destiny, we must called them by their heavenly name.

I encourage you right now, especially for family members, sons, daughters, and spouses who have gone far away from the Lord, call them by their name. Call them in as sons and daughters of God. Call them in as those whom the Lord delights in. Call them according to their purpose and destiny. Don't pray in reaction to the darkness they are pursuing; pray in response to what the Father says about them.

Furthermore, pray for the nations of the earth this way. In the midst of darkness, secularism, atheism, violence, and all manners of demonic activity, call the nations according to how God sees them. Pray they would be nations that are "born in a day" (see Isa. 66:8). Pray they would experience national outpouring of the Spirit, according to Joel 2 and Acts 2. Pray that a glorious church would arise out of each country, pointing the way to national salvation and deliverance (see Isa. 60:1-3).

Watchmen, Arise!

On your walls, O Jerusalem, I have set watchmen; all the day and all the night they shall never be silent. You who put the Lord in remembrance, take no rest, and give him no rest until he establishes Jerusalem and makes it a praise in the earth.

I have set watchmen. The Lord is raising up intercessory watchmen (and watchwomen) in this hour who pray in agreement with God's plans and purposes *until* they become manifest in the nations— beginning with Jerusalem. Many believers have been silent on the topic of intercession because of confusion. It's not praying for the sake of praying; it's not even someone who feels an unusual burden or call to pray. It's prayer that shifts and shapes things in the spirit realm so that natural conditions are impacted. It's relentless. It's everything we read about in these Scriptures. If I had to define intercession, it would be this: militant agreement with the plans and purposes of God in the place of prayer *until* supernatural strategy is revealed from Heaven and measurable shift takes place in the earth.

All day and all night they shall never be silent. Intercessors don't relent in prayer. They continue to pray until what they say becomes what they see. Let's return to the protocol we see outlined in Isaiah 62, though, and begin to place emphasis, once more, on praying for Jerusalem. Absolutely, pray this way for your own nation. Pray this way for your family, for your spouse, for your child, for your breakthrough, for your healing. There is a pattern here that gives definition to what true intercession looks like. But let's not forget, this measure of breakthrough intercession begins with a focus on God establishing Jerusalem and making it "a praise in the earth."

How Do We Participate?

As a response, I appreciated John Piper's perspective as a good starting place: "We should pray for it—that the full number of the Gentiles comes in and that the hardening be lifted from Israel. We should work for it with missions to the nations and witness to Israel. We should put away all conceit and presumption over Jewish unbelievers but realize that God is aiming to save them through our salvation. And we should think clearly and carefully about the land of Israel today."[1]

Pray for the peace of Jerusalem.

> *Pray for peace in Jerusalem. May all who love this city prosper. O Jerusalem, may there be peace within your walls and prosperity in your palaces. For the sake of my family and friends, I will say, "May you have peace." For the sake of the house of the Lord our God, I will seek what is best for you, O Jerusalem* (Psalm 122:6-9 NLT).

Praying for the peace of Jerusalem is far more than just blessing a city. As you pray for this city, you are praying for what will become the capital city of the universe. You are praying that, even now, the Holy Spirit would prepare the nation of Israel for her ultimate inheritance and position among the nations. You are praying for the agenda of the ages to come to manifestation.

Dr. Adrian Rogers further comments: "When you're praying for the peace of Jerusalem, you're really praying for the Second Coming of our Lord and Savior Jesus Christ," because the only time there will be a full manifestation of peace in Jerusalem is when the Messiah returns. But until the Kingdom comes with fullness, we pray, "Kingdom of God, come; will of God, be done!"

What can you do, practically, to participate?

Pray for the turning of the Jewish people.

I want you to understand this mystery, dear brothers and sisters, so that you will not feel proud about yourselves. Some of the people of Israel have hard hearts, but this will last only until the full number of Gentiles comes to Christ. And so all Israel will be saved (Romans 11:25-26 NLT).

For I am not ashamed of the gospel, for it is the power of God for salvation to everyone who believes, to the Jew first and also to the Greek (Romans 1:16).

This is a very interesting subject to pray for, as I believe it's a prophetically fixed event in the timetable of history. We are praying *into* something, not simply for something. We are not praying in hope that something might happen; if anything we are praying for a hastening and great acceleration. We know God's will on the matter. Just as the Scripture reveals the will of God concerning healing, deliverance, salvation, and other items we pray for with great confidence and expectation, likewise, we should pray with equal fervency and boldness for the national turning of Israel.

That said, such a turning will demand a great outpouring of the Spirit. Pray the Lord would raise up prophets in Israel. Pray that Gentile believers, congregations, and communities in Israel would experience a powerful demonstration of God's power and glory.

Pray for power encounters with Jewish people.

As we step deeper and deeper into this outpouring of greater glory, you will notice the Lord bringing more Jewish people across your path. Let me remind you: people are not evangelism projects. We love people because God loves them. We especially love our Jewish brothers and sisters because of the unique role they play in the unfolding of God's plan. That said, the way to salvation for Jew and Gentile is the same. For the Jew to receive eternal life, he or she must receive the free gift of redemption through the work of Messiah Jesus. I believe the reason we have not seen more Jewish people come into the Kingdom is because we have not been operating in the signs and wonders that are our inheritance as Spirit-filled believers. Or, if we have, our focus on signs, wonders, and miracles has been a bit selfish. Could it be that the frequency of the miraculous will increase to the degree that we understand the invaluable role miracles play in the conversion of Jewish people?

That is your assignment. I encourage you, rather than trying to win Jewish people through apologetics or persuasive theological arguments, demonstrate the power of God to them. Pray for their needs. If they are sick, pray for healing. If they need a miracle, ask the God of Abraham, Isaac, and Jacob to stretch out His mighty hand. They understand this. The key is, we are praying *in Yeshua's name*, for He is the key to unlocking the power of God.

Travel to the land of Israel.

What joy for those whose strength comes from the Lord, who have set their minds on a pilgrimage to Jerusalem (Psalm 84:5 NLT).

As of this writing, I have travelled to Israel twice—and I am absolutely convinced that if I visited that precious land one hundred more times in the days ahead, I would still fail to scratch the surface of its significance. Every trip is different. But if you have never gone, might I be so bold as to encourage every follower of Jesus to visit the Holy Land at some point in your lives. Not only does it bring the Bible to life in 3D (as many have rightly claimed), but it connects you, supernaturally, with the plans and purposes of Heaven for that land and its people. Furthermore, you are confronted with the reality that one day, a real Man will split the real sky and descend upon a real mountain (the Mount of Olives).

Pray for the glory of Solomon's temple to be restored…in you!

While at the Western Wall in Israel, I was provoked by the people's intensity in prayer. It's challenging to evaluate the scene that takes place here, at what is also called the "Wailing Wall." So many people crying out, in prayer, believing that their connection to this particular place will give them an advantage or edge with God. Yet, there was something that struck me. This wall has significance because it's believed that it's connected to the Temple and, ultimately, in close proximity to the holy of holies — the place of His Presence.

I prophesy that the manifestation of God's glory in unusual, supernatural, and tangible ways will summon Israel back to Jehovah through Messiah Jesus.

Read Second Chronicles 6 and 7. Time prevents me from doing a more in-depth exposition here, but consider a few portions.

> *Then Solomon prayed, "O Lord, you have said that you would live in a thick cloud of darkness. Now I have built a glorious Temple for you, a place where you can live forever!"* (2 Chronicles 6:1-2 NLT)

This physical temple was simply a shadow and a type for the temple that was to come — you and I, human beings, filled with the glorious Shekinah Presence of God.

Solomon shares the history of the temple project, which originated with David who longed to build a house for the Presence; however, it was Solomon who would complete the assignment.

In Second Chronicles 6:12-42, Solomon prays a beautiful prayer of *dedication* standing before the altar of the Lord. I propose that as we live as a wholly surrendered, yielded, and dedicated temple of God, we will be compatible with glory. As Gentiles do this, Scripture says we will provoke the Jew to jealousy (see Rom. 11:14). As our Jewish brethren do this, I believe it will provoke transformational revival across the Earth. What's the key? The Presence of God's glory resting upon a people.

Here's our prayer, as it was in the days of King Solomon:

> *And now arise, O Lord God, and enter your resting place, along with the Ark, the symbol of your power. May your priests, O Lord God, be clothed with salvation; may your loyal servants rejoice in your goodness* (2 Chronicles 6:41 NLT).

Let's pray together:

> *Lord, arise upon me! May we, Your people, become Your resting place in the earth. We are not content simply have the Spirit live within us, guaranteeing salvation and eternal life in Heaven. We give ourselves entirely to You, the best we know how, so that Your Presence can consume us. I want to be a living sacrifice. Fire of God, fall on me even now. May I live compatible to be consumed by You. Show me areas that need to be more yielded and surrendered to You. Help me not to become introspective and worried about missing it, messing up, and sinning; help me to be more consumed with seeing the Holy Spirit accommodated and welcomed in every area of my life.*

What happens when we live as a dedicated temple to the Lord?

> *When Solomon finished praying, fire flashed down from heaven and burned up the burnt offerings and sacrifices, and the glorious presence of the Lord filled the Temple. The priests could not enter the Temple of the Lord because the glorious presence of the Lord filled it. When all the people of Israel saw the fire coming down and the glorious presence of the Lord filling the Temple, they fell face down on the ground and worshiped and praised the Lord, saying, "He is good! His faithful love endures forever!"* (2 Chronicles 7:1-3 NLT)

We want that. I want to see the fire of God flash down and consume all of those who have given their lives to be living sacrifices, temples whom the glory of God can flow *to* and flow *through*.

25

The Revival
that Never Ends

*Of the increase of his government and of peace there will be no
end* (Isaiah 9:7).

THIS SCRIPTURE IS SURE evidence that God's will is for
Holy Spirit outpouring to continue and increase—*with no end*. Certainly, there will be transition. A day will come when a Jewish Man
splits the sky, sets foot on the Mount of Olives, and begins His rule
and reign. However, this reign on earth will not mean the extinction
of the planet but, rather, the *transition* of the planet.

The wave of God's glory that is coming upon the church needs
to be released into the earth. Revival was never meant to be characterized by a start and end date; it was meant to confront and rede-
fine what we consider to be "normal" Christianity. The powerful,
unusual visitations of God that ignite "revival" will come and go;
the question is, *what will we do with His movement?* Sadly, we see too
much of a revival ebb and flow throughout history. Know that this is
not God's will or evidence of some kind of dispensational theology.

We often like to assign a theological framework to the "ebb and
flow" of the Holy Spirit, when in fact the ebb or decrease is due to
the church mountain neglecting responsibility to release carriers of
God's glory into the other six mountains of society—family, education, government, media, arts and entertainment, and business.

In fact, the very history of revival is defined by outpourings that dynamically started, inevitably waned, and ultimately stopped.

*I believe this next, and consummative, wave of outpouring will be so intense, so dramatic, so glorious that the church will **not** be able to restrain or contain it; the mighty rushing River will be released into the earth!*

I believe the Lord is preparing us for the revival that never ends. The heart of God is for His Kingdom to increase *until* Jesus returns. Why then, does revival ebb and flow, namely in the church? Simple — the church was never meant to restrain Holy Spirit outpouring and keep it to themselves. Revival may be birthed in a church context — not necessarily in a building, but among the community of God — but it's purposed to be released into every sphere of society, that the kingdoms of this world would become the Kingdom of our God and His Christ (see Rev. 11:15). That supernatural governmental shift, where nations are discipled and influenced by the Kingdom, will never take place as long as Holy Spirit outpouring is exclusively defined as extended meetings held within the confines of our church sanctuaries and auditoriums. Yes, we want our services to be characterized by the glorious, intense, and dramatic movement of Holy Spirit. They must be! That's what church *should* look like, but it's *unto something*. Outpouring has an assignment and Jesus is intent on receiving the inheritance of nations (see Ps. 2:8). He will only receive this as His people, filled with the Spirit, go *into all the world* and fulfill His great desire — disciple the nations.

Jesus Is Kicking People Out of the Church!

In a recent vision, I saw the most humorous picture of Jesus *kicking* people out of the church. Okay, so let me give you some context. He was not kicking people out in terms of excommunication or discipline. He was not severing people from vital connection with the body of Christ. I saw Jesus, with a big smile on His face, kicking people out of the institutional church buildings. I saw people getting powerfully touched by the Spirit in these meetings, Jesus evaluating the people who received these encounters, and then, with a smile, giving these individuals swift kicks in the behind, flinging them *out* of the church mountain into their respective mountains or spheres of influence. And yet, this sounds a lot like something Jesus would do. Didn't He say, "*Go therefore and make disciples of all nations*" (Matt. 28:19)?

The River of God must flow *from* the temple in order for it to continue flowing *in* the temple. In other words, the Presence and power of God must be carried into *all nations* in order for us to see the great global agenda of Heaven come to pass. Otherwise, we will continue to simply enjoy periods of renewal behind the four walls of our church buildings with wonderful but limited results. I believe the Lord is turning it up. He's turning up the power. He's turning up the fire. He's turning up the intensity. *Turn it up, Lord!* He's turning it up so that the level of power encounters in His Presence is so strong that there is no alternative but to take what we receive in revival and release it to the other six mountains of influence.

The end objective is beautifully pictured in Ezekiel 47, which this prophetic journey moves toward:

> *The water for them flows from the sanctuary. Their fruit will be for food, and their leaves for healing* (Ezekiel 47:12).

Everywhere the River goes, there is life and healing. I believe the Lord wants us to have a very clear picture of *how* the River is carried into the nations so that its healing work can be accomplished this side of Heaven.

Dutch Sheets shares about a powerful vision he had of the river of God. Perhaps one of the most striking elements was his description of different levels of the river that people were experiencing. As it got deeper and deeper, it reached a point where the Lord told him: "The deeper water is what takes the river to the nations."[1] The greater glory is what takes outpouring to the earth!

The Evidence Is All Around

Back in the 1990s, there were three major moves of the Holy Spirit in America that were purposed to shift the spiritual landscape — the Toronto Blessing, the Brownsville Revival, and the Smithton Outpouring. Of course, there were other notable movements of the Spirit during this time and after — the revival meetings held by Rodney Howard-Browne in Lakeland, Florida; the IHOP Awakening and the Bay (of the Holy Spirit) Revival in the 2000s; the emergence of Bethel Church as a global center for sustained outpouring and exporter of revival culture to the nations, etc.

So, what's coming now? As we prepare for this next (and, most likely, conclusive) wave of Holy Spirit outpouring, I strongly sense that the degree to which the church enjoys the blessing of sustained outpouring will be directly related to the church exporting *people* who are touched by outpouring into the other six mountains of culture.

On a side note, I'm grateful for catalytic thought leaders like Dr. Lance Wallnau who, while they love the move of God, are frustrated with the disconnection between Holy Spirit outpouring and a *dry and thirsty land*. Revival becomes relevant to society when our meetings become portable. We need safe places where people have *space* to encounter God powerfully and dramatically; however, I prophesy that in this next wave of glory, *people* will become portable centers of outpouring and revival, carrying the touch of God outside of the four walls and into strategic spheres of societal influence.

I prophesy that those with significant wealth and influence — businessmen and investors, politicians and media moguls, actors and directors, those who present themselves as dignified and refined — are going to experience undignified, glorious, overwhelming glory encounters in the Presence of God. The church will be a safe space for such meetings to take place — but these will be for the purpose of awakening individuals of influence to the potential of God's Presence within them.

The key to Holy Spirit outpouring in this next season can be found in the following passages of Scripture *in this order*: Psalm 63, Psalm 46, and John 7:37-39.

1. Have Heaven's perspective of your sphere of influence.

> *O God, you are my God; earnestly I seek you; my soul thirsts for you; my flesh faints for you, as in a dry and weary land where there is no water* (Psalm 63:1).

Notice that the psalmist does *not* call the world "lost and dying." Although this is popular language among evangelicals, I do believe we need to change our description of the world and its people, as our description defines our level of interaction. If we see things as lost and dying, it is possible to embrace a hopelessness that robs us of our assignment. It's easy to embrace an escapist approach when we view the world as lost, hopeless, dying, and damned. We'll do our best to win as many people to the Lord as we can, while also hunkering down and preparing for everything to explode like the Death Star. For the Lord would say:

> *See the world, not as lost and dying, but as dry and weary. See the people in your world, who are disconnected from Living Water, not as hopeless, but as those who are thirsty and desperate for the Fountain you carry. Yes, the people, and also the very culture. The world. The very soil and ground, for the whole of creation is groaning and aching, longing for the manifestation of sons and daughters who carry My Solution into dry and weary places. My Solution is outpouring. My Solution is Holy Spirit. My Solution*

is Myself, for You are where you are because I want to be there. You are where you are because I want My Presence and My rule in that place. You uniquely bring people into proximity with Me. Do not disregard your present station and place of assignment. Most likely, it's not where you are going to be stationed forever, for I am the God of glory to glory and changing seasons. However, you will walk in a sense of destiny and fulfillment to the degree that you walk aware of your assignment to carry My Presence and My Kingdom into the place you are currently placed.

2. Recognize that you carry Heaven's Solution into the chaos.

God is our refuge and strength, a very present help in trouble. Therefore we will not fear though the earth gives way, though the mountains be moved into the heart of the sea, though its waters roar and foam, though the mountains tremble at its swelling (Psalm 46:1-3).

Does this sound like the world you presently occupy? A place characterized by fear, anxiety, and trouble? Can you relate to the psalmist's language of mountains falling into the heart of the sea, waters roaring and foaming? Doesn't this feel like life sometimes — if not for you, maybe for those around you? In the midst of the shaking and trouble, what is the solution? What is the answer? The psalmist prophesies the answer in Psalm 46:4, and Jesus clarifies in John 7:37-39.

There is a river whose streams make glad the city of God, the holy habitation of the Most High (Psalm 46:4).

In the midst of all the chaos and calamity, Heaven has a solution — *there is a River.* Now comes the question: *where will this River come from? Out of Heaven? No.*

3. Heaven's River is here.

Back in the 1990s, Vineyard worship released a wonderful prophetic song of praise called "The River is Here." Such an expressive, joyful way to give voice to the words of Jesus in John 7:37-39:

> *On the last day of the feast, the great day, Jesus stood up and cried out, "If anyone thirsts, let him come to me and drink. Whoever believes in me, as the Scripture has said, 'Out of his heart will flow rivers of living water.'" Now this he said about the Spirit, whom those who believed in him were to receive, for as yet the Spirit had not been given, because Jesus was not yet glorified* (John 7:37-39).

We are not waiting for the Holy Spirit to come *down* from Heaven again; rather, Heaven is waiting for the Spirit to come *out* of the church. For the world to be reached, the River must flow *out* of the church. Not church as in the buildings or physical structures, but church as in the redeemed community of God filled with the Spirit of God. The level to which we embrace this next season of outpouring will be dependent upon our awareness of the Presence and Person of the Holy Spirit and how we decide to accommodate His movement in our lives and in our church services. While there is a sovereign element to the Spirit's movement in terms of *how* He moves in a certain context, the fact is that, since the Day of Pentecost, He's been released into the earth and He has been moving. He's been searching for a people who live in tune with Him enough to move *with* Him.

The problem is that the church has desired to restrain the Spirit and call it revival. I'm not talking about restraining the Spirit's supernatural movements and manifestations; I'm meaning that we have wanted to keep revival locked up behind four walls and insist that the world comes to *our* services. Often, the motives are pure — just confused. We truly desire the outpouring of the Spirit, but we neglect to consider the flow of outpouring. It flows *through* so that it can flow *to*. Reconsider Jesus' mandate in Acts 1:8: *"But you will receive power when the Holy Spirit has come upon you, and you will be my witnesses in Jerusalem and in all Judea and Samaria, and to the end of the earth."*

- *"You will receive power."* The you refers to the church, the Spirit-filled people of God on planet Earth.

- *"When the Holy Spirit has come upon you."* This refers to the expression of outpouring.

- *"You will be my witnesses...to the end of the earth."* Right here, Jesus gives us fruit of what outpouring and revival must produce.

So we reflect once again—could it be that we've only played in the "shallow end" of Holy Spirit outpouring, not because God has sovereignly withheld "greater glory" or because we're in some special dispensation, but because we have believed revival was to flow *into the church*, when really it was meant to *flow through the church*. Remember, revival was never meant to have a start and stop date. This only happens when it becomes restricted by buildings, walls, gatherings, and services. Yes, we will continue to gather as a body and have services, but I prophesy that rather than extended meetings, *every* meeting will become an opportunity for dynamic Holy Spirit encounter. What was considered unusual in the bygone days of revival will become the new normal as the people of God become increasingly hungry for the Spirit's movement in their midst.

One Last Instruction: Don't Do What Peter Did!

One last word—if we want to experience a move of God that never ends, that flows with increasing intensity into and through the church *until* the Son of Man returns, we must avoid Peter's mistake at the Mount of Transfiguration. Let's pick up the story, as I believe this holds a powerful blueprint for how we should respond to the outpouring of God's glory in the days ahead:

> *About eight days later Jesus took Peter, John, and James up on a mountain to pray. And as he was praying, the appearance of his face was transformed, and his clothes became dazzling white. Suddenly, two men, Moses and Elijah, appeared and began talking with Jesus. They were glorious to see. And they were speaking about his exodus from this world, which was about to be fulfilled in Jerusalem.*
>
> *Peter and the others had fallen asleep. When they woke up, they saw Jesus' glory and the two men standing with him. As Moses and Elijah were starting to leave, Peter, not even knowing what he was saying, blurted out, "Master, it's wonderful for us to be here! Let's make three shelters as memorials — one for you, one for Moses, and one for Elijah." But even as he was saying this, a cloud overshadowed them, and terror gripped them as the cloud covered them.*
>
> *Then a voice from the cloud said, "This is my Son, my Chosen One. Listen to him"* (Luke 9:28-35 NLT).

Pay very close to attention to *Peter's response*. In the days of outpouring and the demonstration of unusual glory, it's tempting for us to default into old methods and operating systems. When something new hits us, our propensity is to reach back 10, 15, 30 years ago into the halls of what we are familiar with. This is particularly true for the church world. As God moves, we want to build some kind of system around His movement. This would be very similar to the mistake of David we studied earlier — trying to put the Ark of the Covenant on a "new cart."

*The glory will abruptly awaken us from
religious routine, individually and collectively.*

I certainly don't want to stretch the illustration, as the disciples were certainly not going through religious motions while walking with the Savior. However, it did seem like they fell asleep during some very pivotal moments. I prophesy that in the days ahead, the collective hunger and cry of the people of God is going to be the very key that "tears open the Heavens" and ushers in demonstrations of God's glory the earth has not yet seen. These will be jarring, shocking, stunning, and ultimately awakening.

*The shock of the glory will provoke this response:
"What do we do now?"*

While ministering with my spiritual father in South Florida, we had a conference where God's Presence literally canopied the entire building. I had never experienced something quite like it. I'll never forget the very spiritual conversation that ensued. I looked at him; he looked at me. One of us, I can't remember who, asked the following question: "What do we do now?" The Lord highlighted that question and said, "When you ask that question, celebrate—you're entering into a New Era because you're experiencing things you haven't before." This is exactly what was happening to the disciples. They had walked with Jesus faithfully during His earthly ministry, but in this context something was happening that had never happened before. *What do we do now?*

Response #1: We build or maintain an "old wineskin" to contain the new glory.

When the glory of God manifests like this, the tragic reality is that good-intentioned, God-loving people can easily default into methods and systems that worked in the past. This is really what Peter was suggesting. He was reaching back into the Old Covenant, a paradigm he was familiar with, proposing to build tabernacles or tents to accommodate the glory on the mountain. *"As Moses and Elijah were starting to leave, Peter, not even knowing what he was saying, blurted out, 'Master, it's wonderful for us to be here! Let's make three shelters as memorials — one for you, one for Moses, and one for Elijah'"* (Luke 9:33). After all, that was the response to glory "back then" under the Old Covenant. When glory manifested, a tabernacle needed to contain it. But Jesus was moving things in a very different direction, beyond temples and tabernacles. Even here in the transfiguration, you can sense something major is taking place in the spirit.

Response #2: Listen to the voice and do what He says.

Peter was looking back to an old operating system of accommodating God's Presence. However, right here, in the midst of his blunder, we see the key to moving in sync with the Holy Spirit: *"Then a voice from the cloud said, 'This is my Son, my Chosen One. Listen to him.'"* The Father Himself gave us the strategy: listen to Heaven, not yesterday's successful blueprint, operating system, wineskin, church growth method, or even Charismatic methodology. We assume that when God's Presence visits us with that level of intensity, we know exactly what to do—line up the people and pray for them, bring out the sick and pray for healing, prophesy, operate in the gifts of the Spirit, start laughing in the Spirit, etc. All of these are valid manifestations and demonstrations of the Spirit, but they become distracting when they are operating outside of what God is doing *in that moment*. The glory may not be provoking a response of "holy laughter." Maybe it's that weighty *kabod* glory that brings us to our knees in repentance, awe, and wonder. We need to be sensitive, moment by moment, to the speaking voice of a Person called Holy Spirit rather than reach back into the halls of what worked in the past during similar outbreaks or encounters.

When I speak of "the past," I am talking about our methods and operating systems in Christianity; the place we *need* to consult is "the Book," Scripture. When God moves unusually, we need to review the Word and evaluate: "Is this something that God *would do*? Is this congruent and in agreement with His nature?" If not, we don't want any part of it; if so, we want Him to do what He wants to do without interference from our end.

For us to experience the outpouring that will *come out* of the church and bring true Kingdom impact into every sphere of society, we need to live as a people who are on the prophetic edge. With the Scriptures as our foundation and cornerstone, we are summoned to live as pioneers with ears to Heaven. We cannot rely on strategies and schemes that worked yesterday. Tents, tabernacles, and temples may have housed the glory of God in one era, but not today. We rely on the voice that speaks in order to build what He is looking to establish in the earth. Otherwise, we will always go back to what seemed to "work" in a previous era.

26

Moving In and Out of Mount Zion

But you have come to Mount Zion and to the city of the living God (Hebrews 12:22).

WE DON'T NEED another Pentecost; we need to learn how to move in and out of Mount Zion. We are not asking God to send the Holy Spirit again; we are stepping into a realm that the blood of Jesus has bought us present-day access to.

One of the reasons we are not seeing what many call revival is because, on a personal level, we act like we are waiting on something "yet to come." The only *something* yet to come is a *Someone*—the Son of Man who will descend from Heaven just as He ascended. Yes, there are times and seasons of sudden, sovereign outpouring. May we experience more as we move toward the second coming of Jesus! But when it comes to you and I, individually, encountering and experiencing the Presence of God, we don't have to wait any longer. The Holy Spirit is here and He's available! In this chapter, I want us to explore what it means to live as a citizen of a realm called Mount Zion.

This is a message the Lord birthed in my heart in Israel, after we ascended from the Upper Room to the very top of the building. I believe that ascension was prophetic, as the Lord really didn't speak to me in the actual "Upper Room." But I know God completely crashed in on me and Ana when we went up to the *roof* of the Upper Room. Why?

The Lord has been telling me for a while, "I am raising up a community of people who know how to seamlessly move in and out of Mount Zion." This chapter is going to be my best effort to explain what this looks like, how to practically engage this assignment, and how I believe this is the catalyst to unlocking the greater glory of God in the earth.

You Have Not Come to Mount Sinai...and Aren't You Glad?

For you have not come to what may be touched, a blazing fire and darkness and gloom and a tempest and the sound of a trumpet and a voice whose words made the hearers beg that no further messages be spoken to them. For they could not endure the order that was given, "If even a beast touches the mountain, it shall be stoned." Indeed, so terrifying was the sight that Moses said, "I tremble with fear" (Hebrews 12:18-21).

First of all, we are *not* looking back to the "old days." Many New Covenant believers think that what Moses and other heroes of the faith in the Old Testament experienced in God was superior to what we have access to. Not so at all! Martyn Lloyd-Jones explains: "You and I are living in the new dispensation. We are not looking forward to the coming of the Messiah (like those in the Old Covenant), we are not looking forward to Calvary, we are looking back. We have these records in the New Testament, explicit statements, the whole thing unfolded: the Holy Spirit has been given. And yet, I wonder how we compare with the Psalmist, and with Moses? What is the matter with us, my friends? We who like to boast about our superiority over the Old Testament saints (because of the New Covenant)...*how do we compare with them in actual experience?*[1] That's the question: have we, who live in a superior covenant, stepped into that dimension of superior experience?

In the Old Covenant, only the few and elite could experience God, hear His voice, and touch the mountain of God. Hebrews 12 contrasts what Moses experienced with what we have access to. We have *not* come to the mountain Moses ascended — Mount Sinai. Don't think that access to this mountain would be better than what we have available to us today! Remember, Moses was the only one who could ascend to the "glory level." Furthermore, the voice of the Lord was so strong, so terrifying, that those who heard it begged that He would speak no more. Our prayer is, "Lord, speak! Your servants listen!" We desire to hear His voice regardless of what He has to say to us. Truly, it was the hardness of their hearts, produced by sin, that made the people resist the voice of the Lord. If anyone, man or beast, touched the mountain, they would be put to death. There was no touching the Presence or even the mountain upon which the Presence of God was descending. The scene was so startling, even Moses, the friend of God, said, "I tremble with fear."

You Have Not Come to the Upper Room Again

When I was in the Upper Room in Israel, I didn't hear or receive anything from the Lord. Strange, I know! It was only when we went to the roof of the Upper Room, which is one of the highest points on Mount Zion, that God crashed in on us. Why? He knew what my heart was seeking, and He didn't want to confirm something that was obsolete. We don't need another Pentecost. Rather, we need to be a people who ascend into Mount Zion and descend into earth — easily, seamlessly, and supernaturally.

I so cherish the significance of Pentecost and what it means to us today. But friends, we are not waiting or praying for another

Pentecost to come down from Heaven; the earth is waiting for sons and daughters, residents of Mount Zion, to emerge from that realm of glory and bring Kingdom solutions to every arena of crisis and chaos on planet Earth. This is what Creation is groaning for.

> *For the creation waits with eager longing for the revealing of the sons of God. For the creation was subjected to futility, not willingly, but because of him who subjected it, in hope that the creation itself will be set free from its bondage to corruption and obtain the freedom of the glory of the children of God* (Romans 8:19-21).

In its context, this scripture is speaking of sons and daughters who are filled with and led by the Spirit of God (see Rom. 8:14). I love how *The Passion Translation* phrases Romans 8:19: *"The entire universe is standing on tiptoe, yearning to see the unveiling of God's glorious sons and daughters!"* Everything that is redeemable is waiting for people filled with the Holy Spirit to come, show up, and release Kingdom solutions that carry supernatural Presence. The earth is not in travail, waiting for another Upper Room; it's waiting for the carriers of God's glory to show up.

Just remember how Paul prayed. He didn't pray for Heaven to open again and send down the Spirit; he unceasingly prayed:

> *For this reason, because I have heard of your faith in the Lord Jesus and your love toward all the saints, I do not cease to give thanks for you, remembering you in my prayers, that the God of our Lord Jesus Christ, the Father of glory, may give you the Spirit of wisdom and of revelation in the knowledge of him, having the eyes of your hearts enlightened, that you may know what is the hope to which he has called you, what are the riches of his glorious inheritance in the saints, and what is the immeasurable greatness of his power toward us who believe, according to the working*

of his great might that he worked in Christ when he raised him from the dead and seated him at his right hand in the heavenly places, far above all rule and authority and power and dominion, and above every name that is named, not only in this age but also in the one to come. And he put all things under his feet and gave him as head over all things to the church, which is his body, the fullness of him who fills all in all (Ephesians 1:15-23).

Paul didn't encourage us to pray "revival prayers," where the Holy Spirit *comes down again*. How did he call us to pray? Pray that:

- God would give us increased wisdom and revelation of who *He is* through the Holy Spirit (*He* is the Spirit of wisdom and revelation).

- Our hearts will become enlightened and aware of what we have received in the Holy Spirit—God dwelling within us.

- We would know what hope we have been called to, both in eternity and here and now.

- We would grasp the "riches of His glorious inheritance" in us—I believe this has everything to do with the power, authority, and gifts we have received in the Person of the Holy Spirit. This is experientially knowing *Christ in You, the hope of glory* (see Col. 1:27).

- We would discover and operate in His supernatural power—the same *might* that raised Christ from the dead (see Rom. 8:11).

- We would walk in the governmental authority we have received in the spirit over every power, principality, and opposing force to the advancement of God's Kingdom on earth.

- We would function in the heavenly realm dimension that we are seated in with Jesus (see Eph. 2:6), where, in Christ, we are *far above all rule and authority and power and dominion.* This only comes, however, through discovering the knowledge of God because we do not have this rule and authority; Jesus does. It's His, but we are in Him, so we share in this authority.

- We would walk on the earth as the very body of Jesus, recognizing that His Spirit dwells within us. He has qualified and authorized us to continue His works and share in His authority. If all things are under His feet, and we are *in Jesus,* then all things are under our feet.

Common denominator? These are all prayers that ask for an increased awareness to present-tense spiritual realities. *Now* realities. We are not calling something down. We are not waiting for something extra or supercharged to "come" down from Heaven.

I am all for songs or prayers that call for "another Pentecost," or fire falling down, or rending the heavens. Let's just get it straight theologically. We don't need another Pentecost; the first one was more than sufficient for the job. We don't need a Holy Spirit 2.0 or upgrade; we need an upgraded experience of what we have already received. We don't need the heavens to open again; we need to be stewards of the open Heaven Jesus made available through His shed blood and the torn veil.

You Have Come to Mount Zion!

But you have come to Mount Zion and to the city of the living God, the heavenly Jerusalem, and to innumerable angels in festal gathering, and to the assembly of the first-born who are enrolled in heaven, and to God, the judge of all, and to the spirits of the righteous made perfect, and to

> *Jesus, the mediator of a new covenant, and to the sprinkled blood that speaks a better word than the blood of Abel* (Hebrews 12:22-24).

You have access to the place of God's Presence. You don't need to wait for a whirlwind to sweep you up—although God does sovereignly summon people into His glory. The good news is that by faith—a conscious, deliberate, seemingly non-spiritual decision—you can step into this place called Mount Zion.

- Pray for an increased revelation of *Christ in you* through the indwelling Holy Spirit: "Holy Spirit, help me to become more aware of Your Presence in me." This is the first and essential step. Choose to fill your mind with the biblical truths concerning the Spirit of God living within you.

- Next, pray for an increased revelation of you in Christ: "Lord, Your Word says that I am currently seated with Jesus in heavenly realms. I am here on earth, but I am also in Heaven, with Him, hidden in Him. Open my eyes to see this, Lord! I want to live from this place. I want to pray from this realm—heaven to earth. I want to hear the sounds and see the sights of Your world, Lord, so I can translate them into mine."

We have discussed the reality of "Christ in you" a bit, but engaging Mount Zion has a lot to do with operating like you really live seated with Jesus in heavenly realms (see Eph. 2:6 NIV). Consider what is going on around you as you live from this place.

"But you have come to Mount Zion and to the city of the living God, the heavenly Jerusalem." First, the writer of Hebrews compares what we have come into, the Mount Zion of the New Covenant, to the Mount Sinai of the Old Covenant. Zion is not a physical mountain; it is the unseen realm of the spirit that is multidimensional and full

of activity. We are not called to be distracted by the activity in this realm; however, we are expected to be aware of what is taking place and learn how to appropriately partner with it.

"*...and to innumerable angels in festal gathering.*" You have access to the invisible hosts of Heaven, the angels of God. I love the language that is specifically tied to the angelic activity: "festal gathering." I believe that, because of a thin veil between Heaven and earth, the Lord is granting His people greater access to hear the sounds of the angelic festal gathering. Why? I prophesy that the Lord is bringing the worship of earth into agreement with the worship of Heaven, that the songs written and released in the earth realm would be statements of "Amen," agreeing with the words, lyrics, and declarations sung about God around this throne. Such will release the thunder of His throne room into the earth.

"*...and to the assembly of the firstborn who are enrolled in heaven.*" This includes the Great Cloud of Witnesses, along with saints of both Old and New Testaments who are living in Heaven with God. It's important for us, on earth, to recognize that we have extended family in Heaven. Just because one departs the earth through death does not mean that he or she has ceased being part of the Ekklesia, the true church. There is a glorious Heaven and earth harmony that takes place as the prayers of those in the earth are in sync with those who are in Heaven, continuing to pray, with their intercessions all directed toward the Great Intercessor, Jesus. The great cry resounding through both realms is that the Lamb would receive the full reward of His suffering—the souls of humanity and the souls of nations.

"*...and to God, the judge of all, and to the spirits of the righteous made perfect.*" God, on His terms and in His sovereign choosing, can open up an awareness of this realm to us. It's never with the intention that we try to communicate with the dead. For one, those who are in Heaven are living, not dead. Second, why should we seek to communicate with the spirits of the just people made perfect when we have access to the very Spirit of God? Just as a cautionary note, it's vital for the people of God to be more aware of the invisible realm around us. We pray, "Thy Kingdom come," but often are not clued in on what all takes place in the in-breaking of this Kingdom. I don't have definitive mechanical knowledge on how this all takes place. All I know is that in this invisible realm of the spirit, what the author of Hebrews calls the dimension of "Mount Zion," we have entered *into* a host of spiritual activity — angels, the spirits of the just made perfect, blood that speaks, etc.

"...and to Jesus, the mediator of a new covenant, and to the sprinkled blood that speaks a better word than the blood of Abel." When we increasingly recognize the invisible activity going on around us, we discover there is blood that has a voice. The blood of Jesus supernaturally speaks, reminding believers of their redeemed status in the Messiah. When the enemy tries to condemn you, the blood declares "not guilty." Yes, we sin and we absolutely need to repent. But our sin does not change our identity as those whom the blood declares to be in right standing with God, free of guilt, shame, and condemnation. This identity does not license us to sin; far from it! The blood speaks our heavenly identity over us and consistently calls us to walk out lives that are in harmony with that identity.

These heavenly realities accompany you. They are not to serve as distractions, causing us to become spiritually goofy and desiring all sorts of encounters with beings other than Jesus. Rather, we must know what's going on in the invisible realm so we can partner with that activity in the earth. Those who function in the heavenly realms are still assisting us in seeing God's Kingdom purposes accomplished in the earth!

God's Home Address

Outpouring is not coming down from the heavens but out of the Ekklesia, the people of God. Not a building or a tent, not a tabernacle or a box. Not even a "house of worship." For us to access and experience the "greater glory," we need to become grounded in the location of God's home address—inside of redeemed humanity. In less spiritual-sounding words, He lives in you and He lives in me!

> *Don't you know that you yourselves are God's temple and that God's Spirit dwells in your midst?* (1 Corinthians 3:16 NIV)

Paul reaffirms this truth later on in the same letter:

> *Don't you realize that your body is the temple of the Holy Spirit, who lives in you and was given to you by God? You do not belong to yourself* (1 Corinthians 6:19 NLT).

In regard to moving in and out of Mount Zion, the Holy Spirit spoke to my heart and expressed: "I want a people who know how to be in the throne room one minute and the boardroom the next." Too many of us can get lost in Zion, in the glory realm, in the Presence of God and never quite learn how to translate what we see and hear in that supernatural dimension into the sphere of influence we have been called to. This is vital if we are going to truly see an outpouring that impacts "all flesh." Remember, God's great objective is not *all church*, it's *all flesh*.

27

The Coming Glory:
Greater Than We've Ever Seen!

GOD SPEAKS TO US at unusual times. For example, it was October 6, I was eating a turkey sandwich in my favorite Jewish deli, and sovereignly the Lord spoke to my spirit: "No more delay." I couldn't shake the statement. "Lord, do You want *me* to share about this?" I kind of sensed He wanted to go in that direction, but I started naming every prophet and leader I knew who communicated this message far better than I did. I love how sometimes, when we respond to the Lord with complaints and excuses, He doesn't even acknowledge them. He just keeps saying the same thing.

Later that night, my friend and prophet Lana Vawser texted me. It was 10/6, October 6. She told me to look up Revelation 10:6. Now, I am not a prophetic numerologist. I do believe God can and does speak in numbers, but that is not really my field of expertise. I find myself often prophesying by accident, truth be told. When I read Revelation 10:6, I was shocked and stunned, namely by the last statement in the verse:

> *He swore an oath in the name of the one who lives forever and ever, who created the heavens and everything in them, the earth and everything in it, and the sea and everything in it. He said, "There will be no more delay"* (Revelation 10:6 NLT).

No more delay. The great delay in the earth right now is the delay of the manifestation of God's glory. It's not a God-orchestrated delay; it's a delay, as we have been reviewing throughout this book, that will be broken to the degree that we give our lives to hosting and carrying God's glory.

The "Do" of Reformation
Will Break the Delay

The Lord is raising up a people who will break delay by doing what they have been called and assigned to do. Pretty simple. Reformation will be provoked by a people who encounter and do, who pray and do, who engage the spirit realm and do. We don't "do" something, or work, to gain God's favor. Quite the contrary. God in His mercy gave us prophetic words and Kingdom assignments to accomplish. We are called and assigned. We are not working to gain God's favor in order to receive an assignment; we've already been assigned. We simply need to follow through on what we have been called to do.

I see a convergence coming in the body of Christ of three realms of function—prophet, priest, and governor, all pictured in Haggai 1. We will explore this further down the line, but it will be this threefold alignment operating in cooperation and harmony that will translate revival into societal reformation.

Right now, I want to pause and seemingly take a dramatically different direction in this prophetic word, as I believe the Lord has laid it upon my heart to announce that a revival greater than the Charismatic Movement of the 1960s is at hand. I'll explain all of this in a moment, but track with me for a moment here. The Charismatic Movement of the 1960s and subsequent Jesus People Movement of the '60s and '70s were both glorious and also sobering. It was glorious because of Holy Spirit outpouring, but it was sobering because we witnessed an incomplete picture of what God wanted to do in the earth. It was so close. We saw renewal and revival, but revival never translated into reformation. Those who came to the Lord were fed a theology that, in many respects, tolerated delay. While the church's eyes were looking for a soon-coming Rapture of the church, a generation was being discipled by the influences of darkness. The good news is that God redeems abundantly! Any opportunity for societal transformation that was lost or forfeited in that era can be reclaimed and restored with interest in this present hour. The question is, what will we do with this glory when we experience it? Let's explore that, as our stewarding of outpouring is the very thing that can either extend or break the power of delay.

A Coming Revival Greater Than the Charismatic Movement

There is one sure prophetic word concerning the end times that you can stand upon. It's rock solid. In the midst of both dismal prognosticators and enthusiastic futurists, "doom and gloom" skeptics and "everything is getting better" optimists, you can rest on what God Himself said concerning the last days:

> *And in the last days it shall be, God declares, that I will pour out my Spirit on all flesh* (Acts 2:17).

Since the Day of Pentecost, the Holy Spirit has been released from Heaven and has been seeking a compatible resting place on the earth. Yes, all Christians have the Holy Spirit living within them. Theologically we know this. We are regenerated and born again by His effective, supernatural, and sovereign work. At the same time, as Bill Johnson so aptly acknowledges, it's one thing to have the Holy Spirit living within us; it's another dimension to host His Presence to such a degree that He rests *upon* us. A groaning creation is not listening for a people who can articulate a solid pneumatology of the Spirit's quickening work in regeneration; they are *looking* for a people whom God visibly rests upon. I believe such a company is coming forth!

A Movement That Marked
History with Holy Spirit Power

In the 1960s, a movement took place that radically revolutionized church culture. Church history books record it as the "Charismatic movement" or "Charismatic *Renewal*." Regardless of the language we assign to this epoch season in modern church history, one thing is for sure—no one was safe from the Holy Spirit in this time of great outpouring. Nearly every denomination and stream of Christianity felt the rumbling of this powerful move of God, which many would trace back to Episcopal priest Dennis Bennett (who recounts his story in the landmark book *9 O'Clock in the Morning*), who got filled with the Holy Spirit, spoke in tongues, and yet continued to operate in his denominational framework. This proceeded to inspire many other Episcopalian believers to contend for Holy Spirit baptism and also legitimized a unique expression of Holy Spirit outpouring where His supernatural work *could function* in a mainline denominational context. You didn't have to become of the Pentecostal tradition to taste of the power of the age to come. From this encounter onward, Lutherans, Baptists, Presbyterians, and Catholics, among many others, experienced a dynamic season of renewal. It was during this period that some of the great ministries and leaders emerged who gave language to the body of Christ for what God was doing.

God hates division, but He loves uniqueness. During this season of visitation, it didn't matter—pews or chairs, stained glass windows or a living room, organs or a guitar, God was on the move and everything was experiencing fresh life because of His Spirit sweeping through the church. I believe the Lord is ready to do it again in our day. Are we ready? Are we willing?

Why Didn't the Glory Sustain and Increase?

I sense such an urgency to prophesy that even though the Charismatic Renewal is to be celebrated and even looked upon as a blueprint for the days in which we are living, that season of history did have an element of fault. This is not a condemnation of what took place; it was glorious and we would do well to contend for such an awakening again today. However, there was a factor that was absent that, I am convinced, limited the reach of what could have happened. We need to learn from our faults. We need to confront the fault of *that* hour so we don't repeat it in ours. And we are awfully close to repeating history if we don't prophetically course correct. We need to be ready, for I prophesy that the Lord is positioning His people for something that will dramatically exceed the impact, influence, and scope of the Charismatic renewal of the 1960s.

> *Repent therefore, and turn back, that your sins may be blotted out, that times of refreshing may come from the presence of the Lord, and that he may send the Christ appointed for you, Jesus, whom heaven must receive until the time for restoring all the things about which God spoke by the mouth of his holy prophets long ago* (Acts 3:19-21).

Renewal

In the 1960s, we witnessed the Charismatic Renewal, which was aimed at the church. The people of God experienced the Holy Spirit in a dynamic new way and, thus, saw church life infused with His Presence and power. In the 1990s, we witnessed renewal with the Toronto Blessing, which became an epicenter of Holy Spirit refreshing for the nations. Believers came from around the world to receive a touch from the Spirit, and in turn we saw many go back to their respective nations or assume their Kingdom assignments and witness millions receive Jesus.

In this hour in history, I believe the Lord is calling the church to corporate repentance — even identificational repentance. Yes, for our sins — but also, for the specific sin of rejecting the move of the Holy Spirit and trading it for having a good "Christian" reputation. The Lord is calling a generation to identificationally undo this trade (made multiple times throughout church history), repent for being ashamed of the move of the Spirit, and in turn position ourselves for what Malachi prophesied as the Lord coming *suddenly* to His temple (see Mal. 3:1).

Revival

Repentance *from* the church will produce refreshing *in* the church, as witnessed with the Charismatic renewal, the Toronto Blessing, and other wonderful moves of the Spirit throughout the 1900s. The key is learning how to export our times of refreshing, as the "sound" of a church experiencing outpouring is meant to summon the masses, as we saw in the book of Acts. The sound of Holy Spirit renewal should never be insulated; a renewed church should produce revived believers, and revived believers should provoke the unchurched and unsaved to meet Jesus. No, not just "come to church" or come to a meeting, but come to Jesus, and often those who don't know Jesus will be drawn to Him because a revived Christian brought Him into proximity with someone who was asking the question, "Is God really alive?" Renewal should produce a corporate culture in church where "word on the street" is that Someone is actually alive and moving in the midst of "those people."

Holy Spirit renewal should always produce revival, where transformed eternal destinies are the fruit. What's the difference? In this context (Charismatic Renewal) I see renewal as *a time of significant refreshing in the Presence of the Lord,* as described by the Apostle Peter in Acts 3, *which gives birth to souls coming into the Kingdom of God.*

To recap, in the 1960s you had the Charismatic Renewal, which I am fully convinced gave birth, in the spirit, to the Jesus Revolution/Jesus People Movement, which was a bona fide revival. You had renewal and revival—and many called it quits there. This is what we need to course correct in our day if we are going to see the measure of Kingdom transformation God desires to release into the planet. The "do" of reformation will break the delay that's been causing so much frustration in the ranks of God's people.

Reformation: The Missing Key to Sustaining Revival and Seeing Societal Transformation

Many could survey the 1960s and '70s and observe a major failure on the church's part to engage society and culture. In one respect, they would be absolutely correct. When the harvest of souls came into the church during the counter-cultural revolution, as the hippie, free love, and drug culture was being supernaturally invaded by the Holy Spirit, many (mistakenly) assumed this was a sign of a "soon coming" rapture of the church. Instead of a renewed and revived church proactively engaging the ills of society (and there were many present and germinating at the time), the people of God retreated into what Dr. Lance Wallnau describes as the "wilderness." Comparatively, this was very much akin to the 40-year wilderness season that the children of Israel found themselves in following their dramatic deliverance from Egypt.

Why did Israel remain in the wilderness when they could have immediately crossed over into the Promised Land? They were intimidated by the enemy tribes who were occupying the land and saw the opposition as greater in size and scope than God (the God who just delivered them, supernaturally, from Egyptian bondage through a variety of signs, wonders, and miracles). They saw miracles, but the miracles did not transform their thinking, and we know this because they still saw enemy occupiers as bigger than the God who delivered them.

I prophesy that it's time for the church to break out of its prolonged wilderness season. Could it be that the reason we have so many conferences, events, glory gatherings, and even our own "Christian culture" is that, maybe, just maybe, we are scared to confront the forces occupying our nations? We continue to create "other mountains" that separate us from the very clear call of God to give Jesus the nations.

Many are familiar with the concept of the "Seven Mountains of Culture," formulated theoretically by Loren Cunningham (YWAM) and Bill Bright (Campus Crusade for Christ/Cru), and then given revelatory expression by Dr. Lance Wallnau. I am absolutely convinced that these seven spheres need to be engaged by renewed and revived people. Arts and entertainment, business, government, education, family, religion, and politics all make up the "soul of a nation." They are dimensions of created order that are groaning for the influence of the sons and daughters of God who carry the Presence of the Spirit. The problem? Instead of raising up a church to influence these spheres, we continue to create "other mountains." Sadly, these are more "spiritual" mountains that place more distance between an already Holy Spirit-filled church and a world under the influence of darkness — darkness that must be displaced.

In the 1960s, we witnessed a sobering example of what happens when the church abdicates the commission to disciple nations. Instead of carrying God's glory and redemptive strategies into law, politics, media, education, and government, the redeemed Ekklesia decided to give itself to having Bible studies, meeting in homes, reading books plotting out end-times scenarios, and watching *Thief in the Night*. Now, while Bible studies, meeting in homes, and attending church are good and should be encouraged, disengaging from society shouldn't be an option.

The more the Ekklesia withdraws from society, the more a demonic and counterfeit version of history will continue to go uncontested and unchallenged. For the Spirit of the Lord is calling a people who would arise, engage, displace the influence of darkness, and proactively write history in agreement with what the Sovereign King has recorded in the Books of Heaven. God's will *shall* be done in the earth, but to the degree that Jesus' church—His body, His bride, His Ekklesia—says "Yes" to the commission to carry and release glory into the ills of society, that will be the level to which we see the measurable imprint of the Kingdom of God on history. We want to see *His-story* unfold in the earth.

I prophesy that it's time to come out of the "glory wilderness" and displace the darkness occupying the Promise Land!

I'm concerned that, in our day, there is a Charismatic, Spirit-filled "wilderness" that the body of Christ needs to move out of.

In the biblical context, the Promised Land was Israel. Our illustrations of any future Promised Lands should never, ever downgrade or displace the significance Israel both had and has to the Lord. For the sake of this illustration, though, I believe the Lord is calling His people out of a wilderness cycle, where we've had meetings, services, conferences, and even glory gatherings. We continue to press in for greater "refreshing" in the church, but we are not seeing that refreshing translate to the world around us. Why? May our cities, regions, and even nations look different because of the presence of a glorious church.

Crossing over from the "wilderness of glory" into the promised land of displacement, dispossessing, and occupation—this is where the Charismatic Renewal and Jesus People Movement missed it. Those moves of God are to be forever celebrated for their impact on souls and even the advancement of the church in that season; sadly, though, the culture of that generation was abdicated to darkness, for every sphere of influence that was outside of the church was considered off-limits to the church because the church was bracing and preparing for an "any moment secret Rapture."

The key missing dimension that was absent in the 1960s and '70s was reformation. I am convinced that our gracious God is extending an opportunity to this generation to see renewal and revival translate into reformation — where society is measurably impacted by the Presence of the Ekklesia.

In fact, in a recent prophetic experience, I was gripped by this. I don't want my daughter, or her children, or her children's children looking back upon this present hour and noticing the absence of the Ekklesia's influence in the pages of history.

A Haggai Moment: A Convergence of Priest, Prophet, and Governor

In the second year of Darius the king, in the sixth month, on the first day of the month, the word of the Lord came by the hand of Haggai the prophet to Zerubbabel the son of Shealtiel, governor of Judah, and to Joshua the son of Jehozadak, the high priest (Haggai 1:1).

For "revival" to translate outside the wilderness of our Charismatic camp and become societal transformation, I see the Lord converging what we see pictured in the book of Haggai, a spiritual alliance of prophet, priest, and government (I think we can expand government to anyone occupying a position in different societal spheres of influence). In our context, here is what I believe the Spirit is saying to the church right now:

In order to build a structure that carries His glory — fashioning a dwelling place for God *in the earth* — there must be intersection in these three realms.

The *prophet*, Haggai, represents the prophetic voice the Lord is raising up in this hour. It's that "messenger anointing" we see pictured in Malachi 3:1, where words of the Lord are released that prepare the way for a "sudden coming" to His temple. It's not one lone-ranger prophet who claims to have a monopoly on hearing from the Lord; this is the opposite of what we will be seeing, so beware and be warned. I see a chorus or collective of prophets functioning in healthy alignment with other expressions of the church (Ekklesia, five-fold ministry), declaring a word that, although it may have different expressions or attributes, it's calling the people of God into a uniform reality. It's preparatory in nature. It's saying, "If you truly desire a visitation, let alone a habitation of God in the church and ultimately in the nations, *this* is how you need to position yourselves." There are things we need to repent of, let go of, and turn away from. Likewise, there are superior realities we need to taste of and turn toward. The prophetic voice of this hour will not be cranky and angry, nor will it be sunshine and lollypops; this collective of prophets will call the people of God *out of the inferior* for the purpose of calling them into *the superior*.

The *priest* could represent church leaders — those who need to receive and respond to the word of the Lord delivered through the prophetic collective. Why does it seem like we have heard reputable prophetic voices repeating the same words, year after year, season after season? The Lord recently showed me that prophets will *prophesy*. An obvious revelation, yes, but consider the greater picture. Prophets prophesy. They hear or see and then give voice to the message they received in the spirit. Why don't we see more prophetic words come to pass? Simple. No one is partnering with them. The "priests" — leaders in the church mountain — need to learn how to respond to prophetic words by partnering with them. God sovereignly gives words to His prophets, but the people of God, particularly church leaders, need to be good stewards of these words, not simply by saying "I receive that," but by reordering and reorienting life to accommodate the messages from Heaven being prophesied.

The *governor* represents Seven-Mountains activism. Just for the record, this is not Christian dominionism, where believers assert themselves as leaders in societal takeover. I see "dominion" being expressed this way: a company of people filled with the Holy Spirit aim toward ascending the high places of societal influence to assert dominion, not through a natural overthrow, but having authority in the spiritual airways. The one who lives under the Spirit's influence is the one most qualified to have influence. The Lord desires to raise up a company of Spirit-filled leaders who break the cycle of shifting atmospheres. Right now, Christians have been taught victorious strategies to shift atmospheres that have been under the influence of darkness. We need to study and implement these tools for victorious warfare, yes, but the Lord desires to raise up those who are the ones who *set the atmosphere*. Yes, the Lord says "set, not shift." Those who ascend the high places will displace darkness, most certainly, but once darkness is dislodged from the high places, it's time for those places to be given to the Holy Spirit. This actually serves those who are under your influence, be it a company or an entire mountain of influence, for I see anointing flowing from the top down. I see the river of God flowing down off those occupying and operating in these "governmental" positions shaping environments of peace, love, joy, gentleness, goodness, and every life-giving attribute that expresses the imminent Presence of God's Kingdom. It's about cleansing darkness in the unseen realm so that those in the natural realm directly benefit from environments under Kingdom jurisdiction, for the Kingdom of God is righteousness, peace, and joy in the Holy Spirit (see Rom. 14:17).

I see righteousness — what does this look like? First and foremost, it looks like an environment where it's, for lack of a better word, easier for people to discover right standing with God through the work of Jesus. What's all of this Seven Mountains ascending-to-the-high-places activism really for? One of the key motivations is the creation of environments conducive to people being able to connect with God through Christ Jesus, discovering that the blood of Jesus has made right standing with the Holy God possible. But furthermore, I see the manifestation of righteousness taking place. Righteous decisions. Righteous motives. Righteous, not meaning that the people are perfect, but they are operating in agreement with how God Himself would operate in that place.

I see peace — what does this look like? The peace of God creates a solid, unshakeable people. In the midst of chaos, individually and societally, in the boardroom and in the headlines, it's possible for people to be anchored in peace. Peace doesn't pretend away problems; it simply rests in the stability of a superior Answer.

I see joy — what does this look like? Imagine entire companies, schools, even cities where they are known for "joy." It is possible. If there could be "great joy in the city" in Samaria (see Acts 8:8), is it possible for us to see this manifestation of joy in our midst today on this same scale — and greater? Yes, as the Holy Spirit who moved in Samaria is the same Spirit moving today. As I reviewed that portion of Scripture, I felt the Lord highlight to me the *why* of joy. Why was there so much joy in that city? The statement in verse 8 has a context:

> *Now those who were scattered went about preaching the word. Philip went down to the city of Samaria and proclaimed to them the Christ. And the crowds with one accord paid attention to what was being said by Philip, when they heard him and saw the signs that he did. For unclean spirits, crying out with a loud voice, came out of many who had them, and many who were paralyzed or lame were healed* (Acts 8:4-7).

As the enemies of joy were confronted, the city of Samaria was broken open for the Kingdom of God. I see a direct connection between the bold demonstration of signs and wonders and entire cities being opened to receive the Gospel.

This is what it looks like when the Kingdom of God has influence and dominion in spheres of influence — *righteousness, peace, and joy in the Holy Spirit reign!*

For us to see transformation, there must be a three-fold convergence of prophet, priest, and governor; otherwise, we will continue to believe and perpetuate the lie that the ultimate expression of God's movement is renewal in the church and revival among the lost. There is a third dimension that determines the destinies of nations — reformation. How will the move of God be translated into government, education, arts and entertainment, business, politics, and every other sphere of influence? By a Spirit-filled community of people who know how to receive prophetic strategies from the Throne Room, one moment, and release them into the "board room" the next.

28

Transferable Glory

THIS COMES DOWN TO a question: *what will we do with the glory?* Ana and I have co-authored this section, with Ana taking the first part and me doing the second.

Ana

How Do We Sustain the Glory of God?

May we be people who always have expectation and faith for God to do unusual things. I am 100 percent sure that expectation and faith are two ingredients that are necessary for us not just to have a one-time touch from God, but to sustain and move in the glory of God. Take a moment and just think about this picture.

Moses cried out to God: "*Show me* Your glory!" He had expectation and hunger for God to reveal Himself and so he asked for more. Also, this is coming from a man who saw a pillar of glory by fire and cloud and watched as God split the Red Sea wide open. Yet Moses cried out for *more!* May we be a people who desperately want to see a move of God, not just for the movement but from the place of wanting to know Him more. This is what set Moses apart:

> *He made known his ways to Moses, his acts to the people of Israel* (Psalm 103:7).

Why did God reveal His ways to Moses? Simple. Moses sought Him for that purpose:

> *Now therefore, if I have found favor in your sight, please show me now your ways, that I may know you in order to find favor in your sight* (Exodus 33:13).

Just look at how God and Moses interacted:

> *The Lord descended in the cloud and stood there with him as he called upon the name of the Lord* (Exodus 34:5 NASB).

What I love about Moses is we can chart his journey. He starts out as this man who at first says, "Who, *me?* I can't lead these people out of slavery. I'm insufficient—I have a stutter!" Then we watch as he steps into faith and boldly declares: "Let my people *go!*"

He stretches his hand over the sea, and the Lord splits the sea wide open! *Wow.* Then time after time again, we see Moses crying out to God to break through as the Israelites complain or disobey God (see Exod. 33:12-13).

His humility and complete dependence on the Lord is why I believe God met *"face to face"* with Moses, *"as a man speaks to his friend"* (Exod. 33:11) Therefore, Moses could stand in the glory. Face to face he met with God as a friend. Let your mind wrap around that for a second. "As a friend." *Wow!* *"I am the vine, you are the branches; he who abides in Me and I in him, he bears much fruit, for apart from Me you can do nothing"* (John 15:5 NASB).

Friendship is cultivated out of a place of intimacy. The closest friends I have are the ones I have invested the most into. They are the ones to whom I say, "No matter what, I want to remain close to you." This is what Moses had with God. It's from this place of desiring intimacy and remaining close to Him that we are able to remain in the glory. We pursue His heart and love above all else—above a calling, platform, mantle. We long for deep connection with Jesus — to meet face to face with Him, just for the sake of getting to know Him more.

This ability to remain close to Him *requires sacrifice and investment* often. Letting go of our fleshly desires and things that don't really matter, guarding our time, and pursuing Him above everything else — then we can abide and remain. Investing in spending time with Him, reading and meditating on the word of God, praying daily like God really hears and answers our prayers, worshiping and adoring Him even when we don't feel like it, repenting for our sins and turning away from them, asking Him to cleanse us again and again, taking time to just simply be with Him to get to know Jesus personally — all of this is an investment into our relationship with Him.

As we fix our eyes and focus on the King, we will become more like Him. As we become more like Him and desire the things He wants, sin becomes more repulsive to us and we press in to live a life that is *"worthy of the calling"* (Eph. 4:1). *"Blessed are the pure in heart, for they shall **see** God"* (Matt. 5:8). So, let's do everything we can to *remain pure!*

We can stand in the glory of His Presence because our eyes and hearts are locked upon the Creator. As we fix our gaze on Him we become grounded in our identity; knowing His love for us, we are not easily shaken (see Eph. 3:17-18). The more we get our eyes off of our own problems and everyday struggles and focus them on Jesus, the more our lives are transformed. From the inside out, He comes and transforms us in His love. He pours His love over us, and we are made new.

This is what Paul describes in Second Corinthians 3:18:

> And we all, with unveiled face, beholding the glory of the Lord, are being transformed into the same image from one degree of glory to another. For this comes from the Lord who is the Spirit.

I have a friend who says flexibility is the extra fruit of the Holy Spirit! If we want to sustain the glory of God, we have to remain flexible to His agenda in whatever way He moves—even if it looks different from the past moves of God. We want more of the Holy Spirit, so we cannot quench or try to control Holy Spirit. A quote from *The Chronicles of Narnia* describing Aslan comes to mind: "'After all, he's not a *tame* lion.' 'No, but he is good.'" When Holy Spirit moves and the glory of God falls, people respond differently depending on the way they were made. The key point is they respond to the Spirit, whether we like it or not. So we cannot try to control Holy Spirit and put Him in a box, saying, "I only want You to move like this, on my terms, in the way that makes *me* comfortable." Control grieves the Holy Spirit and stops the flow and movement of the glory. This is why Paul warns, *"Do not quench the Spirit"* (1 Thess. 5:19). *The Passion Translation* phrases it this way: *"Never restrain or put out the fire of the Holy Spirit."*

Transferable Glory

Remember, Moses spoke to God face to face, like a man speaks to his friend (see Exod. 33:11). Moses also was one who contended for the glory of God. *"Show me your glory"* he requested of the Lord (Exod. 33:18).

May this encourage all of us to keep pursuing God and not settle for where we are in our experience of Him. Moses saw and experienced a lot, but still he burned to behold and encounter more. There is always a level of more, and sometimes we do have to contend for it.

As Moses walked down Mount Sinai, it says that his face shone because of speaking with God (see Exod. 34:29). There is a point where our experience of tasting God has to have some sort of external reflection. The more we behold Him, the more we will become like Him, and then the more it should be transferable.

Arise, shine, for your light has come, and the glory of the Lord has risen upon you (Isaiah 60:1).

Isaiah tells us what to do with the glory — *arise* and *shine*. It has to come out of us and have a measurable impact on the world *out there* that is experiencing darkness. God answers the cry for more when He knows that we will go down the mountain and radiate His glory into the darkness.

I am convinced that the veil between Heaven and earth is getting the thinner as we approach the return of Christ. What separates us from the heavenly realm is becoming thinner. More and more people are finding themselves able to encounter Jesus unlike ever before. God is pouring out His Presence exponentially across the earth, as He is desiring to call in every person from every corner of the earth into the Kingdom. "Return home!" He beckons. Earth is not actually our forever home. We were created for much greater things. One taste of Heaven and you quickly realize what could be and should be.

As a carrier of God's glory, you are an atmosphere shifter. Wherever you are, you can walk in and release the glory of God into that environment. Pass it on. Pass the glory and love of God on to someone near you who is needing it today. The next wave of glory that is coming, I am convinced, is much larger than we have ever seen before. It's big enough to usher in the great prophesied harvest, along with preparing nations for the great end-time division. On one side, there will be goat nations, those hostile to the Lord, and yet on the other side Jesus says there *will be* sheep nations that welcomed Him and His people. The level of glory we need to save the souls of people and transform the souls of nations cannot be restrained by four walls; it must be released to shift the atmosphere of culture!

It won't be one location of revival, but rather individuals all across the globe carrying revival within, willing to let the glory of God spill out of their lives to cover the world.

Your Job, His Assignment

Did you know God entrusted you with a great responsibility? The more authority He gives us, the more responsibility we have. The more glory, the more we're entrusted with. All of us are given a mandate from the Lord.

Mark 16:15 says, "*Go into all the world and proclaim the gospel to the whole creation.*" I realize that not everyone reading this has a call on their life to be a preacher. We all are called by God, though, to share the news of Jesus and love of Jesus with the world. Whatever world you are in—whether that be at home with the kids, at the office, or out on the field repairing maintenance lines—wherever you are, you are a representative of Jesus to the world. Your very presence in that place shifts the atmosphere as you carry Christ within you.

As we get a touch of His glory, then we desire for Him to get all the glory. All our personal desire for glorification gets stripped away when we come face to face with our Creator. The Kingdom is at hand! (See Mark 1:15.)

After I experienced the glory of God that day in the Jordan River, I couldn't wait to tell people about Jesus! I remember approaching a store owner in Israel after I had left my phone in his shop accidentally. "Do you know the Lord? Do you know Jesus?" I asked him.

"Yes ma'am. I am a Jew. Of course I know this Jesus," he responded.

"But do you know Him? Like, do you talk to Him daily?" I persisted.

"No ma'am. I am not a religious man." The conversation went on, and with ease I led that store owner to ask Yeshua to come into his life and heart as His Savior, and then he got baptized in the Holy Spirit right there in the middle of the shop! Praise God! I was so excited that next I bumped into one of our bus drivers who was drinking at a bar. Grabbing a coffee, I asked to join him. We then got into a discussion all about Jesus and different theologies, which led to him deciding that he wanted to know what "this Holy Spirit" was all about.

You are a representative of Him. As we encounter Him, we can't wait to tell others about Him. That's transferable glory!

Larry writing.

We Will Encounter and Walk in the Greater Glory When...

We will see God's glory cover the earth to the degree that the people of God who make up this entity called *the church* accept their assignment to cover the earth. It's one thing to learn how to move *in* Zion, to flow in the supernatural and engage the realms of the spirit, but it's another thing entirely to *be the outpouring of God* in the sphere you have been called to. Ninety percent of the church is not called to minister *in* the church.

It's time to yield and surrender to the call and assignment of God like Isaiah did. He encountered the glory, which is one dimension, but in order for the glory to *fill the earth* Isaiah had to carry and translate his encounter.

I love the following practical instructions from Ana that show us what it looks like to walk in the greater glory of God.

Ana writing.

We Die...and Then Die Some More to Our Flesh

In Luke 9:23, we see the following: "*Then he said to the crowd, 'If any of you wants to be my follower, you must give up your own way, take up your cross daily, and follow me'"* (NLT) In *The Passion Translation,* Jesus' words are translated as follows: *"you must disown your life completely, embrace my 'cross' as your own, and surrender to my ways."*

Ouch! Even though this scripture is so over-taught, I'd like to unpack it in a way that relates to how to step in and sustain the glory of God. Because really, for the glory of God to come, there has to be 100 percent of dying to our flesh.

We Love Beyond...

Loving isn't always easy is it? Jesus commands us to love our neighbor and also our enemies — but have you ever thought about loving when you're exhausted and completely extended, or when it's inconvenient?

I look at the Scriptures and see many times when Jesus would finish ministering to the large crowds and try to slip away to get some time to rest and restore and hear from the Father. Yet the crowds kept following Him. Out of compassion He would perform miracles.

> *Departing from there, Jesus went along by the Sea of Galilee, and having gone up on the mountain, He was sitting there. And large crowds came to Him, bringing with them those who were lame, crippled, blind, mute, and many others, and they laid them down at His feet; and He healed them. So the crowd marveled as they saw the mute speaking, the crippled restored, and the lame walking, and the blind seeing; and they glorified the God of Israel* (Matthew 15:29-31 NASB).

Don't read this incorrectly. It is so valuable and important to get alone time with the Lord. Even Jesus would slip off to spend time alone and pray with the Father. We just need to discern when He's calling us to slip away, like Jesus, or when He's calling us to draw from that inexhaustible glory within and minister out of His Presence, not our weakness.

Love does cost something, though. I have heard the Lord say to me before, "Will you love when you're tired, when it's inconvenient, when it costs you something, when it's hard?" It's part of dying to our flesh. Will you love when it costs something?

I'll never forget when I prayed for a lady in Nepal and God did one of the most incredible miracles I have ever personally experienced! It was a wet, muddy day and my husband and I went to the slum village that lived under the bridge to pray for people. Our translator motioned for us to come pray for a lady in her home, which was a structure consisting of plastic tarps and cardboard boxes.

Ducking into her home, I asked her how I could pray. Shockingly, she lifted up her shirt and exposed her stomach that had a gaping hole in it. I saw her insides oozing out.

"Oh God, I don't do ooze!" was my inner complaint to God.

Then I heard, "You do now! I want you to hug her and don't let go until she does," He responded back to me.

So, I asked through the translator if I could hug her. We hugged for what felt like an awkward amount of time, as she sobbed tears on my shoulders. I could feel the ooze of her stomach pressing against my own shirt. But I continued to hug her nonetheless and pray.

Finally, she pulled away and smiled right at me. That moment forever marked me. As she smiled at me, I suddenly saw the face of Jesus smiling back at me through her for just a few seconds. She then lifted up her shirt, and the gaping wound was completely gone! *Jesus did it!* He totally healed her; despite my complaining spirit and unbelief, *He* did it! It cost me my pride, my shirt, my time—but it was all worth it.

Loving beyond your own strength and partnering with what He wants to do is how we personally can walk in the glory of God.

We Give 100 Percent Obedience

Recently I was having coffee with a prophetic friend of mine, and he said something that so resonated with my heart. He said, "I don't even have time anymore to *not* be fully obedient. If God says jump or go, I'm gonna go. If God says wait, I'm gonna wait!"

I play a game with my kids as a little fun prophetic-activation activity. At this writing, my kids are three and five, so I know my oldest child understands what we are doing, while the youngest just goes with it and I believe seeds are being planted! We load up in the car, turn it on, and then ask Jesus where we are supposed to go. We literally will ask Him, "Do we turn right now or left? Do we go down that street or to that parking lot?" I know it might sound crazy, and also like a waste of good gasoline, but I am trying to teach them at a young age how to hear the voice of God and how to move where He says to go. You would be amazed at the divine setups of the Lord we have experienced together doing this activity. We have prayed for healing for many people in stores, prayer-walked through a park, given someone a gift or prophetic word, etc. It's simply doing what He says or shows.

The truth is, I want to be where God is moving. I want to be doing what is on His heart. Jesus said, *"Truly, truly, I say to you, the Son can do nothing of Himself, unless it is something He sees the Father doing"* (John 5:19 NASB).

Therefore, I must lay down my agenda and embrace His. That includes running on His timeline. What my friend meant that day in the coffee shop was simply this: the season we are living in right now — where God is pouring out His Presence at a very rapid pace and also the harvest of souls that's being prepared — we don't have time anymore to worry about being comfortable. It's time to jump when He says jump; it's time to go when He says *go*. Living in the glory means that we do our part to make sure the point of connection between us and the Father is never broken. Living in the glory means we stay intimate with the Lord. As we stay connected to Him, we will hear Him and obey Him with ease.

We Rest in Trust

"Do you trust Me? Do you really trust Me?" I have heard Him ask me time and time again as I am being stretched.

I remember when my husband and I were in Mozambique, Africa doing the IRIS Harvest School with Heidi and Rolland Baker. Toward the end of the school a family member of mine became very ill, so much so that we felt the Lord shift our plans and ask us to go back home for a season. There is one flight that leaves Mozambique each week and that week's flight was completely booked full. There was absolutely no way, looking at it from the natural standpoint, that we could get home. "God's gonna do it!" I kept saying in my mind. "I don't know how, but He's going to do a miracle here!"

We arrived at the airport and got in line. When we went up to that counter, I remember looking and seeing a handful of angels standing up at that ticket counter with us. We explained our situation, the stewardesses granted our tickets, and other people were not allowed on. Still to this day I think back on that situation and think, *but God!* As I walked up to that ticket counter, with no possible way in the natural we were going to make that plane, I heard that small voice: "Do you trust Me?"

As we live in the glory of God, we are stretched beyond our limits—*yes!* Our faith muscles are constantly being worked. We are pushed to take on new territories we never even dreamed were possible on our own. And yet the ongoing wrestle remains—will we trust Him at all costs? Can we rest in trust when we can't see the outcome? I'm challenged by this myself even now.

> *Lord, restore our ability to rest in You. Bring us back to that place of purely trusting in You with everything. Some of us have gone through loss during our lifetime. Help us to see that You were there through it all. Help us to trust in You with our lives and with our whole hearts.*

It's a daily walk and journey, isn't it? Laying down our control and leadership and learning to lean into the Father and trust that He has what's best for us in mind.

Back to Larry.

We Surrender to God's Process

Finally, you need to surrender to God's assignment and the place or process He *currently* has you in. Don't devalue anything you are presently doing, writing it off as menial or mundane, for the Lord is processing you. Maybe you feel called to be a voice to the nations in government or a light to the culture through Hollywood or an innovator in technology—and right now, you are attending school or working a job that seems as far away from the fulfillment of that dream as humanly possible. There is no shortcut to becoming a revolutionary.

I know we look to the left and to the right and see many examples of people out there on the front lines changing the world. Know that anyone who is changing the world legitimately for God, their "spotlight" was the result of years, if not decades, of being undiscovered, hidden, and in a state of process. Why? If you are elevated or promoted before you are processed, that which is meant to bless you and ultimately bless others will destroy you and be no good to anyone else. God knows what He is doing. Trust Him and trust His processes. He is looking for how you steward the glory right here, right now. He is looking for yielded, consecrated, dedicated lives. Lives who don't prize the spotlight but burn to see Kingdom transformation in every sphere of society.

This is what is coming…

29

The Isaiah 6 Commission

MAY THIS FAMILIAR PORTION of Scripture give you prophetic perspective on how God is commissioning people in His glory, even today!

> *In the year that King Uzziah died I saw the Lord sitting upon a throne, high and lifted up; and the train of his robe filled the temple. Above him stood the seraphim. Each had six wings: with two he covered his face, and with two he covered his feet, and with two he flew. And one called to another and said:*
>
> *"Holy, holy, holy is the Lord of hosts; the whole earth is full of his glory!"*
>
> *And the foundations of the thresholds shook at the voice of him who called, and the house was filled with smoke. And I said: "Woe is me! For I am lost; for I am a man of unclean lips, and I dwell in the midst of a people of unclean lips; for my eyes have seen the King, the Lord of hosts!"* (Isaiah 6:1-5)

The prophet Isaiah encountered the glory realm of God. I do not believe it's possible for us to *go out of Zion* until we *go up into Zion*. We don't have anything to offer the world unless we receive it from Him, His realm. Why? The world is scrambling to seek out solutions; they are failing. They may identify temporary fixes, but true solutions that will transform societal chaos and cultural crisis are found in the throne room. At an individual level, it's the Presence and power that thunders from the throne room that heals disease, sets the demonized free, and brings people into a saving relationship with Jesus. The same is true for cultural transformation. Society is sick and culture is demonized. It needs Holy Spirit solutions, which are only found in the glory realm—Heaven. I prophesy that in this hour, many reformers and revolutionaries are going to have dramatic supernatural visitations from the Lord, encountering His Presence in transformational ways. You are going to learn how to seamlessly move from Zion into your sphere of influence—from the throne room to the board room. This is what happened to the prophet Isaiah. First, He encountered the glory of the living God.

> Then one of the seraphim flew to me, having in his hand a burning coal that he had taken with tongs from the altar. And he touched my mouth and said: "Behold, this has touched your lips; your guilt is taken away, and your sin atoned for."
>
> And I heard the voice of the Lord saying, "Whom shall I send, and who will go for us?" Then I said, "Here I am! Send me" (Isaiah 6:6-8).

What is our response to the glory? "Here I am, send me." Conferences and events are great. Revival meetings are wonderful. People *need* to have outlets and opportunities to have an Isaiah 6 encounter. But such a touch of God must be stewarded if it's going to become transformation.

And who is qualified to be a "sent one" on behalf of the King? Not the perfect. Not the religious. Not the ones who have their "act together." Consider Isaiah. He has an encounter with the glory of God and how does He respond?

> Woe is me, for I am undone! Because I am a man of unclean lips, and I dwell in the midst of a people of unclean lips; for

my eyes have seen the King, the Lord of hosts (Isaiah 6:5 NKJV).

Clean lips didn't qualify Isaiah to be used by God. It was his "undone" state that positioned him to be a "sent one." How are we undone? By beholding the glory of the Lord. *"In the year that King Uzziah died **I saw the Lord**"* (Isa. 6:1).

Religious obligation is never enough to dispatch "sent ones" into their mission fields. Isaiah 6 does not begin with Isaiah waking up one morning and mustering enough spiritual grit to go out and do something great *for* God. No, the account begins with an encounter where Isaiah beholds the glory of God and is utterly wrecked. In response to such an encounter, how could we *not* become sent ones?

God Gives the Most Influence to Those Who Live Under the Influence

The Lord told me that He is looking for people who live *under the influence* of the Holy Spirit to give influence to. Imagine with me, just for a moment, environments that are under the leadership, jurisdiction, and authority of men and women who live under the influence of the Holy Spirit. By default, those environments and the people operating within them are being impacted — whether they know it or not — by the Holy Spirit.

Ascend to the High Places

Don't run away from career ambition. It's only a bad thing when personal fulfillment and selfish gain are the end results of you ascending the "corporate ladder." But if the desire of your heart is to have influence and leadership so that you, in turn, can be an influencer and a leader for the sake of Kingdom expansion, go after it. Seriously. The people of God need to stop worrying about being contaminated by the world. As yielded vessels and living sacrifices, we must run toward everything in society that is redeemable and declare: "Come back to God!" Partner with the processes of God. Grow. Learn. Become educated. Demonstrate your desire to rise to the top of your trade or career by putting in the work. I've heard it said that God adds His supernatural to our natural. In other words, God will accelerate that which you put your hand to in serving the Kingdom. However, sitting on the sidelines does not position us for that measure of supernatural amplification. God will amplify those who are on the move, for they are moving with God inside of them. By default, this means that if you are moving with the Holy Spirit living within you, then *you are a move of God.* You are the move of God your job is waiting for. You are the move of God your school is waiting for. You are the move of God the earth is waiting for!

What Could the Seven Mountains Look Like?

I have the utmost respect for thought leader Dr. Lance Wallnau. I am convinced that he carries the missing component for revival and the worldwide demonstration of God's glory. We act, sometimes, as if Joel prophesied an outpouring of the Spirit to *all church.* Scripture does not say that. Joel prophesied that *all flesh* would experience a supernatural collision with God through the Holy Spirit. "*And it shall come to pass afterward, that I will pour out my Spirit on all flesh*" (Joel 2:28). If "all flesh" are meant to experience this outpouring, by default, we — the church — need to go to where "all flesh" are. By and large, they are not coming to, or sitting in, our modern sanctuaries.

Martyn Lloyd-Jones commented that "many secular historians are ready to agree that it was the evangelical awakening in the time of Whitefield and the Wesleys that probably saved the country from an experience such as they had in France in the French Revolution. The church was so filled with life and with power that the whole of society was effected." This is sure evidence that glory is in our midst: society will start to look different.

Here is a problem, however, that restrains the church from being an agent of supernatural transformation in society, the *Seven Cultural Mountains*. My friend, prophet and author Beverley Watkins, puts it like this: right now, the church is somewhat getting on board with the idea of changing culture, but the problem is the church is trying to transform culture without first being transformed itself. The church, operating in old paradigms, operating systems, and wineskins, will not be fit to change culture. Why? The church will be trying to make culture more like religion instead of partnering with God to see the kingdoms of this world becoming the kingdoms of our God and His Christ (see Rev. 11:15). In other words, God is not going to use the church to transform the culture *if* the church is trying to get the world to look more and more like a dysfunctional religious system. The church must first rediscover her assignment and identity, and as she does she will be equipped and empowered to disciple and deploy seven-mountains change agents. The people of God will truly discover the purpose of God for nations and culture as they learn to engage this realm called "Mount Zion" or the Mountain of the Lord. It's only when we know what God's world looks like that we start to discover what *this world* could and should look like.

The Church Mountain

This must be defined by the culture of Mount Zion. It's a place of discipleship, community/family, and sending. It's a place where Isaiahs are given opportunities to encounter the Presence of the Lord and become "sent ones" into the spheres of influence they are assigned to. Likewise, it's a place that disciples and builds up these sent ones so they can be effective Kingdom ambassadors in their places of assignment. The old paradigm of the attractional, "bring them here" model is becoming increasingly obsolete. It will not accommodate nor sustain Holy Spirit outpouring. Even the old model of "revival meetings" where you come to a church for special, extended, sustained meetings will not work. I believe the local church is the key place for Holy Spirit outpouring to take place on a regular basis—the key is, we will experience continued outpouring *into the church* as we send and deploy people *out of the church.*

The Family Mountain

I prophesy that the reestablishment of healthy families will declare solid biblical definition to a culture in anarchy and chaos. Everything is in the process of being redefined, from gender roles to what constitutes marriage to when life begins. More than anything, sin is being redefined, and one of the chief places this redefinition is aiming at is the family. As the Spirit of God moves in power in our midst, we are once again reminded that God is not some distant, cosmic spectator; He is real, near, and cares very much about what our lives look like. If He is real, then what He says matters, and if what He says matters, then we must uphold *His definition* for the family unit and believe that is the only path to life and vitality among humanity. It's the family that models what Heaven on earth looks like through relationship dynamics.

The Government Mountain

The "seven mountains" paradigm does not advocate Christian dominionism or theocracy. When Jesus' followers have influence or leadership in these spheres, it does not mean that every single person will be converted to Christianity. It does, however, mean that those who are advocating for life, sanity, and righteousness are leading, and the Scriptures tell us that *"When the righteous are in authority, the people rejoice: but when the wicked beareth rule, the people mourn"* (see Prov. 29:2 KJV). People who are filled with Holy Spirit must have leadership in government because they will have access to supernatural prophetic strategy on how to lead nations, create laws, and ultimately cause people to flourish. There is no problem too big for the Holy Spirit. The thing is, we need to really hone in on the present location of the Spirit. He's not in Heaven, waiting to be called down; He's in us, waiting for our engagement. We cannot run away from the government mountain because of corruption; if anything, corruption or darkness should provoke believers to run toward these "gates of influence." The presence of darkness demands an increased manifestation of glory. If a sphere/mountain of influence appears to be dominated by darkness, let that be a summons to the church to engage it with the wisdom, strategy, solutions, and power of the age to come.

The Education Mountain

Those operating in this sphere are literally responsible for molding the minds of the next generation. One could make this observation concerning all of the "seven mountains," but perhaps it's education that is most directly (and often adversely) shaping the way a generation thinks, believes, and lives. We need trained, educated, and Spirit-filled professors teaching in secular universities. We need those who carry the glory functioning in administrative positions in our schools, influencing curriculum development. During the 1960s and '70s, on the heels of the Charismatic Renewal and Jesus People Movement, there was an erroneous teaching that crept into Christianity basically discouraging young people from attending college because of the possibility of an "any moment" return of Jesus. I am not against living in the light of Jesus' return, but I am against us doing it at the expense of thinking long-term. We should do both. What we are faced with in the realm of academia today is, partially, the result of a church that did not engage its assignment to run toward darkness several decades ago. The good news is that God redeems lost time. Even though it would seem like this mountain of influence was "lost" in the '60s and '70s, I am convinced that should revival begin to break out on university campuses, on-fire students have the ability to turn the tide. Lance Wallnau commented that revival would have to begin with the students; professors would get fired for these convictions, but an impassioned student community, ignited by the glory, would be unstoppable.

Arts and Entertainment

In many ways, the artists are the prophets of this generation. The Lord spoke to me very clearly concerning His strategy for Hollywood. I believe He is intentionally placing prophets and intercessors in artisan hotspots—namely Hollywood, Nashville, Chicago, New York, London, and others. Why? He told me this: "I want them to clear the airways." I believe that as intercessors pray and do warfare, while prophets declare the purposes of God over these areas, even the unrighteous who seek to *create art* will do so out of sanctified spiritual airspace. A lot of what we see today in film, television, music, and the arts, unfortunately, has been birthed out of people partnering with the demonic realm. The Christian solution has not been satisfactory, as we have either resisted popular culture entirely or have created a Christian subculture where everything is "Christianized." We have Christian movies, television, music, books, etc. This is fine, but will never make a measurable dent on popular culture—the influencers who are actually shaping global mindsets and "norms." We must embrace the call to the film, television, theater, and music industries as a missionary would an assignment to a people group or nation that is hostile toward the Gospel.

Media

Media should be a separate entity from *arts and entertainment*, because the arts denote fiction and entertainment, while *media* should be the outlet through which truth, news, and facts are communicated for the purpose of delivering current information. I believe the Lord is raising up truth tellers to once again pursue careers in news media. Journalism. Magazines. Yes, this industry has gotten very dark and corrupt. All the more reason that those who carry God's glory should have a place of influence in this mountain. Glory will always expose and cast out darkness. More glory means the more darkness will be challenged and pushed back. Here is the issue: those who carry glory often remain in environments where the glory is celebrated. In other words, those who radiate with the glorious Presence of God like to stay in safe places. I know I do! I like to stay where the glory is free to flow and move, people are getting touched by God, and it's a wonderfully "open" place for the Spirit of God to fall. But the Lord says, "I am making the church an open place once again, so that you are equipped and empowered to boldly carry glory into the *closed, dark, and hostile places!*" Media and journalism certainly fit this description. But rather than run away from them, we must do the opposite and make sure the people of God, filled with the glory of God, can shine the light of God in these dark places and that truth would prevail.

Business

For a long time, we have heard about a "great transfer of wealth" coming to the body of Christ. I have no doubt this is Heaven's desire; I am just concerned that we are not stewarding this prophetic summons correctly. Could it be that we are waiting for money to come out of Heaven when, in fact, the Master has given you and I gifts, talents, abilities, acumen, expertise, and supernatural access to the greatest strategist ever, the Holy Spirit? I believe wealth will transfer into the Kingdom of God when believers learn how to function as both kings and priests. It's not an "either/or" identity; I believe the Lord is looking for those who know how to powerfully minister before the Lord—going in and out of Zion and then using the supernatural intelligence they have received in the throne room to function as "kings" in the "boardroom."

The Fire Is Falling and Commissioning Builders

In this season of Isaiah 6 encounters when the glory once again fills the community of believers, I see gatherings, meetings, and environments where God powerfully falls on people, and as He falls He releases mantles, commissionings, and assignments. They will not be traditional, for this language has always been used in respect to church ministry. The Lord is calling His people to build His house in the earth. We are His house, but we are called to build His house. His objective is to fill the earth with His glory, to see "all flesh" experience the outpouring of the Spirit. How will this happen?

"Sent ones" will be marked for Hollywood and government, law and medicine, education and science. I see dynamic encounters with God thrusting people into the harvest fields of secular universities, the entertainment industry, politics, and other "dark places." The mission field is expanding. Yes, it will continue to be unreached people groups in other nations, but it will also be unreached people groups who are under the demonic spell of societal strongholds.

For those filled with glory will always have the upper hand over darkness, for light dispels darkness. Those under the influence of the Holy Spirit are called to have the greatest influence. Don't find it strange for God to release media mantles on people during a time of outpouring. Don't find it off if there are moments in a gathering when the prophetic word comes out: "I see the Lord extending a scepter to those who feel called to government and politics."

Should Revival Last Forever? No.

We want to close with an invitation. Revival was never meant to be normal. Furthermore, revival as history records it is not sustainable; reformation is. Different leaders have defined revival as a period of unusual divine visitation. I would agree with this.

Do you know what revival has done for two thousand years of church history? It pushes against the wineskin and operating system of Christianity. God visits with such intensity, not to establish "extended church meetings," but rather to change the way we do life and, ultimately, what the expression of Christianity looks like. Will we receive His work? Will we adapt and adjust to what He is doing? Will we surrender to the unique revelations of God that are unveiled through every outpouring of the Spirit?

Concluding with some final words from Dr. Lloyd-Jones, I want to encourage you—the glory is available now! Don't wait. Don't wait for "all flesh" to experience it before you have an Isaiah 6 encounter. It's not coming; it's not one day, someday. I believe there is an impartation on this book to stir such hunger and desperation in your heart that you will be, like Moses and like Isaiah, an apprehender of His glory. And as you touch Him, reach out to Him, and encounter Him, I believe you will become a sent one!

> To what extent are we aware of a desire for God himself and for a knowledge of the glory of God? I imagine that this is the highest peak of faith. Moses, you see, is no longer asking for particular blessings. He has done that, but he does not stop at that, he has gone beyond blessings, he has gone beyond the gifts, he is not seeking God for himself. He does not despise the gifts, it is rather that, because of the gifts, and because of the glimpses he has received of the glory of God in the matter of the gifts, now forgetting himself, and all gifts and blessings, he just has this longing for God himself and for the glory of God...this, then, is the ultimate, the end of the true seeking for revival. The prayer for revival is, ultimately, a prayer based upon a concern for the manifestation of the glory of God.[1]

Prayer to Experience the Glory

Father, I come to You in the Name and finished work of Jesus. I thank You that the blood speaks on my behalf. I'm not waiting for You to touch me; on the basis of Your word, I will touch You. Just like the woman with the issue of blood in Luke 8, I press through to touch You. I am entering into Your Presence. I am drawing near to You.

According to Hebrews 4:16, I am coming boldly to a real dimension in the spirit called the "Throne of Grace." I come into Your Presence, not because of what I've done or not done. I am not qualified. My works don't qualify me, it's only by the blood of Jesus that speaks a new identity over me. The blood declares I am righteous and in right standing with You. By faith, I step in. I enter Heaven.

Even now, Holy Spirit, make me increasingly aware of Christ in me and me in Christ. Open my eyes to these realities. May I experience them, not just know about them.

According to Hebrews 12:22, I have already come to this place in the spirit — where I can encounter Your glory. I am not waiting for it; I am there already because of the work of Jesus. Open my eyes to the unseen activity around me so I can partner with it, so Your will can be done in the earth.

Right now, I step in. I enter in. I don't wait for God to come down; I go up.

I step in, by faith, into a real place called Mount Zion.

Father, I ascend Your holy mountain.

I come into Your manifest Presence because of Jesus' blood, that place behind the veil.

And Lord, show me how to come in and go out. May I encounter the greater glory so I can steward it, carry it, and release it. May I be like Isaiah — touch me so I can be a sent one. Undo me, Lord, in Your Presence. Overwhelm me. Do whatever You need to do, and do it in Your way, on Your terms.

Right now, I dedicate myself afresh to be a living sacrifice. The best I know how, I surrender control of my life, my rights, my ways, and my thoughts to You. Like the Temple in Solomon's day, I dedicate myself to Your use. And even now, just like with Solomon's temple, may Your fire fall afresh on my life and consume me as an offering.

In Jesus' Name, Amen!

*I made a consecration of my life that I had never made
before, when I saw that it was absolutely possible for me to
so yield my life, my body, as a living sacrifice — a sacrifice
so consecrated to Him that the name of God almighty may
be glorified through the life of a sinner saved by
the grace of God.*

Kathryn Kuhlman

Notes

3: Becoming an Altar

1. David Martyn Lloyd-Jones, *Revival: Can We Make It Happen?* (Marshall Pickering, 1992), 221.

5: Why We Need the Glory

1. Ed Silvoso, *Ekklesia* (Bloomington, IL: Chosen Books, 2017), 25.

2. Ibid., 55.

6: Open Up the Gates

1. One can differentiate a vision of the mind from an open vision in that a vision of the mind is more like a spontaneous mental picture, while an open vision is literally, physically being caught into a vision that one sees with the actual eyes. For a fantastic introductory resource on these different aspects of the prophetic, I recommend Kris Vallotton's *Basic Training for the Prophetic Ministry*.

2. Gordon Lindsay, ed., *The John G. Lake Sermons: On Dominion over Demons, Disease, and Death* (Dallas, TX: Christ for the Nations, 1986), 68.

3. A.W. Tozer, *Rut, Rot, or Revival* (Camp Hill, PA: Wingspread Publishers, 1993), 15.

4. Michael L. Brown, *Whatever Happened to the Power of God?* (Shippensburg, PA: Destiny Image, 1991), 18.

5. One example of such preaching in the ministry of evangelist George Whitefield: "Such a commotion was surely never heard of, especially about eleven o'clock at night. It far outdid anything I ever saw in America. For about an hour and a half there was such weeping, so many falling into deep distress, and manifesting it in various ways, that description is impossible. The people seemed to be smitten in scores. They were carried off and brought into the house like wounded soldiers taken from a field of battle. Their agonies and cries were deeply affecting." This is recorded in Albert D. Belden, *George Whitefield – The Awakener* (London: Sampson Low, Martson & Co., 1940), 65.

6. The classic biography of St. Francis, the Fioretti, records that "because the true servent of Christ, St. Francis, was in some things almost a second Christ given to the world for the salvation of the people, God the Father made him in many of his acts conform to His Son Jesus Christ." Fioretti 7, in *Little Flowers, Legends and Lauds,* ed. Otto Karrer, trans. N. Wydenbruck (London: Sheed & Ward, 1947), 183.

7. We see that "Seymour wholeheartedly accepted (Charles) Parham's doctrine concerning tongues, even though he had nor experienced this phenomenon himself...of all the topics Seymour preached on, none sent more shockwaves through the community than his advocating of glossolalia as a sign attending baptism with the Holy Spirit. Seymour preached the new Pentecostal doctrine using Acts 2:4 as his text." As documented by Vinson Synan and Charles R. Fox, Jr., *William J. Seymour: Pioneer of the Azusa Street Revival* (Alachua: Bridge-Logos, 2012), 33-34.

7: Getting Back to Normal

1. Francis MacNutt, *The Nearly Perfect Crime: How the Church Almost Killed the Ministry of Healing* (Grand Rapids, MI: Chosen Books, 2005), 91.

2. Eddie Hyatt, *2000 Years of Charismatic Christianity* (Lake Mary, FL: Charisma, 2002), 15-23.

3. Vinson Synan, *The Century of the Holy Spirit* (Nashville, TN: Thomas Nelson, 2001), 18.

4. James L. Ash Jr., "The Decline of Ecstatic Prophecy in the Early Church," *Theological Studies* 37 (1976): 227.

5. Henry and Melvin Blackaby, *Experiencing the Spirit: The Power of Pentecost Every Day* (Colorado Springs, CO: Multnomah, 2009), 47, 51.

11: Consult the Lord First

1. Robert Morris, *The God I Never Knew* (Colorado Springs: Waterbrook, 2011), 20.

2. Wesley L. Duewel, *Revival Fire* (Greenwood, IN: Duel Literature Trust, 2001), 12.

12: For the Glory to Come, Fear Has to Go

1. Lloyd-Jones, *Revival*, 166.

14: The Glory and the Fear of the Lord

1. Arthur Wallis, *In the Day of Thy Power* (Fort Washington, PA: CLC Publications, 2010), 119.

17: What Have These Trades Produced?

1. Lloyd-Jones, *Revival*, 24.

2. Kilian McDonnell and George T. Montague, *Fanning the Flame: What Does Baptism in the Holy Spirit Have To Do With Christian Initiation?* (Collegeville: Liturgical Press, 1991), 16.

3. Jon Mark Ruthven, *On the Cessation of the Charismata* (Tulsa: Word and Spirit Press, 2011).

4. *Old Testament Survey*, 396.

5. Charles Spurgeon, *The Abiding of the Spirit, the Glory of the Church*, accessed June 13, 2018, https://www.blueletterbible.org/Comm/spurgeon_charles/sermons/1918.cfm?a=911001.

6. S.A. Bent, compiler, *Familiar Short Sayings of Great Men*, 1887, accessed on June 13, 2018, http://www.bartleby.com/344/20.html.

18: What Unplugged the Power?

1. Rodney Stark, *The Rise of Christianity* (New York, NY: Harper Collins, 1996), 14.

2. Randy Clark, *There Is More!* (Grand Rapids, MI: Chosen Books, 2013), 157.

3. Jonathan Goforth, *By My Spirit* (Minneapolis: Bethany Fellowship, Inc., 1964), 9.

4. Randy Clark and Bill Johnson, *The Essential Guide to Healing* (Bloomington, IL: Chosen, 2011), 95.

5. MacNutt, *The Nearly Perfect Crime*, 79.

6. Jack W. Hayford and David S. Moore, *The Charismatic Century* (New York, NY: Warner Faith, 2006), 24.

7. MacNutt, *The Nearly Perfect Crime*, 85.

19: The Trade of Constantine's Era

1. Jeff Oliver, Pentecost to Present: *The Holy Spirit's Enduring Work in the Church* (Newberry, FL: Bridge Logos, 2017), 116.

2. Chrysostom, John, *On First Corinthians*, 36; Patrologia Graeca, 61:312, 313: CI 288-289.

3. Eddie Hyatt, *2000 Years of Charismatic Christianity* (Orlando: Charisma House, 2002), 38.

4. Hyatt, 34.

5. Hyatt, 34.

6. Hyatt, 36.

7. Ibid.

20: What Hinders the Spirit's Flow in Our Midst Today?

1. Vinson Synan, *The Century of the Holy Spirit* (Nashville: Thomas Nelson, 2001), 18.

23: Israel, the Glory, and the Coming Great Move of God

1. Adrian Rogers, "Can We Hasten The Second Coming Of Christ?" Love Worth Finding, accessed March 28, 2019, https://www .oneplace.com/ministries/love-worth-finding/read/articles/can -we-hasten-the-second-coming-of-christ-15204.html.

2. John Piper, "All Israel Will Be Saved," Desiring God, February 29, 2004, accessed March 28, 2019, https://www.desiringgod.org/ messages/all-israel-will-be-saved.

24: Relentless Prayer

1. Piper, "All Israel Will Be Saved."

25: The Revival that Never Ends

1. Dutch Sheets, *The River of God* (Ventura, CA: Renew Books, 1998), 25.

26: Moving In and Out of Mount Zion

1. Lloyd-Jones, *Revival*, 215.

29: The Isaiah 6 Commission

1. Lloyd-Jones, *Revival*, 214-216.

About Larry Sparks

LARRY SPARKS is publisher for Destiny Image (destinyimage
.com), a Spirit-filled publishing house pioneered by Don Nori Sr.
in 1983 with a mandate to *publish the prophets*. Larry is fueled by
a vision to help the church community create space for the Holy
Spirit to move in freedom, power, and revival fire, providing every
believer with an opportunity to have a life-changing encounter in
the Presence of God. In addition to publishing, Larry is a regular
contributor to *Charisma Magazine*, conducts seminars on revival,
hosts regional *Renewing South Florida* gatherings, and has been fea-
tured on Sid Roth's *It's Supernatural!*, TBN, CBN, the ElijahList, and
Cornerstone TV. He earned a Master of Divinity from Regent University and enjoys life in Texas with his beautiful wife and beloved
daughter.

lawrencesparks.com